IDEOLOGY AND UNCONSCIOUSNESS

IDEOLOGY AND UNCONSCIOUSNESS
Reich, Freud, and Marx

IRA H. COHEN

1982
New York University Press
New York *and* London

Library of Congress Cataloging in Publication Data

Cohen, Ira H., 1950–
Ideology and unconsciousness.

Bibliography: p.
Includes index.
1. Ideology. 2. Subconsciousness. 3. Personality
and politics. 4. Reich, Wilhelm, 1897–1957.
5. Freud, Sigmund, 1856–1939. 6. Marx, Karl, 1818–1883.
I. Title.
BF698.9.P6C63   306   81-22478
ISBN 0-8147-1383-1   AACR2

Manufactured in the United States of America

To my parents, Harry and Kay

CONTENTS

INTRODUCTION

REICH is the central figure in this study because of his efforts to merge two of the most powerful theoretical traditions of modern times, psychoanalysis and Marxism. There have been other attempts to bring together Marx and Freud, it is true, but none as systematic and comprehensive as Reich's. Unfortunately, by the time Reich immigrated to America he abandoned this project in favor of his biophysical research into bions and cosmic orgone energy. This work generated a storm of controversy and consequently, Reich is better known to American audiences for orgone boxes than for his penetrating social theory.

Orgonology is such an unconventional and speculative theory that those who have taken sides in the legal and political battles it generated have tended to see Reich as either a martyr or a charlatan. Yet Reich's contribution to social theory is much too significant for us to allow him to be stereotyped as either a savior or an imposter. The hoopla surrounding his later work must not deter us from a thorough examination of his early work.

Reich's efforts to bring together Marx and Freud were a response to fundamental problems within each tradition. As a psychiatrist Reich was attracted to Marxism when he confronted the limitations of psychoanalytic theory and therapy. Neurosis was so widespread as to be untreatable on an individual level. What relief the analyst could offer the patient often required the patient to accept and adapt to living conditions which were painful and unnecessarily severe. To Reich, the point was to change these conditions and to allow the patient to develop psychologically without the conflicts and impediments they provoked.

As a political activist, Reich was not satisfied with existing explanations of why working-class people accepted and espoused

ideologies which clearly conflicted with their social interests. Marxists explain this in terms of the actions and interests of the ruling
class. The dominant ideologies of our era embody the interests of
capitalists. They reify social relationships and abstract social factors
from their context, thereby obfuscating the class conflict and
exploitation inherent in the structure of capitalist social relationships. They present social trends and processes as natural laws
which are impervious to human actions. By precluding the possibility of qualitative change, they maintain and reinforce the
position of the privileged classes, which then disseminate these
ideologies with a forceful enthusiasm. The coalescence of workers
in a class gives them the opportunity to overcome this ideological
obfuscation. Their position in the relationships of producing and
exchanging commodities gives workers the potential to alter their
relationships with their bosses. This, in turn, creates the possibility
for workers to become class conscious. However, the Marxian
theory of class consciousness and ideology says little about why
this imputed consciousness does or does not develop in a particular
worker. At most, it claims that workers may be confused by
ideology.

Reich's early writings (between 1927 and 1936) mark the most
significant attempt to shed light on the reason workers become
confused by ideology. There are conflicting influences on the
consciousness of workers, some which lead to the development of
class consciousness, others which militate against it. Yet it is not
simply a matter of exposing workers to the appropriate influences.
The development of consciousness is not only a passive process.
There are psychological factors within each person which attract
him or her to certain ways of looking at the world, and his or her
place within it. These psychological factors are socially conditioned.
To understand why people become motivated by ideologies which
are in conflict with their own social interest, we must understand
their interests and those expressed by the ideologies. We also must
understand the way in which human needs are socially conditioned
and expressed unconsciously within the individual's psyche.

Although Reich was a psychoanalyst prior to becoming a Marxist,
the method of his political psychology and the issues on which he
focuses are derived more from Marx than Freud. Reich uses the

Freudian theory of the unconscious to develop a psychological supplement to the Marxian theory of ideology: his theory of character structure. Emotions as well as ideas are socially conditioned. Character is the way in which the individual is preconditioned to react to his environment.

It is my aim to summarize and evaluate Reich's theory of character structure, but not until I have laid the ground for placing his work within each of the traditions from which he draws: the Marxian theory of ideology and class consciousness, and the Freudian theory of the unconscious. This requires that we delve into these traditions. Each offers more than Reich uses. Each is comprised of a complex set of concepts and relationships which cannot be reduced to those of the other. Each, when rigorously pursued, reveals its own limits.

A systematic presentation of the relationship between consciousness and social life, and consciousness and unconsciousness, is necessary both to appreciate Reich and to go beyond him. The synthesis of Marx and Freud that he offers is firmly grounded in each tradition. His theory of character structure shares many presuppositions with each. Yet many readers, due to the structure of intellectual specializations, will approach Reich with a much more comprehensive knowledge of one than the other. Furthermore, both Marxists and Freudians are notorious for their propensity to proliferate conflicting schools of thought on major issues. The form of the final synthesis must be conditioned by the schools that are stressed. In Parts I and II of this study I will reconstruct the traditions from which Reich draws, but I will not attempt to limit myself to Reich's words or implicit ideas. I will attempt to preserve the conceptual and theoretical richness of each system while presenting each in terms that allow for dialogue with the other.

In Part I, I focus on a school of Marxian theory which defines a structure of social relationships and identifies within it the determinants of ideology, class consciousness, and social activity. I refer to this school as critical Marxism because it stresses nondeterministic relationships in a historically specific mode of explanation. In Chapter 1, I outline the methodological principles involved in this type of explanation. I reconstruct the method of

Marx's social research in which he breaks down social factors to their basic units: socially structured relationships between people. Chapter 2 is concerned with identifying the relationships which define and condition working class life. In Chapter 3 I identify the sources of working class consciousness in workers' struggles to improve their condition. Also, I compare the Marxist-Leninist strategy with Reichian Sex-Pol strategy for developing class consciousness. I argue that the Sex-Pol strategy, informed by a political psychology of class consciousness, creates various possibilities for leaders to recognize and develop class consciousness in the workers and to attack the social and psychological sources of ideological consciousness.

At this point the Marxian theory of class consciousness must be complemented by a depth psychology, There are several reasons for turning to psychoanalysis. Psychoanalytic theory provides an insight on human needs and motivation. It explores how psychological processes of which the thinker is unaware condition conscious thought. Psychoanalytic theory is similar to Marxism in its method of explanation. Marx developed a method of conceptualizing social phenomena in terms of the social relationships entailed within them; Freud, a theory of how social relationships are internalized by the individual.

Part II explores Freud's theories of unconsciousness and the internalization of social authority. In psychoanalytic theory individuals not only confront their environment but incorporate it within themselves. Social experience conditions psychic development, but the psyche, via its relatively autonomous internal processes, appropriates these experiences. In Chapter 4, I make these processes explicit and evaluate the extent to which Freud's theories of the psyche are a critical mode of explanation which explains basic factors in terms of social relationships. Although there is much in Freudian theory that can be used in critical social research, there is much that can not. Freud's conception of the relationship between the individual and his environment embodies certain ideological views. How these views pervade his group psychology and social theory I discuss in Chapter 5. Like the social contract theorists before him, Freud constructs a state of nature in which "human nature" could be seen more clearly. He embeds this primeval state in the human psyche to explain the necessity for the leviathan of civilization. Such a view of social processes could lead only to an adaptationist ideology.

Reich understood the processes of psychological development described by Freud as the processes by which the dominant social relationships are reproduced within the individual as a corresponding character structure. In Part III, I summarize and evaluate Reich's theory of character structure as a framework for analyzing the social obstacles to the development of working-class consciousness. Reich attempted to explain both the ideological consciousness and imputed revolutionary consciousness of workers in terms of the social relationships of working-class life. The most compelling example of this was Reich's timely and penetrating analysis of German national socialism. This analysis suggested that extreme nationalism and racism could politically motivate a frustrated population whenever a rigid patriarchy and extreme repression of impulses molds the requisite character structure. What Reich failed to appreciate was how the manipulation of impulses, no less than direct repression, could result in the psychic reproduction of authoritarian relationships. Chapter 7 is concerned with locating the source of this shortcoming in Reich's description of the libido. The study concludes with a discussion of the relationship between political psychology and political activity. Political activity is necessary to transform the existing character structure and its social basis. Political psychology can inform political activity and broaden the struggle against the exploitation inherent in commodity production and exchange.

I must express my gratitude to those people without whose assistance this work would not exist. My research was initiated in two seminars on political psychology by Tom Denyer and Cedric Robinson. Both directed me to relevant sources and discussed with me ideas and texts. Tom must be singled out for reading every draft of this study and suffering through many false starts to various sections. More than once it was his advice which allowed me to overcome a cumbersome position or awkward presentation. Sondra Koff allowed me great latitude in pursuing my interests in political psychology at a time when they were still developing. Marilyn Kent's patience and support, proofreading and typing assistance, were indispensable. Bertell Ollman offered encouragement, support, and invaluable advice at a time when I thought there was no interest in this project. Of course, I alone am responsible for any shortcomings the reader may perceive.

I

MARX: CONSCIOUSNESS AND SOCIAL LIFE

The chief defect of all hitherto existing materialism . . . is that the thing, reality, sensuousness, is conceived only in the form of the object or of contemplation, but not as human sensuous activity, as practice, not subjectively. . . .

The materialist doctrine that men are products of circumstances and upbringing, and that, therefore, changed men are products of other circumstances and changed upbringing, forgets that it is men who change circumstances and that it is essential to educate the educator himself. . .

Karl Marx, "Theses on Feuerbach"

1

THE CRITICAL METHOD

ONE of the aims of Marx's social research was to overcome the influences of ideology in social life and our understanding of it. Marx's perspective was developed from concepts and formulations which expressed the basic relationships of class societies. He identified the relationship between workers and capitalists as the fundamental social relationship of capitalist societies and consequently, as fundamental to understanding contemporary ideologies. He explained workers' movements in terms of the workers' class interest and evaluated the extent to which workers were developing an explicit consciousness of their struggles. He located in the conditions of working-class life determinants of both ideological thought and the possibility of overcoming it.

In Part I of this study, I present a Marxian perspective on the relationship between the conditions of life and people's understanding of them. I am concerned in this chapter with reconstructing the methodological principles involved in this perspective. I refer to the method I present as the critical method because it is a mode of explanation which stresses the mutual conditioning and interpenetration of social factors and their historical development. In Chapters 2 and 3 I apply this method to some important issues in the study of class and class consciousness. First I identify the working class through its economic, political, and social relationships and activity; then I consider the relationship between class interests, the social and political activity of workers, and the development of class consciousness.

My reconstruction of Marx's method will begin from his premises. I then will demonstrate how Marx made explicit the preconditions of the general trends and processes of social life by examining the forms of human activity from which these trends and processes were generated. Methodologically, Marx achieved this by identifying a system of social relationships and explaining each factor that entered into his analysis in terms of that system. Marx considered the primary productive and reproductive relationships of society, and the relationship of human labor to the material means of satisfying human needs, to be the most fundamental social relationships. These relationships constitute the material base of society. The logic of Marxian inquiry is dialectical rather than formal, stressing the interrelations and historical development of social life. I will discuss in turn each of these aspects of the Marxian method.

PREMISES

According to Marx, the premises of his method "are men, not in fantastic isolation and rigidity, but in their actual, empirically perceptible process of development under definite conditions." The first premise of all human history is "that men must be in a position to live in order to be able to make history." Thus, a fundamental condition of history is the production of the means for satisfying the essential needs of hunger, thirst, habitation, clothing, among other things, that is, the production of material life itself.

As they continually produce the conditions of their lives, humans also propagate their kind. This results in relationships between men and women, parents and children, that is, the family. Although the family, in the earliest stages of social development, was the primary relationship, it became subordinate to other social relationships when needs and the population increased.

Throughout history there has existed a "materialistic connection" between men which is determined by their needs and mode of production. "A certain mode of production or industrial stage is always combined with a certain mode of co-operation or social stage, and this mode of co-operation is itself a productive force."[1]

The means of satisfying primary needs, the creation of new needs, the dominant type of family, and the division of labor are the four aspects of the primary historical relationships. They form the basis on which our social, economic, and political institutions and ideologies evolve. Institutions are nothing more than persistent and structured patterns of human interaction; ideologies, the expresssion of the way we understand the interactions of human beings with one another, with nature, and with the products of these interactions. Actually, ideologies are misunderstandings of these interactions, failures to understand the social structure in terms of human activity and relationships. In the dominant ideologies of a society the society's institutions appear as opaque, self-contained objects, independent of the actions of the individuals of the society. Ideological understanding, then, takes the existing historical form of the primary relationships for granted, thus implicitly or explicitly accepting them as necessary conditions of human existence. As such, ideological thought serves the interest of the dominant socioeconomic class which has the most to gain by the preservation of the existing form of primary relationships.

In contrast, Marx's critical method conceptualizes each social factor in terms of the primary relationships it presupposes. The logic Marx based his work upon can be reconstructed as a pattern mode of explanation.[2] Marx explains a social factor by placing it in the pattern of relations identified by his theory. But, given the premises from which he begins, Marx's model is not an abstract and formal one; it is a substantive model of society and the relationships it identifies are the social relationships between individuals within the institutional framework of that society. Since society for Marx is, "man himself in his social relations," the subject matter of this model is not just "society" but society conceptualized relationally. As Bertell Ollman stated, "Every factor which enters into Marx's study of capitalism is a definite social relationship."[3] Marx's relational conceptualization of the social structure is the subject of the next section.

THE PATTERN OF SOCIAL RELATIONSHIPS

Critically conceived, the relations between social factors, which are based on the existing form of the social relations between individuals, are not contingent but rather internal to each factor. A factor cannot be defined if it is abstracted from the relationships it entails. Marx offered the following example:

> A Negro is a Negro. He only becomes a slave in certain relations. A cotton spinning jenny is a machine for spinning cotton. It becomes capital only in certain relations. Torn from these relationships it is no more capital than gold in itself is money or sugar the price of sugar.[4]

A black person is a slave only within the relationships of a social system that applies its property law to human beings. A machine becomes capital only when its owner purchases the labor power of another to run it, creating in the process surplus value. As long as the social relations of slavery or capitalism exist, these relationships are intrinsic to each component of the system. But although intrinsic, they are not necessary. The slave can be emancipated and capital expropriated. They exist as such only within the reality defined by the present system of relationships. Reality is always only a product of the proceeding intercourse of individuals, that is, always a historical moment.[5]

The expression of these factors in concepts which abstract them from these relationships cannot describe adequately either the factors themselves or the total social system which they comprise. As an example, Marx cites the work of political economists:

> The simplest economic category, e.g., exchange value, presupposes population, a population moreover which produces under definite conditions, as well as a distinct kind of family, or community, or state, etc. Exchange value cannot exist except as an abstract unilateral relation of an already existing organic whole.[6]

The problem with the categories of political economy, like those of history and social science, is that in order to use them, we must take for granted a social structure which the concepts allow us to understand only vaguely. It is only within the context of this structure that the empirical content of these concepts can be evaluated.

In Marx's critical method, concepts frequently are used to stress one-sided aspects of the subject matter, yet their systemic meaning contains information of the total system by virtue of the relationships they entail.[7] Thus the same concept may be employed alternatively to express different partial truths. This has led some critics to claim that there is an inconsistency in the way Marx uses some of his most central concepts such as ideology and class. But this inconsistency involves nothing more than maintaining the complete, systemic import of the concept in face of each particular application. In Marx's words, "The concrete concept is concrete because it is a synthesis of many definitions, thus, representing the unity of diverse aspects."[8]

Furthermore, Marx methodically used different concepts to describe the same relationships from different aspects. For example, while the worker sells his "labor power" to the capitalist, this labor power exists for the capitalist as "variable capital." This expresses the fact that what exists for the capitalist as an object exists for the worker as his own activity. "The subjective essence of private property, as activity for itself, as subject, as person, is labor."[9]

Many critics claim to perceive a lack of rigor in Marx's method. This is not the case. Rather, these critics fail to recognize that Marx refused to explain phenomena with abstract precision. Every factor is explained in terms of the primary social relationships. These relationships are never relationships of a population in general. Population is an abstraction if one disregards the classes of which it is composed. Classes remain empty terms if one does not know the factors on which they depend, such as wage labor, and capital.[10] That is, conceptual rigor requires that we explain each social factor not in terms of personal but rather structural relationships, for the fundamental life activity of human beings only occurs in the context of definite social structures.

Accordingly, the worker is related to the employer not as one individual to another but as the representative of one class to that of another:

> ... the worker, whose source of livelihood is the sale of his labor power, cannot leave *the whole class of purchasers, that is, the capitalist class*, without renouncing his existence. He belongs not to this or that capitalist but to the *capitalist class* and moreover, it is his business to dispose of himself, that is, to find a purchaser within the capitalist class.[11]

The relation between worker and capitalist is the fundamental characteristic of the division of labor in capitalism. The social relations of production in their totality constitute society at a definite stage of historical development. As moments in the development of humankind the totality of productive relationships are both a prerequisite and consequence of the change and development of the material means of production.[12] Accordingly, to understand a society relationally is to understand it in terms of the material means and social relationships of production, that is, its material base.

Let us now examine what it means to explain social phenomena in terms of the material base.

THE MATERIAL BASE

Despite its fundamental role in his system, none of Marx's concepts are more ambiguous than that of the "material base." Before stating that "the totality of these relations of production constitutes the economic structure of society, the real foundation, on which arises a legal and political [and ideological] superstructure", he claimed that the productive relations themselves are appropriate "to a given stage in the development of their material forces of production." In the same passage, he referred to the conditioning element of socio-historical processes as "the mode of production," "social existence," "the economic conditions of production," and "material life."[13] As Ollman has pointed out, "Not only do these expressions have different referrents . . . but some of them appear to include in their meaning part of the reality which Marx says they 'determine.'"[14] For example, the productive relations may be expressed in legal terms, that is, superstructural terms, as property relations.

Some readers of Marx have sought to avoid the ambiguity of Marx's formulation of the material base by interpreting it as meaning that changes in the societal superstructure are mechanistically brought about by changes in the productive technology.[15] But this seems to be an empirical hypothesis rather than a methodological principle. Statistical time-lapse studies can be designed to ascertain its validity. The materialist conception of history then is reduced to an empirical position which can be tested by behavioral methods. As such, not only is the complexity of Marx's method lost, but the interpretation clearly is incompatible with the historiography outlined in Marx's basic premises.

How, then, is the ambiguity that arises over the concept of the material base to be resolved? The crucial questions are: What exactly is included in the material base "and in what sense is it said to determine [or condition] these other factors"?[16]

The solution to the first problem is suggested, I believe, by Marx's statements that capital is "not a thing but a social relation between persons mediated through things," that capital itself "is a social relation of production." Consequently, when Marx speaks of contradiction in material life in terms of "the conflict existing between the social forces of production and the relations of production,"[17] we are not to understand this as a conflict between two distinct realms of technology and social structure, but rather two interpenetrating parts of material life. The material means of production never are considered in general, but only as they exist for living human beings producing within a given social structure. The instruments of production embody the social relationships through which they are employed. But these relationships are relationships of people to the instruments of production as well as to each other.

This interpretation is compatible with the premises from which we began. Only by placing living individuals as they are engaged in the life processes of society at the core of the material base can we make intelligible some otherwise confusing statements of Marx. For example, when Marx claims that theory can become a material force when it seizes the masses or that personal powers (relationships) are transformed through the division of labor into material powers, he clearly is assigning a fundamental role to the social relationships within which individuals produce, although these relationships always are mediated through the instruments of production.[18]

This leads us to the problem of describing the process of determination or conditioning in the relationships between the material base and other social factors. Describing this relationship as one of causality or correlation may seem to be the most obvious solution to the problem, but it is not adequate. The concepts of causality and correlation describe relationships between discreet variables which may be defined as dependent or independent. The concept of determination in the critical method describes a process which occurs within a relationship of manifold interconnections and complex mediations. The most varied fields of human activity, as Istvan Meszaros states

> ... are not simply "built upon" an economic basis but also actively structure the latter through the immensely intricate and relatively *autonomous* structure of their own ... for if economics is the "ultimate determinant," it is also a "determined determinant"; it does not exist outside the always concrete historically changing complex of concrete mediations ... [19]

In the critical method, determination by the material base means that the relationships of social life conform to a pattern which is delineated by the relationships of the activity through which material needs are satisfied and new needs are created. In the course of their material life humans create social, political, and economical institutions and ideologies, the content of which is derived from the historically specific organization of the primary social relationships. But just as the primary relationships are obscured by their mediation through things (as in capital) so do these institutions appear to exist as independent objects which develop according to autonomous, natural laws.[20] Thus the individual's own deed "becomes an alien power opposed to him, which enslaves him instead of being controlled by him."[21] The individual can participate in social life only within the condition of alienation. The dominant ideologies will express this alienation.[22]

Alienation is not to be confused with the objectification of human activity in general; it is, rather, the specific form of this objectification within a specific set of social relationships. Objectification is a precondition of social activity and human history. Since the life processes of human societies, the way in which human beings satisfy their needs through interaction with nature, is always expressed through their instruments and relationships of production, objective social forms must emerge through which this activity occurs. It is only when human interaction with nature is mediated through historically specific forms of material life (Meszaros' "second order mediations") that alienation occurs.[23]

In the contemporary social structure, the source of alienation is to be found in the capitalist division of labor and process of commodity production. In capitalist production, the worker's own products are accumulated as the property of the owners of the means of production, thereby increasing the capitalists' power over the workers.[24] The power of social institutions and ideologies to appear as alien entities over which humans have little, if any, control, is derived from the power of the one class over the other. Furthermore, this alien appearance can become a real force. Since these institutions and ideologies have an effect on the individuals who are at the core of material life, they have a very definite repercussion on material life itself.

So, although the institutions of commodity production and our ideological understanding of them are derived from the material base, their exact forms cannot be explained in terms of cause and effect. Rather they are products of the conditions of material life mediated through the concrete, historically changing, complex of social, political, ideological, and economic structures created in the course of material life. This process cannot be explained in terms of intervening variables in which one variable is correlated with another which, in turn, is correlated with a third. Nor is it a matter of a two-way interaction between variables. In the complex process of mediation, a general factor is actualized through another factor, which gives to it a more specific expression. This is not a causal sequence between independently existing variables but an extremely complicated, systemic process between interpenetrating factors. It can be explained only by a mode of inquiry based on a logic of systemic completeness and historical process. Marx saw the works of Hegel as the most sophisticated expression of such a mode of inquiry. Hegel's dialectic provided Marx with the means of methodically representing social reality in terms of factors which are related as essential components in each other's relations.[25]

THE DIALECTICAL MODE OF INQUIRY

Dialectics is an approach to the study of problems which concentrates on looking for relationships not only between different entities but between the same one in different times.[26] Accordingly, Marx's historical-relational view of society is itself dialectical and the fact that I have gone so far in my discussion of Marx's method without as yet considering dialectics is not meant to imply otherwise. The discussion is so structured as to avoid the fallacious notion that the dialectic is an a priori construct foisted upon the subject matter. First I have explicated Marx's perspective on human society. Now I will present the dialectic as an essential component of the method of social research which begins from that perspective.

In discussing the role of dialectics in critical methodology we are confronted with the two difficult problems: When is it used (what assumptions are entailed in its application) and how is it used (what are its postulates of inquiry)? These two problems are the basis for the following discussion.

According to Hegel:

> Method is the consciousness of the form taken by the inner spontaneous movement of the content of Logic ... The necessity of connection and the immanent origination of distinctions must show themselves in the discussion of the subject matter, for they are part of the self-development of the concept. The one and only thing for securing scientific progress—is knowledge of the logical percept that Negation is just as much Affirmation as Negation.[27]

Here we see that, for Hegel, the dialectic is the movement of the self-development of a subject and the method for understanding that movement. As such it grasps "The necessity of connection and the immanent origination of distinctions." The struggle of differences is resolved in a negation which "is just as much Affirmation," that is, a synthesis or negation of the negation.

However, the dialectical process that Hegel described is the "self-development of the concept." In other words it is the process by which thought propels itself forward (the movement of thought abstracted from material life). To Marx, this method was a mystical shell which contained a rational kernel. It presented the "general form of working in a comprehensive and conscious manner."[28] But the kernel had to be shucked before it could be used.

Hegel's dialectical method is an attempt to create a substantive methodology. It ". . . is meant to conform to the actual structure of reality, conceived as a process in which the logical subject unfolds itself into its own predicates." Hegel, Marx claimed,

> . . . grasps the self-creation of man as a process, objectification as loss of the objects, as alienation and transcendence of this alienation, . . . he therefore grasps the nature of labor and conceives objective man as the result of his own labor.[29]

Yet Hegel, according to Marx, observed only the positive side of labor or "abstract mental labor." The problem, as Marx perceived it, was that Hegel inverted the subject and predicate of the process he was describing. "Hegel makes of man a man of self-consciousness, instead of making self-consciousness the self-consciousness of man, i.e., of real man as he lives in the world of objects."[30]

Hence, for both Marx and Hegel the dialectic is the movement of the self-development of a subject which acts upon itself. It is the method by which that subject becomes aware of itself as a subject in the process being studied. The difference is that in Hegel the subject is the World Spirit and the dialectic is one of thought. In Marx, the subject is the human species as it exists in particular social structures and the dialectic is one of social activity. The rational kernel is reached when the dialectical process is seen as the self-creation of humankind through its materially necessary activity.

Dialectics embodies the activity of the self-developing subject. However, if history is reduced to a set of general laws, then there is little room for a human subject in this process. At most, humans can be agents through which these laws are actualized. Instead of the self-development of the subject acting upon itself, history becomes the natural development of the historical object. As in the old materialism criticized by Marx, reality is perceived only in the form of the object, not as human sensuous activity, or practice. Through their social activity, people have the ability, as Lenin commented on a passage from Hegel, to change external actuality and overcome its necessity.[31]

In this reconstruction of Marx's method, the dialectic is not an a priori construct or general law of motion, but a set of postulates for the presentation of the movement of the self-development of subject.[32] As such its application is limited to this type of process. Before it can be applied to a particular subject matter it must be shown that within that subject matter a process of self-development is occurring.

In examining social phenomena, dialectics incorporates our ability to change social reality into our understanding of it, and enables us to understand social reality as a process so that we may act critically upon it. As such it stands in contradistinction to formal logic, for the latter is not suited for the investigation of the interconnections and internal development of social processes. The law of contradiction ($- (A \cdot -A)$) precludes recognition that a social factor contains that which it is not. In formal logic, paradox is described as absurb. Yet in social analysis we are confronted with many seemingly contradictory and paradoxical situations (for example, an individual holding contradictory positions on issues, an increase in economic indicators co-occurring with an increase in unemployment). We cannot assume, a priori, that contradictions and paradoxes are not analyzable.

Formal logic is limited to the abstract analysis of self-contained static entities ($a = a, a \neq b$). Its application certainly has brought about an increase in our knowledge of historical processes, yet the process itself, all our detailed information notwithstanding, may remain beyond our comprehension. Without a logic of interconnection and internal development, the trends and tendencies of the moment can be understood only as "laws" and "mechanisms" of human society. Reality confronts us as an objective given, and our research assumes a contemplative stance. The progressive self-development of human life within an increasingly humanized environment exists only as a normative ideal (and as such distinct from scientific consideration) rather than as a historical potentiality which can be actualized through social activity.

What is needed is a logic for understanding social processes and a framework for describing them. It is in this regard that Engels' general laws of dialectics (which were a restatement of Hegel's formulations of the dialectical development of the concept) prove their value. Engels himself enumerated these as:

> The law of the transformation of quantity into
> quality, and vice versa.
> The law of the interpenetration of opposites.
> The law of the negation of the negation.[33]

Engels formulated these principles as ontological laws. In the discussion of the content of these dicta, which follows, they are understood not as general laws of the motion and development of nature and society (as Engels intended them) but as a set of methodological postulates by which we understand, describe, and develop our ability to act upon the processes and connections that exist in the social world. That is, they are understood not as structures of reality but rather as interpretive aids to our knowledge of reality. The content that Engels imputed to them thereby is revised somewhat, but their application in social analysis remains essentially the same.

What is lost in the breadth of applicability of Engel's dicta with this revision is gained in the logical cohesion of the reconstructed method. If, in the course of Marx's work, his materialist conception of history emerged from his criticism of the Hegelian method, his critical humanist perspective was logically prior to Hegelian dialectics as a component of his method. Marx once wrote to Engels that ". . . to bring a science by criticism to the point where it can be dialectically presented is an altogether different thing from applying an abstract ready made system of logic to mere inklings of such a system."[34] Marx's own work on Hegelian dialectics was concerned more with revealing human history to be a process in which we create and recreate the conditions of our lives through the forces produced by our materially necessary labor, and with overcoming the abstractness of Hegel's idealistic conception of this process, than with establishing clear-cut methodological precepts. The historical-relational view of society was the means by which Marx developed, through criticism, his theory of human society to the point where it could be represented dialectically. Engels' dicta are treated here as representations which capture a moment of applied dialectical logic.

The historical-relational view of society reveals that each social factor is a relation. The factor is composed of all the elements of the relation, some or all of which may be contained in other factors. That a factor contains that to which it is related is expressed by the postulate of the interpenetration of opposites. An example of this postulate is found in Marx's conceptualization of the relationships of production. Conceived of statically, labor and capital confront each other as distinct, opposing entities. Conceived of relationally each is contained within the other. Labor is contained within capital as variable capital; capital is contained within labor as the instruments of labor. Each factor as a relation involves opposition and conflict. With this postulate of mutual interpenetration, dialectics enables us to present each factor from different vantage points and to follow it "out of and into the particular forms it assumes at different times."[35]

The logic of universal interaction and mutual interpenetration is antithetical to the usual way of viewing things as either (A) . . . or (B). The methodological significance of this is most obvious in contrast to the procedure of considering each factor in an interaction as either a cause or effect. Understood dialectically, interaction between factors occurs not as the effect of one distinct factor upon another, but as the result of the mutual interpenetration of factors, within the interconnections of the total process. Cause and effect, " are merely moments of universal reciprocal dependence, of (universal) connection, of the reciprocal concatenation of events. . . ." Causality is only a small particle of universal interconnection.[36] Cause and effect are concepts which may be applicable to individual cases. But as soon as we consider the connections of the individual case with the total process, cause and effect run into each other, eternally changing places "so that what is effect here and now will be cause there and then, and vice versa."[37]

A factor exists as a relation and, consequently, requires for its existence the existence of its own opposition. That is, we cannot conceptualize a moment of reality without at once thinking of that to which it is related, the context within which it exists, in short, of that which it is not. Development occurs as the resolution of this opposition, as the process, in thought and reality, in which the one moves into the other. This is expressed in the postulate of the negation of the negation. The application of this postulate is not, as commonly believed, the mechanical juxtaposition of thesis-antithesis-synthesis. Rather, the negation of the negation is the logic of the historical development of the self-contradictory relation into something qualitatively new, and the means for describing that development. The development of the relationship is resolved in a synthesis which "(1) exhibits something qualitatively new, (2) preserves some of the structural elements of the interacting phases, and (3) eliminates others."[38]

The emergence of a qualitatively new factor is a function of quantitative change in at least one of the components of the relation. Yet it is also more than this. Quantitative change in a component at one point may alter the relation within which it exists so that the relation is qualitatively different than it was before. This is summarized in the postulate of the transformation of quantity into quality. For example a worker may incrementally increase his possession of the commodities necessary for production. As long as he uses these commodities himself, they exist as instruments of production and entail only the relationship between them and the producer. Once the accumulation reaches the point where the possessor is able to purchase the labor power of others as commodities and employ them as variable capital in the production of surplus value, the instruments of production are qualitatively transformed into capital, entailing the relationships between capitalist, means of production, and laborer. The point at which this transformation occurs is always a function of the total process. In the example given, it will differ in different stages of capitalist production and different spheres of production, according to their special and technical conditions.[39]

A process, similar to that described above, occurs in the development of working class consciousness. Demands for reforms in the organization of work are the manifestation of a trade union consciousness—a consciousness which does not go beyond the existing social structure. Incremental change can occur in the militancy and substance of workers' demands (such as demands for higher wages, shorter hours, and better workplace conditions) without a qualitative change in the worker's consciousness taking place. Qualitative change will be brought about when workers' demands go beyond the limits of reform that are permitted in the existing social structure, and are recognized as such. At this point, an incremental change in consciousness becomes a qualitative change. (This process will be examined in Chapter 3.)

While the materialist conception of history provides critical Marxism with its subject matter (human society) and perspective (the historical-relational view of society), these dialectical postulates provide the logic of its perspective and the means for describing its subject matter. The historical-relational perspective on society, as developed previously, itself expresses the manifold interconnection and mutual interpenetration of the components. It conceives social development as the resolution of internal contradictions and the emergence of qualitatively new social forms. Hence these postulates are contained within it, implying that dialectical logic is being applied.

Whether we begin from an empirical investigation in which social factors are conceived as social relations developing within a particular social structure (or substantive pattern of relations) or a philosophy in which history is conceived as the self-development of the human subject, we start from the same place: The subject matter of social research is the processes by which the conditions of life are created and recreated through the forces and relationships produced by our materially necessary labor. The critical method expresses simultaneously the structural and historical dimension of these processes and allows us to understand each component within the context of the process.

In this chapter, I have attempted to reconstruct Marx's method as an attempt to explain social patterns. Marx considers social relationships within a particular social structure. The critical method requires that we explicate the fundamental relationships of society. Each factor is examined in its relation to others, as it actually exists in a network of relationships and not as it is abstracted for analysis. The whole society is always manifest in each component through the relationships which comprise it, so our examination of each component should yield information on the entire social structure.

The critical study of political consciousness is concerned with developing an understanding of why people accept the institutions and ideologies which obfuscate their role in socio-historical processes. The necessary development of an exploited working class within the relationships of the capitalist production process does not imply the development of class-conscious workers. Workers live within a structure of political, social, and cultural relationships as well as economic ones. These different sets of relationships can have conflicting effects on the way workers understand their class position.

In the next chapter, I describe the effects of these sets of relationships on the development and self-development of the working class. In Chapter 3, I consider how Marxists have attempted to locate the sources of class consciousness in working-class life and argue that to understand the process of the social conditioning of consciousness, we must recognize the psychological processes by which workers internalize social relationships.

NOTES

[1] Robert C. Tucker (ed.), *The Marx-Engels Reader* (New York: W. W. Norton & Co., 1972), pp. 119–121 (The German Ideology).

[2] The model of theory generally accepted by social scientists is the heirarchical deductive model. According to Abraham Kaplan, "The hierarchy is a deductive pyramid in which we rise to fewer and more general laws as we move from conclusions to the premises which entail them." In the pattern model of explanation "Something is explained by identifying it as a specific part in an organized whole." Kaplan, *The Conduct of Inquiry* (Scranton, Pa.: Chandler Publishing Co., 1964), pp. 298, 327–346.

[3] Ollman, *Alienation: Marx's Concept of Man in Capitalist Society* (Cambridge: Cambridge University Press, 1971), pp. 14–15. The quote from Marx is cited on p. 16.

[4] Tucker (ed.), op. cit., p. 176 (Wage Labor and Capital).

[5] Ibid., p. 157 (The German Ideology).

[6] Marx, *A Contribution to the Critique of Political Economy*, ed. Maurice Dobb (New York: International Publishers, 1979), p. 206.

[7] Ibid., p. 12. See also Carl G. Hempel, *Fundamentals of Concept Formation in Empirical Science, International Encyclopedia of Unified Science Series*, vol. 2, no. 7 (Chicago: University of Chicago Press, 1952), pp. 36–37, 43–47. Although Hempel's views are couched in terms of the hypothetico-deductive model of explanation, Hempel too stresses that a concept must have systemic as well as empirical import.

[8] Marx, *Critique of Political Economy*, p. 206. For a critical discussion of Marx's critics, see Ollman, op. cit., p. 6.

[9] Marx, *Economic and Philosophic Manuscripts*, contained in Fromm, *Marx's Concept of Man* (New York: Frederick Unger Publishing Co., 1970), p. 119.

[10] Marx, *Critique of Political Economy*, p. 205.

[11] Tucker (ed.), op. cit., p. 171 (Wage Labor and Capital). Emphasis in original.

[12] Ibid.; and Marx, *Capital*, vol. III (New York: International Publishers, 1967), pp. 818–819.

[13] Marx, *Critique of Political Economy*, pp. 20–21.

[14] Ollman, op. cit., p. 7.

[15] Ollman discusses the works of critics who do this. Referring to their interpretation as "Marxism as Fundamentalism" he draws out the assumptions it entails. See Ollman, op. cit., pp. 6–9. But some advocates of Marxism have been equally mechanistic. For a critique of Soviet "historical materialism" see Helmut Fleischer, *Marxism and History*, trans. Eric Mosbacher (New York: Harper & Row, 1973), pp. 38–45.

[16] Ollman, op. cit., p. 6. Actually, Ollman refers to the "mode of production" rather than "material base" but in Marx's works the former term usually refers to the productive relations. When talking more comprehensively of productive forces, we avoid confusion by using the latter term.

Although I quote Ollman's formulation of the problem, and although my reconstruction of Marx's method draws from his work, the reconstruction in the text is formulated in my terms. I emphasize this because of the difference between my position and Ollman's on two important issues of critical methodology. Ollman believes that the conception of reality as relations and the dialectical mode of inquiry are valid for natural objects (Ollman, op. cit., Chapter 3), and natural science (Chapter 5), respectively. I prefer the position of Lukacs that the dialectic is a method for the study of social processes. Lukacs, *History and Class Consciousness*, trans. Rodney Livingstone (Cambridge: MIT Press, 1971), p. 24. I believe that the difficulty involved in Ollman's position is indicated by the distinction he makes between Marxism as a science and the natural sciences (Ollman, op. cit., p. 67). The logical extension of his position would be to posit the Marxian method as *the* method for both natural and social sciences. Since I am reconstructing the method as a method of social analysis, to discuss this further would be to tread unnecessarily on a metaphysical quagmire. Besides, I find little fault with Ollman's explication of Marx's method as a method of social analysis.

[17] Marx, *Capital*, quoted in Lukacs, *History and Class Consciousness*, p. 49. My edition of *Capital* translates the same passage as "a social relation between persons established through the instrumentality of things," *Capital*, vol. I (New York: International Publishers, 1967), p. 766. However, in the present context the difference is not that great and the concept of mediation, as we shall see shortly in the text, better conveys the methodological principles I am seeking to develop. See also Tucker (ed.), op. cit., p. 177 (Wage Labor and Capital); and Marx, *Critique of Political Economy*, p. 21.

[18] Tucker (ed.), op. cit., p. 18 (Contribution to the Critique of Hegel's *Philosophy of Right:* Introduction), and p. 161 (The German Ideology).

[19] Meszaros, *Marx's Theory of Alienation* (New York: Harper & Row, 1970), p. 115.

[20] Besides the obvious references to the quote previously cited in the text and documented in note 17, Marx says, in discussing the commodity as the form of the products of human labor within capitalist production, that

> A commodity is therefore a mysterious thing simply because in it the social character of men's labour appears to them as an objective character stamped upon the product of that labour: because the relation of the producers to the sum total of their own labour is presented to them as a social relation, existing not between themselves, but between the products of their labour (*Capital*, p. 72).

[21] Tucker (ed.), op. cit., p. 124 (The German Ideology).

[22] Engels said that "ideology is a process accomplished by the so-called thinker consciously, it is true, but with a false consciousness," Tucker (ed.), op. cit., p. 648 (letter to Franz Mehring, July 14, 1893).

Some examples of the expression of alienation in dominant ideologies are found in Marx. Religion is the representation through human imagination of human and natural power expressed as forces alien to humankind. In political economy the products of human labor confront humankind as the external condition of private property. When human beings develop their own powers through modern industry, the representation of them as alien objects become increasingly less adequate. Thus Luther annuls "external religiosity while making religiosity the internal essence of man" and Adam Smith reveals labor to be the source of private property, thereby annulling "wealth external to man and independent of him." But neither can overcome the alienation of material life. Luther annuls religious externalization only by turning the alienated products of religious thought into expressions of a universal human essence. Smith could conceive of labor only within the capitalist system of production, that is as alienated labor which depends on private property for its expression. Thus private property is incorporated into the essence of man.

Similarly, Marx tells us that in Hegel's epoch-making system, history is understood as the self-creation of man within the condition of alienation. "The philosopher, himself an abstract form of alienated man, sets himself up as the measure of the alienated world." (*Economic and Philosophic Manuscripts*, contained in Fromm, op. cit., pp. 120, 173–174).

[23] For example, no production is possible without an instrument of production, even if this instrument is simply the hand. It is not possible without past accumulated labour, even if this labour is only the skill acquired by repeated practice and concentrated in the hand

of the savage (Marx, *Critique of Political Economy*, p. 190. See also Meszaros, op. cit., p. 79).

[24] Marx states that

The worker becomes poorer the more wealth he produces. . . . Labour does not only create goods; it also produces itself and the worker as a commodity. This simple fact implies that the object produced by labour, its product, now stands opposed to it as an alien being independent of the producer" *Economic and Philosophic Manuscripts*. Contained in Fromm, op. cit., p. 95.

[25] Ollman, op. cit., p. 34–37.

[26] Ibid., p. 52.

[27] Hegel, *Science of Logic*, cited in Lenin, *Philosophical Notebooks*, Howard Selsam and Harry Martel (eds.), *Reader in Marxist Philosophy* (New York: International Publishers, 1971), p. 329.

[28] Marx, *Capital*, p. 20.

[29] Lichtheim, *Marxism: An Historical and Critical Study*, 2nd. ed. rev. (New York: F. A. Praeger Publishers, 1973), p. 7; and Marx, *Economic and Philosophic Manuscripts* in Fromm, op. cit., pp. 177.

[30] *Economic and Philosophic Manuscripts* in Fromm, op. cit., and Marx, *The Holy Family*, quoted in Lukacs, op. cit., pp. 189–190.

[31] Tucker (ed.), op. cit., pp. 107–108 (Thesis on Feuerbach); Selsam and Martel (eds.), op. cit., p. 351 (Lenin's Philosophical Notebooks).

[32] Acton, in an article critical of the Marxian method, claimed that dialectical materialism is the logic, epistemology, and ontology, of Marxism while historical materialism is its ethics, politics, and philosophy of history. As such dialectical materialism is seen as an a priori construct on which Marx's theories of society, politics, economics, and history are based. Acton, "Dialectical Materialism," *Encyclopedia of Philosophy*, vol. 2, ed. Paul Edwards (New York: Macmillan Publishing Co. and Free Press, 1967).

Engels says that "Dialectics is nothing more than the science of the general laws of motion and development of nature, human society, and thought." Selsam and Martel (eds.), op. cit., p. 136 (Anti Duhring). Although there is evidence to suggest that Marx, at least in part, shared Engels' views (see Ollman, op. cit., pp. 52–53; and Marx, *Capital*, p. 309n), the establishment of general laws of motion negates the primacy of social activity that Marx sought to establish in his critique of Hegel. My reconstruction of the critical method seeks to avoid this inconsistency of Marx's and Engels' logic and is consistent with the following statement by Marx:

Of course the method of presentation must differ from that of inquiry. The latter has to appropriate the material in detail, to analyze its different forms of development, to trace out their inner connexion. Only after this work is done can the actual movement be adequately described (*Capital*, p. 19).

The relational view of society and the historical quality of the primary relationships allowed Marx to do the former. The dialectic is employed for the latter.

33 Selsam and Martel (eds.), op. cit., p. 123 (Dialectics of Nature).

34 Ibid., p. 109n. (Letter to Engels, 1858).

35 Ollman, op. cit., pp. 67–68.

36 Selsam and Martel (eds.), op. cit., p. 337 (Lenin's Philosophical Notebooks).

37 Tucker (ed.), op. cit., p. 618 (Socialism: Utopian and Scientific).

38 Sidney Hook, *From Hegel to Marx* (Ann Arbor: University of Michigan Press, 1962), p. 61.

39 Marx, *Capital*, p. 308.

2

THE RELATIONSHIPS
OF CLASS

CLASSES, specifically labor and capital, constitute the fundamental categories of Marxian economic analysis. They are also the fundamental categories of Marxian historiography, although what is emphasized here is not as much the class relationships of productive activity as the relationships of social and political activity. What distinguishes these two contexts is that they isolate different (but overlapping) relationships involved in the activities of classes.

E. P. Thompson explains class as "something which in fact happens (and can be shown to have happened) in human relationships." We cannot conceive of classes in terms of political, social, or economic structures without reference to the activity of the living individuals involved in the relationships of class. Class is not a "structure" or a "category" but

> . . . class happens when some men, as a result of common experiences (inherited or shared), feel and articulate the identity of their interests as between themselves and as against other men whose interests are different from (and usually opposed to) theirs.[1]

In Thompson's study of the development of the English working class, he uses the term "class" to refer to a complex of historical relationships and activities rather than to a category to which individuals may be assigned with absolute precision. The strength of Thompson's study is the detail with which he describes the activity through which the English working class formed itself as a class. The problem with Thompson's work is that the general characterization of class that he attempts to formulate assumes part of that which his study is intended to explain, namely, the activity through which shared experience is articulated into an identity of interests. The English working class of the eighteenth and nineteenth centuries, Thompson's model of the working class, indeed may have articulated an identity of interests as a result of common experiences. But immediately after he characterizes class in terms of shared experiences and the articulation of an identity of interests, Thompson himself suggests that the working class is exploited in the process of capitalist production whether or not it expresses its opposition to this exploitation. Furthermore, this articulation does not result automatically from the common experiences of workers. Thompson offers a lengthy description of the long and arduous struggles through which English workers came to recognize their mutual interests.

In this chapter I will advocate a somewhat revised version of Thompson's formulation of class. I will argue that the common experiences of workers do result in an identity of interest between themselves and against the owners of the means of production. All workers are made to endure economic, social, and political inequities as a result of the structural imbalance in their relationship with the owners of the instruments of labor. Many workers will develop an awareness of these inequities. But the perception of inequality in itself is not (and need not lead to) the articulation of an identity of working class interests and of the conflict between the interests of workers and the interests of capitalists. Rather than being a precondition of class, this articulation is a component of class consciousness.

Class involves the relationships between classes as well as the relationships between members of the same class. These relationships condition the experiences of the individual. Analysis of the activities of the members of a class allows us to understand this conditioning and to relate seemingly diverse experiences. To speak of a working class in capitalist society is to refer to people whose experiences are conditioned similarly by their comparable position in the structure of social relationships, most fundamentally the social relations of productive activity. Political economies concentrate on examining the relationships of the labor process; sociocultural histories of class, such as Thompson's, study the activity of the class within and in response to its socially conditioned experience. Working-class life is characterized by the structural relationships of both its productive and sociopolitical activity. In this section, I will consider in turn each of these aspects of working class life. I will emphasize, within each, the exploitative and oppressive nature of the relationship between the buyers and sellers of labor power.

THE WORKING CLASS AND ECONOMIC ACTIVITY

According to Marx, the worker who must sell his labor power to the capitalist engages in the labor process only as a commodity to be used by the exploiting agent of capital. The function of directing and superintending the labor process is alienated from the worker and carried out by capital. "Hence the productive power developed by the labourer when working in cooperation, is the productive power of capital."[2]

For Marx this experience was typified by the detailed labor of the early industrial factory. He observed a qualitative difference between the division of labor in detail of the factory, and the division of labor in general (the separation of social production into its main divisions) and in particular (the splitting of those into species and subspecies) of society. "The division of labour in the workshop implies concentration of the means of production in the hand of one capitalist; the division of labor in society implies their dispersion among many independent producers of commodities.[3]

Marx observed that if capital is to consume most efficiently the labor power it has purchased, it must decrease the amount of labor power unproductively consumed, such as time spent changing or moving from one task or function to another. Through the constant separation and fragmentation of tasks, work is transformed into different detailed operations which are repeated by the worker for the duration of his shift. In addition, a contemporary characteristic of the capitalist division of labor is the tendency continuously to separate the less-skilled roles of the labor process from the more-skilled roles, while keeping separate the different work roles from the role of control and supervision of the enterprise as a whole.[4] This is done to optimize the employer's (be it an individual capitalist or a capitalist corporation) profits.

Since the wages of more-skilled workers generally are higher than those of less-skilled workers, it is wasteful to use more-skilled labor to perform tasks that less-skilled workers can perform. Consequently, the labor process is divided into a series of detailed operations and the worker participates in the process only through an alienated, fragmented role. It is the worker's dependence in the process of production, his being molded into a highly specialized but not necessarily skilled operative, and the assumption of control of the work process by the capitalist rather than the immediate producers, that characterizes the productive activity of the worker in industrial capitalism.

The owners of the early industrial factories organized the production process for the purpose of accumulating capital. They purchased labor power to transform materials into different commodities which could be sold at a cost considerably higher than the cost of production. The production costs were kept down by consuming labor power as efficiently as possible, that is by transforming the worker into a detail worker, and extracting surplus labor.

If in the middle of the eighteenth century these conditions prevailed in manufacture and other productive industries; they are now more pervasive. An essential characteristic of the capitalist organization of work is that it increasingly expands to include diverse enterprises. Capital is accumulated not only through the production of surplus value but also through the absorption or sharing in the distribution of the economic surplus. As the productivity of labor increases, the number of workers engaged in productive industry decreases. This decrease has been even more dramatic for agricultural workers. The capitalist organization of work expands to absorb this labor elsewhere. Tracing this mass labor, we will be led, as was Harry Braverman:

> . . . into branches of nonproduction, entire industries and large sectors of existing industries whose only function is the struggle over the allocation of the social surplus among the various sectors of the capitalist class and its dependents.[5]

As the rate of production increases, so does the number of commercial enterprises. Capital organizes for its profit the work process in those enterprises (or branches of industry) concerned with most efficiently consuming labor power (management), absorbing or realizing the economic surplus (sales, finance, marketing), or sharing in the surplus through the direct marketing of labor power (services). The capitalist must purchase labor power and the same process of fragmenting roles, separating more-skilled from less-skilled tasks, and creating the detail worker, occurs. For example, the management of a modern corporation is not performed by a manager nor even a staff of managers. It is the function of a management department or office, which is, as Braverman noted, "An organization of workers under the control of managers, assistant managers, supervisors, etc." Braverman goes on to state that:

> Management has become adminstration, which is a labor process conducted for the purpose of control within the corporation; and conducted moreover as a labor process exactly analogous to the process of production, although it produces no product other than the operation and coordination of the corporation.[6]

Similarly in the service occupations we see the same process of fragmenting skills which in the end destroys those skills (ultimately preserving only the skill of control and supervision of the enterprise as a whole at the upper echelons of corporate positions). The service worker is no longer a personal servant employed to enrich the capitalist's leisure but has become a detailed worker employed to create profit for the service enterprise. The work experience of the service worker has more in common with the factory operative than the personal valet. Indeed, many perform functions virtually indistinguishable from those performed by workers classified as productive workers. For example, the service worker in the restaurant carries on tangible production similar to the laborer in the food processing industries. The service worker in transportation performs a function similar to the laborer who moves materials around the factory or construction site. Laborers are employed in production to clean and prepare goods for their first use much like the service performed by janitors, chambermaids, and dishwashers.[7]

The expansion of the capitalist organization of work to these diverse enterprises results from a shift in the system from com-

petitive to corporate capital. The corporation is the institutionalization of the capitalist function.[8] Work done within the corporate
structure, be it that of the operative in the factory, the secretary
in the office, the clerk in the bank, or the service worker in the
restaurant or hotel, takes place within conditions similar enough
to consider these different workers as a class. The corporate
organization of work is the common denominator which reduces
it to the repetition of routine operations and alienates the worker
from control of the enterprise.

If the corporate organization of work alienates the work roles
from the control of the enterprise as a whole, it must create roles
for this very function. The institutionalization of the capitalist
function means that the function of control and direction of the
process is no longer carried out by an individual capitalist but
becomes incorporated into the structure of work roles. The
function of capital is accumulation and an upper echelon of
managers are responsible for this function. It matters little whether
these managers own shares in the enterprise or are simply extremely highly paid employees. That they function as capitalists
making the decisions and taking responsibility for the accumulation
of capital and control of the work process is more fundamental to
their position than their formal or juridical status as "owners" of
the enterprise.[9] (However, the latter cannot be discounted as a
fundamental source of individual motivation.)

It is not my intent to offer a thorough and comprehensive
theory of class, one that would allow us to assign all the middle
strata of corporate workers and other categories of workers to a
distinct class. Such a theory requires the examination of many
factors that I have not even mentioned (such as the international
division of labor, racism, and sexism) which would fill at least a
volume by itself. Rather, it is my intent only to identify a working
majority which is constituted as a class by a similarity of work
experiences. Those, already identified at the more fragmented,
routinized, and lower paid positions, are that majority. In addition,
many of the technical and professional jobs at the middle levels
display, to varying degrees, working-class characteristics.[10] The
routinization of work, exclusion from control of the enterprise,
and appropriation of surplus labor for the production, absorption,

or realization of surplus value, identify the working class in its economic activity. Differences in the forms of work people do and economic differentiations subdivide workers into factions of the class, but they do not dissolve the relationship of these people into different social strata.[11]

The working class is formed by the relationships of commodity production and exchange. Yet working-class life is characterized not only by these relationships but by relationships between workers as well. Workers may form cooperative and interdependent relationships at work. Outside of work they participate in a variety of political and social activities from which a working-class culture or identity may develop.[12] We now turn to the active role workers may play in forming themselves as a class.

CLASS CULTURE AND SOCIOPOLITICAL ACTIVITY

The working class, which suffers a common exploitation in its economic activity, must engage in political activity to overcome this. This is so because the state is the guardian of property laws which legitimates the relationships between labor and capital. But the state itself rests on social institutions and organizations ("civil society") which function to ensure the consent of the populace for the existing social, economic, and political relationships. Although we can isolate the spheres of economics, politics, and civil society for the sake of analysis, they are closely interrelated.

Whereas the distinction between the state and civil society is as old as classical liberal theory, Antonio Gramsci, writing in the early half of this century, was the first to adopt it to analyze class. For Gramsci modern civil society corresponded to "the function of hegemony, which the dominant group exercises throughout society." This is in contrast with the function of direct domination by the state. By hegemony, as one commentator noted,

> Gramsci meant the permeation throughout civil society—including a whole range of structures and activities like trade unions, schools, the church and the family—of an entire system of values, attitudes, beliefs, morality, etc., that is one way or another supportive of the established order and the class interest that dominates it.[13]

This theory that ideas favorable to the dominant class are transmitted through the institutions of civil society is not a theory of the socialization of the individual to society in general, but a critical theory of the maintenance of class domination. It emphasizes that class relationships need not be involved directly in the institutions of civil society for the latter to function in support of the former. These institutions socialize a labor force and prepare it "to enter the workplace and treat it as a natural institution that stands over and above the creative action of the workers themselves." Without this socialization, "it would be necessary to continuously make legitimate to every generation of workers the social divisions within the labor process or else to simply control them through force."[14]

Though the relationships of class need not be directly involved in institutions performing this hegemonic function, advanced industrial societies are characterized by the increasing involvement of class relationships in the institutions of civil society. The development of a mass consumer culture which relates large aggregates of individuals through the media of mass communication and the interactions of the commodity market has led to the erosion of many traditional institutions and their authority. Just as capital organizes more and more work activity into detailed operations, so too, does it organize more and more sociocultural activity into the market relationships of commodity consumption. This process is described by Braverman.

> . . . as the social and family life of the community are weakened, new branches of production are brought into being to fill the resulting gap; and as new services and commodities provide substitutes for human relations in the form of market relationships, social and family life are further weakened.[15]

Transactions on the commodity market convert goods or services into exchange values and actualize their surplus value. The quest for profits leads to the marketing of more and more commodities. This extension of the commodity market proceeds from two sources. On the one hand, given modern work patterns and lifestyles, family, friends, neighbors, and community become less significant as the functions they once performed are taken over by the commodity market. Food and clothing, which were once provided from within the household, are now produced outside of the family and for the enrichment of capital. Recreation and amusement are now offered by the mass media, professional sports, a sporting goods and facilities industry, and hobby-equipment firms. Security is purchased from the insurance industry; the care of the old, the sick, and the handicapped has increasingly been institutionalized.[16] On the other hand, besides expanding market relations to satisfy diverse needs, new needs are created for new products. This function is performed by the all-important advertising industry. Modern advertising goes far beyond informing the consumer of the commodity and its practical utility. The commodity is represented as "a matrix of economic achievement and social status." The need for status symbols is cultivated by the mass media, which transmits an attractive vision of the middle-class consumer lifestyle and emphasizes the values and norms essential for it. Not only does this create the market for new commodities, but it makes alienated labor tolerable, as the means of deriving satisfaction through consumption.[17]

So while it erodes the authority and functions of more traditional institutions and relationships, the new mass culture takes over from them the hegemonic function of adjusting the individual to the institutions of class domination. That participation in mass consumer culture cuts across class lines is not a negation of the class structure of society. Rather, this participation serves the ideological function of obscuring class relationships. In the labor process, workers are placed in direct relationship with other workers. The capitalist organization of work imposes upon them similar conditions. Many workers have organized to improve and reform these conditions. Yet these organizations cannot lead to the development of a class culture or community as long as the working class participates as part of a mass in the hegemonic culture. If the working class is to overcome the domination of capital, it must challenge capitalist political, social, and cultural hegemony directly. "If socialism is to assert its ideological hegemony, it must create its own culture . . . as an integral part of a total revolutionary process; in doing so, it must build upon embryonic currents of cultural protest and revolt."[18]

These currents of revolt are to be found in the social, political, and cultural activities of the working class; that is, in the activity of the class as it struggles to produce and reproduce its daily life beyond the limits imposed by capitalist hegemony. If classes are formed in the work process and the productive relationships which structure it, they form themselves in these social struggles. For instance, the English working class began to form itself even before its work activity was characterized by the conditions of the industrial factory.[19]

The English working class in the early decades of the nineteenth century was comprised of people who worked in their homes and small workshops, be they craftsmen, mechanics, journeymen, or laborers. Rural workers, suffering from enclosure, eventually were pauperized or displaced from the land, and many of both of these groups were employed in larger factories and mills. Thompson describes how these workers, even before the turn of the nineteenth century, developed a radical culture in the working-class areas of the growing towns. Artisans and laborers, through their societies and unstamped newspapers, led the struggle against the stamp act and government censorship. These underground publications were read by a large portion of artisans and laborers whose literacy was a result mainly of their own efforts. To label this struggle for literacy and a free press as "petty bourgeois" or a manifestation of "bourgeois individualism" is to distort the reality involved. This was the struggle of the working class. They expropriated the tradition of freeborn Englishmen, "adding to the claim for free speech and thought their own claim for the untrammeled propagation, in the cheapest possible form, of the products of this thought." In short, it was the struggle of the workers against the social hegemony of their exploiters.[20] Of course, they also struggled against class domination in the economic realm. Workers formed the "friendly societies" and eventually, the unions and reform and socialist movements through which they struggled against the exploitation and insecurity which characterized their work.[21]

The point Thompson is making is that the experiences of class cannot be understood adequately merely by describing the various work categories—no matter how sophisticated that description may be. "The working class made itself as much as it was made."[22] It acted within and reacted to the conditions imposed upon it. It organized and institutionalized its activity and the relationships entailed in it. It created a class culture. There existed between those who participated in this activity and culture a unity which characterized them as working class even if their jobs or occupations could not be so clearly described. In this respect a relationship could be formed between those industrial, commercial, and service workers, identified as the working class in the previous section, and the lower echelons of the professional and technical workers. The petty bourgeoisie who find their economic situation more and more precarious and participate in the cultural community of their working class neighbors can relate themselves to the working-class struggle against capitalist hegemony.

However, it does not seem as if there is anything inherent in the social position of the working class or these other classes which will propel them toward anticapitalist activity. The working class may constitute itself as a militant and well-organized pressure group within capitalist societies and still stop short of struggling to transform those societies. For example, in most western European countries workers and their allies have organized themselves into such groups as Workers' Councils, and Labor, Social Democratic, and Communist parties. At the same time socialism throughout the west "has become a means by which workers obtain a redress of grievances within capitalist society, rather than an instrument for its transformation." Ironically, by seeking to be legitimate participants in the political process, working-class political organizations tend to legitimize the system even while professing a desire to transform it.[23]

In other words, workers can form themselves into a class through social, political, and cultural activity and still not emerge as a revolutionary social force. Collective activity, while necessary, is not a sufficient condition for overcoming the empirical conditions which constitute workers as a class. These conditions cannot be transformed incrementally by adding together more and more reforms. They must be attacked directly in theory and practice. That is, workers must become conscious of the relationships and factors which result in their exploitation and act to change them, or they will be locked into a struggle for reform in which they constantly will be forced to defend the moderate gains they achieve. In the next chapter, I will be concerned with locating in workers' struggles the sources of this imputed consciousness.

SUMMARY

The working class can be studied from the perspective of capital or the perspective of workers. A working class is formed by the development of the capitalist labor process and the commodity relationships assumed within it. The number of people whose jobs take on working-class characteristics is constantly increasing as capital expands to organize more and more enterprises as sets of detailed operations. If workers are to overcome the exploitative conditions of work, they must overcome the political and cultural factors which maintain and reinforce the relationships of the labor market. Accordingly, workers constitute (or fail to constitute) themselves as a class through their political and cultural struggles. Yet workers may act collectively against capitalist hegemony and exploitation and still stop short of the activity necessary to overcome that exploitation and hegemony. Workers must become conscious of the structure of relationships which condition their lives in order to transform those relationships.

NOTES

[1] Thompson, *The Making of the English Working Class* (New York: Pantheon, 1963), p. 9.

[2] Marx, *Capital*, vol. 1 (New York: International Publishers, 1972), p. 333.

[3] Ibid., p. 355. See also pp. 351–355.

[4] Ibid., pp. 339–350; Braverman, *Labor and Monopoly Capital* (New York: Monthly Review Press, 1974), pp. 78–81; and Robert E. Tucker (ed.), *The Marx-Engels Reader* (New York: W. W. Norton & Co., 1972), p. 188 (Wage Labor and Capital).

[5] Braverman, op. cit., p. 255.

The concept of economic surplus is introduced in Baran and Sweezy, *Monopoly Capital* (New York: Monthly Review Press, 1968), pp. 9–11. See also the appendix to the work, "Estimating the Economic Surplus" by Phillips, pp. 369–384. The concept is also used by Braverman, but, whereas Baran and Sweezy included in this concept the utility of the commodities produced, Braverman explicitly rejected this. Rather, Braverman used the concept of surplus to describe the absorption by other branches of industry of the surplus value produced in manufacture. Braverman, op. cit., pp. 251–257. See also Jacoby's review of *Labor and Monopoly Capital* in *Telos*, no. 29 (Fall, 1976), 200.

For statistics describing the changing composition of the U.S. work force from 1920 to 1970 see for example Albert Szymanski, "Trends in American Class Structure," *Socialist Revolution*, no. 10 (1971–1972), p. 104 (Table 2) and p. 107 (Table 3).

[6] Braverman, op. cit. p. 267.

[7] Ibid., pp. 360–361. The process of proletarization of service workers is described by Braverman in Chapter 16; of clerical labor, Chapter 15; of corporate subdivisions intended to absorb social surplus or realize surplus value, Chapter 12.

[8] Baran and Sweezy, op. cit., p. 44. Chapter 2 of their work is concerned with the corporate supersession of the individual capitalist.

[9] James develops this position in his critique of the economy of the Soviet Union. See "Excerpts from State Capitalism and World Revolution," *Radical America* vol. 4, Special Issue (May 1970), 28.

[10] Statistics cited by Braverman, op. cit., p. 379, indicate that the categories of manual laborer, clerical, service and retail sales workers, when added together, constitute not only a majority of the working population but an *increasing* majority, from 50.7 percent of the population in 1900 to 69.1 percent in 1970. Statistics cited in Szymanski, op. cit., p. 107, indicate a similar trend, 52.4 percent to 70.9 percent. That these figures are slightly higher is at least in part a result of the inclusion of foremen in the "craftsmen" category of manual labor. These new working-class jobs result in no improvement of wages for workers. According to the Bureau of Labor Statistics, the commercial factions of the working class receive a lower weekly wage than the industrial factions (Braverman, op. cit., p. 297). If only the yearly wage of male employees are considered, clerks and sales workers fare slightly better than operatives and laborers (Szymanski, op. cit., p. 116, Table 11). However, two-thirds of those employed as clerks or retail sales persons are women, who have been traditionally lower paid (ibid., p. 110, Table 6).

A majority of the 12.9 percent of the population identified as professional and technical employees will be found in positions which have working-class characteristics (only an additional 1.5 percent of professionals and technical workers are independently employed). These employees generally are involved in the direction of the enterprise as a whole. Given the twofold nature of capitalist production, production of use values and exchange values, the process of direction is also twofold. The coordination and unity of the process essential for the creation of use values is a function of the collective worker. The additional control and surveillance of the process necessary to realize surplus value for the corporation, is a function of capital. See Carchedi "On the Economic Identification of the New Middle Class," *Economy and Society*, vol. 4 (1975), 43. Both these functions are found in varying degrees, in various professional, technical, managerial, and supervisory roles, with the lower echelons (even at the level of management, corporate organization is heirarchical) performing more of the functions of the collective worker, and the upper echelons performing exclusively the function of capital (Carchedi, op. cit., p. 33).

Furthermore, many of the tasks performed by professional and technical workers are susceptible to the process of fragmentation, separation of more-skilled and less-skilled occupations, and routinization. The existence of research staffs and paraprofessional workers is one manifestation of this. The necessity of these positions for the collective worker, and the fragmentation and routinization of the tasks they perform, gives the lower echelons of professional and technical workers, and even some managers and supervisors, characteristics of working-class roles. In addition, many of these positions become

> part of a mass labor market that assumes the characteristics of all labor markets, including the necessary existence of a reserve army of unemployed exercising a downward pressure on pay levels (Braverman, op. cit., p. 408).

This is not to suggest that professional and technical workers form a "new working class," in the sense of "Their gloss, presumed advancement, and superiority to the old" (Braverman, op. cit., p. 26). Workers in these categories amount to only a small fraction of the work force and fill positions which take their characteristics from the functions of both capital and the collective worker. If the working-class characteristics tend to impress themselves at the lower echelons, it is unlikely that these positions will emerge as a leading faction of the working class.

[11] Poulantzas "On Social Class," *New Left Review*, no. 78 (March–April 1973), 38.

[12] Aronowitz, *False Promises* (New York: McGraw-Hill Book Co., 1973), p. 413.

Thompson conceives of working class culture as the basic collective idea and the corresponding institutions, manners, habits of thoughts, and intentions which arose in response to certain common experiences (Thompson, op. cit., p. 423).

[13] Boggs, *Gramsci's Marxism* (London: Pluto Press, 1976), p. 36; and Gramsci, *Prison Notebooks*, trans. and ed. Quinton Hoare and Geoffrey Nowell Smith (New York: International Publishers, 1971), p. 12.

Though Marx speaks of civil society in "On the Jewish Question" and *The German Ideology*, he uses it in the same way as his liberal predecessors and includes within it economic relations and activity. Civil society includes all those social arrangements the individual participates in as a "private person". (These references may be found in Tucker (ed.), op. cit., pp. 32–33, 127.)

For Gramsci, however, civil society is a realm distinct (but not separate) from both political and economic activity. With the latter as the material base of society, politics (the state) and civil society form the two super-structural levels. Though both are imbued with the class relationships which structure economic life and in turn function to legitimize and maintain those relationships, the activities which are carried out in these realms have lives of their own and do not mechanistically follow development in material life. Thus the political and civil hegemony of capital must be dealt with directly if class domination is to be overcome.

[14] Aronowitz, op. cit., p. 60.

[15] Braverman, op. cit., p. 277.

A wealth of sociological literature exists on mass culture and mass societies. A good summary and bibliography can be found in the editor's introduction to Eric and Mary Josephson (eds.), *Man Alone: Alienation in Modern Society* (New York: Dell Publishing Co., 1962).

However, much of the literature cited in this collection fails to recognize the structural relationships among workers and between workers and capitalists. Mass society is characterized not by an alteration of these relationships but by their obfuscation. This obfuscation is achieved not only by the transmission of dominant ideologies through the mass media, but through daily practice as well. In the chapter on the fetishism of commodities in *Capital* (pp. 67–84), Marx described how commodity relations reify the essentially human relationships of production and the market. The increasing pervasiveness of this process with the development of capitalism and its effects on working-class consciousness, is described in Lukacs, *History and Class Consciousness*, trans. Rodney Livingstone (Cambridge: MIT Press, 1971), pp. 83–209.

The interaction between, on the one hand, the atomization of workers and the cultural devaluation of work with development of Taylorism, and on the other, the increasing pervasiveness of a national consumer culture, is described in Alt, "Beyond Class, the Decline of Industrial Labor and Leisure," *Telos*, no. 28 (Summer 1970), 55–80. The conclusion of this article is that monopoly capitalism shifts the source of social relations, culture and ideology from the class structure of work to a mass culture of consumerism.

[16] Braverman, op. cit., p. 276. For a history of the devaluation of the family as an institution of production of goods and services, and its reduction to a unit of a mass-consumer culture (as well as a buffer between the members and an increasingly atomized mass society), see Ryan, *Womanhood in America* (New York: New Viewpoints, 1975). (Ryan concentrates on the devaluation of the woman's role as a result of these changes.) In Parts II and III, I will describe the role of the family as a transmitter

of social ideologies in connection with the psychological theories of Freud and Reich.

Aronowitz considers the hegemonic function performed by mass culture. He discusses several films and TV shows as instances of the transmission of dominant ideologies and conservative images of working-class life. He also proposes that some of the music associated with the 1960s counterculture arose from the protest against the hegemony of mass culture (see Aronowitz, op. cit., Chapter 2). However, he believes that in general the "New Workers," even while more militant than their older counterparts, are bound to the offerings of mass culture in their leisure activity (Chapter 8).

For a consideration of types of American popular music which makes a serious effort to convey working-class experience, see Lipshitz, "Working People's Music," *Cultural Correspondence*, no. 2 (1976), 15–33. Lipshitz concentrates on the class awareness of country and western music but also discusses blues and some rock music.

[17] Aronowitz, op. cit., p. 96. For a consideration of the role of advertising in creating new needs as an essential function of mass production and marketing, see Ewen, *Captains of Consciousness: Advertising and the Social Roots of the Consumer Culture* (New York: McGraw-Hill Book Co., 1977). From a similar viewpoint, Tod Gitlins argues that on TV, advertisements are the message, the programs are the package. Gitlin, "16 Notes on Television and the Movement," *Tri-Quarterly*, no. 23/24 (Winter–Spring 1972).

[18] Boggs, op. cit., p. 60.

[19] See Thompson, op. cit., whose work goes to great lengths to demonstrate this; and Hammond and Hammond, *The Rise of Modern Industry*, 3rd ed. (London: Methuen & Co., 1947), pp. 104–109, 206–207.

[20] The creation of this early radical artisan culture is the subject of Thompson, op. cit., pp. 711, 732, and Chapter 16 Section 1. The importance of radical-democratic politics in the formation of the English working class is stressed also in Hobsbaum "Labor History and Ideology," *Journal of Social History*, vol. 7 (Summer 1974), 374; and Abendroth, *A Short History of the European Working class* (New York: Monthly Review Press, 1972), p. 14.

Others have recognized the participation of the working class in these struggles, but have denied that a specifically working-class culture was developed through this participation. Malcolm I. Thomas argued that the participation of workers in these struggles was an indication of their selfish, sectional, self-interest, not collective concern. *The Town Laborer in the Industrial Revolution* (London: B. T. Batsford Ltd., 1974), p. 186–193. But Thomas himself described the development of an unstratified, undivided working class in the industrial towns as early as 1819 (pp. 60–61). Thomas also failed to appreciate the full range of sociocultural activity described by Thompson. A similar position is taken by R. Currie and R. M. Hartwell in a review of *The Making of the English Working Class in the Economic History Review*, 2d series, vol. 18 (December 1965), pp. 663–643. These authors support their position not through an examination of activity involved, but by attempting to disprove the assumption of a decrease in the quality of life of the working class during the industrial revolution. They claim that Thompson's argument depends on the assumption of a decrease. But since Thompson describes radical working class activity which preceded the industrial revolution, the assumption hardly seems as central to his argument as Currie and Hartwell claim.

However, those who claim that a radical opposition was being expressed by working-class activity at that time, do tend to hold a pessimistic interpretation of the industrial revolution; those who claim that assimilation desires and self-interest were being expressed, an optimistic interpretation. The issue between the optimists and the pessimists is whether the standard of living of workers, as measured by quantitative and qualitative indicators, increased or decreased during this period. For a summary of the debate, see E. J. Hobsbaum and R. M. Hartwell, "The Standard of Living During the Industrial Revolution: Discussion," *Economic History Review*, 2d series, vol. 6 (1963/64), 119–143.

[21] Thompson, op. cit., pp. 418–424, 807–832. Included in these movements are the chartists and owenites. Thompson describes the struggle which occurred between workers and middle-class reformers for the control of progressive social movements. He also notes that a significant part of the early union movement was socialistic, demanding not just higher wages but abolition of the wage system.

[22] Ibid., p. 194.

[23] Aronowitz, op. cit., p. 51; and Abendroth, op. cit., p. 58. Andre Gorz made a similar observation in relation to trade unionism in "The Working Class and Revolution in the West," *Liberation*, vol. 16 (September 1971), p. 32.

3

THE DEVELOPMENT OF CLASS CONSCIOUSNESS

Marx observed many trends in the development of capitalism through the middle of the nineteenth century and predicted what might happen in the future. Among other predictions, he expected that there would be an increasing concentration of capital, recurring economic crises, the growth and recurrent dislocation of the proletariat, and an increasing global dominance of commodity production and exchange. At this time these projections seem essentially to have been correct. Yet Marx's forecast of the development within industrially advanced societies of a human agent of social transformation has still to occur.

In classical Marxian theory, the human agent, which was to bring about social change, was to be a class which had a vested interest in the historical supersession of capitalist social relationships, but also which was located strategically within the structure of relationships so as to be able to transform them. This class, the industrial proletariat, was to become the human agent of historical change as soon as it became conscious of itself as an exploited class and conscious of its collective ability to transform the empirical conditions which constitute it as a class. I stress that workers must become conscious of their exploitation and collective potential before they can begin to improve the conditions of their alienated human existence. That is, workers must become class conscious if working class activity is to move beyond the immediacy of capitalism.

In this chapter, I examine the relationship between working-class consciousness and working-class life. In the first section, I argue that class consciousness is not something which comes about spontaneously or automatically. Workers may develop various kinds of awareness of their social position. However, an organized leadership is necessary to develop an understanding of class relationships throughout the working class. In the second section I compare two strategies for developing working-class consciousness: that of the Marxist-Leninists and that of Reich's psychoanalytically oriented Sex-Pol movement.

CONSCIOUSNESS AND CLASS

Marx claimed that the social conditions of working-class life would lead the worker to develop the consciousness of his exploited position and historical potential. Marx also described conflicting social influences that could interfere with the development of this consciousness. He examined how ruling-class interests were manifested in the dominant ideologies of a society and how these ideologies obscured the class structure of society, thereby impeding the development of working-class consciousness.[1]

It was perhaps Georg Lukacs more than any other theoretician who developed the epistomological implications of Marx's theory of ideology. Lukacs claimed that the socially dominant ideologies accept as inevitable the class structure of the moment before attempting to explain the social problems that emerged. This acceptance of the class structure is detectable in the conceptual structure of ideologies as the reification of social relationships and the fragmentation of the social structure as a whole. That is, ideologies disguise the social relationships at the base of society as relationships between things. Within ideologies observable trends and processes are abstracted from the structure of social relationships which is their precondition. These trends and processes are understood instead as natural laws of social development. The major social problem as formulated within this perspective is not the restructuring of social relationships, but the more efficient administration of the existing trends and processes.[2] Clearly, this is a perspective which is biased toward the interests of the ruling class.

The empirical consciousness of the working class suffers from this reification and abstraction. This is true of both workers' immediate responses to particular issues and their more comprehensive political, economic, and social attitudes and orientation. There are contemporary empirical findings which can be interpreted to support Lukacs' formulation. For example most Americans may favor the policies of low-cost health care, full employment, and the establishment and maintenance of safety standards in the workplace. But they do not consider their potential to organize and implement these policies. Instead they wait for or urge the government to pursue these policies, perhaps working within pressure groups or supporting sympathetic candidates. Yet many of these same people say that government has gone too far in regulating and interfering with private enterprise.[3] Presumably this indicates that, whereas large majorities favor government action on the above-mentioned issues, they would like the government to act within the structure of the commodity market, without transforming its essential features. Accordingly, class antagonisms are not broached as such. Rather, the issue is whether or not the government should offer immediate relief from the most blatant and harmful consequences of the fact that people are organized into social classes. In other words, the contradiction between working class and ruling-class interests is ideologically obfuscated and working class activity is accommodated to the existing social structure seeking, at most, reforms which can be achieved without altering the inherently exploitative relationship between classes.

To counteract the effects of ideology, the exploited class should be encouraged to understand the conditions of the existing social structure in terms of their own interests. This could lead them to recognize the possibility that they could transform the class structure through their own actions. It is this understanding that Lukacs referred to with the phrase "imputed class consciousness." The development of class relationships within capitalism makes the emergence of this consciousness possible. The position of the working class within capitalism makes it the imputed bearer of this consciousness.

To Marx this imputed consciousness was not merely something which was to emerge with the further development of the material forces of production. Rather, it was something he perceived as existing within the workers' movement of his time. In the period of industrial capitalism during which Marx wrote, the contrast between the life of the capitalist and of the worker was more obvious and immediate than it has since become. Marx thus perceived the consciousness of the workers to be only quantitatively different from the consciousness of the Communist intellectuals, who were able to understand theoretically the proletarian movement and to articulate its goals and courses. Although the Communists are "practically the most advanced and resolute section of the working class parties of every country, that section which pushes forward all others," the intellectuals and workers could communicate and work together because of their common revolutionary perspective.[4]

But it seems that Marx, caught up in the political fervor of his times, overestimated the proletariat's existence as a revolutionary force. In fact, it is probably fair to say that Marx read into the struggle of the working class against capitalist exploitation and hegemony his consciousness of the proletariat's historical potential. The working class was forming itself into a class, but it was hardly constituting itself as a revolutionary force. Workers would develop into a class because they became aware of the fact that there was arising a conflict between classes. However, the workers would not resort to revolution unless a revolutionary class consciousness evolved. Anthony Giddens distinguishes conflict consciousness from revolutionary consciousness as follows:

> Class conflict consciousness: where perception of class unity is linked to a recognition of opposition of interests with another class or classes.

> Revolutionary class consciousness: a recognition of the possibility of an overall reorganization in the institutional mediations of power, and a belief that such a reorganization can be brought about through class action.[5]

People become aware of the fact that there is a conflict between classes when members of the exploited class engage in diverse and organizationally unrelated struggles. Giddens' terminology of "an opposition of interests with another class or classes" is applicable because, within these struggles, the fundamental relationships of labor and capital are fragmented into relationships between factions of labor and factions of capital. Yet these struggles are essential for forming the class into a class. As Marx claimed, the diverse economic and political movements of the working class are the means of developing the organization necessary for the emergence of the working class as the hegemonic political force.[6]

Revolutionary consciousness is the consciousness of a class which has developed a community of interest and whose factions are organizationally related for an "overall reorganization in the institutional mediations of power." This consciousness may develop from the diverse struggles of workers, but the process of its development is not a mechanical or automatic one. It develops only through class activity within and in reaction to the conditions of its existence. The class has a revolutionary potential, but this does not mean that it must turn into a revolutionary force. In other words, workers may or may not develop an awareness of their social position, which may or may not lead them to act in conformity with their class interests. The effects of social conditions on consciousness may be to strengthen bourgeois hegemony. Marxists have long attempted to explain this phenomenon. As early as 1858 Engels noted that the English working class was becoming "more and more bourgeois." Almost a quarter century later, while echoing the same idea, he attributed this to the fact that "workers gaily share the feast of England's monopoly of the world market and the colonies".[7]

Lenin, of course, was to develop this idea in his famous work on imperialism.[8] Lenin believed that the imperialist policies of the advanced nations tempered the contradictions between labor and capital by giving the capitalist a source of surplus value in addition to the indigenous proletariat. This resulted in a deradicalization of the proletariat in the imperialist nations. Thus the proletarian revolution in the industrial countries would have to be preceded by antiimperialist revolutions in the colonial nations. Capitalism would break down initially in its least developed, not most advanced, sectors. There is no doubt much truth in this thesis. The antiimperialist struggle has been waged more militantly by the workers and peasants of the colonial and exploited nations than the class struggle has been fought by the proletariat of the industrial nations. But the antiimperialist struggle is a nationalist as well as a class struggle.

The thesis that workers in the industrially advanced societies have been co-opted by better living conditions is, at best, only a partial explanation of the variations in class consciousness among these workers. For example, the history of the American working class shows that, although workers may have won higher wages, militancy has not declined. On the one hand, the working class is not especially militant in times of economic crisis. Indeed workers during a depression become more conservative in their activity for fear of losing their jobs.[9] On the other, there is no obvious correlation between the level of skills and wages and the militancy of workers.[10] As Lukacs observed,

> The experiences of the revolutionary struggles have failed to yield any conclusive evidence that the proletariat's revolutionary fervor and will to fight corresponds in any straightforward manner to the economic level of its various parts. There are great deviations from any such simple, uniform parallels and there are great divergencies in the maturity of class consciousness attained by workers within economically similar strata.[11]

The working class is mostly involved in an economic struggle. Furthermore, the class does not act collectively, only factions do. The activities of the factions reflect not only their exploitation but the strength of their organizations and security of their employment. The organization of the working class expresses the fragmentation of workers and institutionalizes it.[12] Hence we still are confronted with the problem of transforming a consciousness that the workers have a conflict with capitalism into a consciousness that they are a class. They must unite the struggles of diverse factions into one struggle for socialism. Perhaps Lenin was correct in arguing that the working class could not unite on its own but only as the result of an external stimulus, the political party. But this argument raises the problem of the relationship of the party to the class and the role of each in historical transformation. For the Leninist conception of the party to fit in with the movement of the proletarian revolution, it must provide a means whereby the more conscious workers can raise the consciousness of their comrades while rataining the class as a whole as the historical subject. The danger to be avoided is the substitution of the party (or of a bureaucratic state apparatus) for the class. The problem is whether a political party can perform a leadership role and mediate the development of working-class consciousness without becoming an alienated elite with little organic relationship to the activity of the working class.

The leadership function is essential for the development of the class as an articulate social force. This is not to suggest that workers cannot act spontaneously or need to have discipline imposed on their actions. Political crowds and movements can and have acted in a spontaneous and well disciplined manner. They may even formulate a political program. Yet a capable and responsive leadership also seems to be necessary if the movement is to be effective.[13] The task of the political party is to develop a responsive leadership, while developing class consciousness within the class rather than within an elite. In the next section, I compare different strategies for developing the consciousness of workers.

THE SEX-POL AND VANGUARD STRATEGIES FOR THE DEVELOPMENT OF CLASS CONSCIOUSNESS

The role of the party as the leader in achieving class awareness is basic to the Marxian program. The *Communist Manifesto* stressed the need for the party to coordinate the diverse movements of the working class on a national and international level, and to propel these toward a united struggle against capital.[14] Nevertheless the relationship between the party and the class, and the way in which the party's leadership is to be exercised, has been a major source of division within the Marxian socialist movement. Orthodox Marxist-Leninists have understood the party as a self-conscious agent of the revolutionary proletariat's struggle. According to the orthodoxy, a segment of the working class must organize itself independently from the majority of workers to lead the struggle against capitalism. Historically this orthodoxy has dominated the organized Marxist movement, although there have been, in fact, many challenges to it. Here I will single out one which highlighted the need for a political psychology in Marxian theory and practice, the German National Association for Proletarian Sexual Politics or Sex-Pol movement. Led by Reich, this movement of workers and intellectuals in Weimar Germany accepted the leadership of the party while attempting to develop a new strategy for the development of working-class consciousness. It was concerned with locating the sources of class consciousness in the life experience of workers, rather than in a scientific theory of leadership. If these sources were not apparent as yet, Reich suggested that it was because Marxists have looked for them with too circumscribed a perspective.

In this chapter, I will compare the Leninist and Sex-Pol programs for the development of class consciousness. The Leninist strategy focuses its activity against property and the state. As the enforcer of property law, the state asserts the interests of the class of owners over the class of workers. An elite group of workers and intellectuals constitute themselves as the vanguard of the workers and struggles for control of the state in order to use it to transform the relationships it currently upholds. The Sex-Pol strategy is to organize the struggles of civil society under the auspices of the working-class party. The comparison that follows is concerned with making explicit the different conceptions of class consciousness and strategies for political activity that are expressed in these two programs.

THE MARXIST-LENINIST PARTY

The Marxist-Leninist party is based on the belief that capitalism can be transformed only by a self-conscious working-class movement, but that left to their own devices most workers will not develop the consciousness necessary for such a movement. Lenin noted that the consciousness directly emanating from economic and political struggles is a trade-union (or conflict) consciousness. Development of this consciousness could be brought about only as the result of a stimulus developed outside of the mundane struggles of the working class.[15]

Class-conscious workers and intellectuals would have to organize themselves as a highly disciplined and centralized political party to become the external stimulus which would bring revolutionary consciousness to the workers. Whereas the activity of the working class is circumscribed by capitalist hegemony and the immediacy of the struggle for reform of work conditions in the capitalist labor process, the party institutionalizes the struggle against the structure of capitalist social relationships and all its manifestations. It meets the ideological hegemony of the ruling class with detailed examinations of the structure and consequences of class relationships.

The party is crucial in the historical process because its members collectively constitute the only revolutionary influence on society. As such, a party is the vanguard of the proletariat, the only part of the class which is aware of itself as a class and as a historically significant force. The party counters the ideological backwardness of the workers with its own advanced theory. In other words, "The party is assigned the sublime role of bearer of the class consciousness of the proletariat and the conscience of its historical vocation."[16] According to this view, it is not the position of the proletariat which enables it to become conscious of its historical potential but the existence of the proletariat which enables the intellectuals to develop a knowledge of the movement of history. The divorce of the class and its imputed consciousness is completed in the following passage from Lenin:

> . . . the theoretical doctrine of social democracy arose quite independently of the spontaneous growth of the labor movement; it arose as a natural and inevitable outcome of the *development of ideas* among the revolutionary socialist intelligentsia [emphasis added].[17]

From the quote given above it is a short step to see the revolutionary intelligentsia as not just the embodiment of class consciousness but as the revolutionary force itself. This is a step that Lenin, his claim that the fundamental task of the party is to educate the workers notwithstanding, seemed unable to avoid. His party served to separate the professional revolutionaries from the working class.

Lenin's organizational theory was a response to the historically conditioned underdevelopment of the Russian working class and the despotic conditions that prevailed there. But the putative success of Lenin's movement and its world historical significance led many Marxists to universalize this theory and to take it as a model for socialist movements in industrially advanced societies. This development has made the problems with this position particularly apparent.

The attempt to establish a vanguard party within the conditions of advanced capitalism is, in effect, a rearguard action. Marx, in his own time, already had warned against a similar tendency:

> The emancipation of the working class must be the work of the working class itself. We cannot, therefore, cooperate with people who openly state that the workers are too uneducated to emancipate themselves and must first be freed from above by philanthropic big bourgeoisie and petty bourgeoisie.[18]

There is no reason to assume that revolutionary intellectuals could emancipate the working class more effectively than philanthropists might. It was the function itself that Marx rejected. The action of a revolutionary intelligentsia cannot be substituted for the action of the working class. Yet it seems as if Lenin was correct in maintaining that class consciousness does not, and will not, develop spontaneously, or automatically from the life experiences of workers. How then, is this consciousness to be brought about? This is the question socialists must answer if their vision is to become a historical reality.

Reich claimed that if the party leaders examined the association between capitalist social relationships and the personal problems of workers, the antecedents of class consciousness might be found in the workers' own understanding of their problems. Reich convinced the German Communist party (KPD) to organize a section for the implementation of his program to provide for the sexual and psychological problems of working-class men and women. The program included the establishment of centers to which workers could come for advice on sexual hygiene, birth control, and abortion, and for lectures and discussions on the relationship between psychological problems, sexual repression, and class hegemony. Reich previously had organized similar centers in Vienna. Through the KPD, the Sex-Pol activists carried their program to the workers and Communist youth groups, and seemed to have received a favorable response.[19]

THE SEX-POL MOVEMENT: POLITICIZING EVERYDAY LIFE

Reich believed that a socialist party's efforts to develop class consciousness would be in vain if the leadership of the party did not recognize class consciousness when it emerged. This proposition is not as cynical as it may sound. If the leadership of a socialist party expects the workers' understanding of social relationships to be the same as their own, they will be deeply disappointed. More importantly, such a leadership will be unable to recognize and develop those attitudes and ideas of workers which are of a potentially revolutionary nature, let alone to recognize and develop their own attitudes on the bases of the workers' insights. Those who have developed a critical understanding of the world must appreciate the distinction between their own theoretical under-standing and proletarian class consciousness. This means that socialists must stop viewing class consciousness as something which is either present or absent and realize that in every worker, "It is present as a number of concrete elements which in themselves do not yet constitute class consciousness (i.e., simple hunger) but which in conjunction with one another, could become class consciousness."[20]

As Reich explains, hunger is not yet class consciousness; a brick is not a house. But if hunger leads a person to recognize and to resist the conditions which made him hungry, then class conscious-ness is in the process of developing. Trade-union consciousness is not yet revolutionary consciousness but the former does contain the seeds of the latter. However, these seeds must be cultivated carefully, if they are to bear fruit.

Reich saw the revolutionary leadership not as the agent of working-class consciousness but as the practical mediation by which the antecedents of class consciousness that existed within the working class were cultivated. He thus avoided the pitfalls of a theory in which class consciousness is seen as developing sponta-neously, while rooting consciousness in the experiences of workers. The practical implications of this are manifested in the new but carefully circumscribed role Reich assigned to the socialist leaders:

> The task of leadership is not "to carry the Communist program to the masses" or "to make the masses into class conscious militants"; its most important task, besides studying the objective historical process, consists in developing the revolutionary instincts which are already there.[21]

To do this the socialist leaders would have to understand the workers' way of life and way of viewing the world better than they now do. They would have to realize that their own worldview is a highly specialized one, and one that is not easily accessible to people other than those whose major concern is political or social theory. Although a revolutionary leader must know what surplus value is, Reich thought it sufficient for the worker to know "how much profit for the entrepeneur he is producing with his labor. That is class consciousness."[22]

Thus, although a detailed knowledge of the process of capitalist production is indispensable to the socialist movement as a whole, it is not necessary for each worker to possess this knowledge. A revolutionary consciousness begins to emerge when the worker believes that the means of production belong not to the holders of deeds, but to those who produce. However, this revolutionary disposition must be channelled properly. Reich was impressed with the fact that some anticapitalist workers stood alongside sections of the middle class and leaders of German industry as Hitler's staunchest supporters. For anticapitalist feelings to be transformed into class consciousness they would have to be developed into an awareness of the responsibilities involved in being one's own master, and a preparedness for that added responsibility. "The actual takeover of power in factories must be preceded by concrete preparation for the takeover in the mind. . . . This and only this deserves to be called 'arousing class consciousness.'"[23]

The idea of people assuming responsibility for their own lives marks Reich's contribution to the concept of class consciousness. It must be emphasized that this is a responsibility which is to be exercised in every sphere of life. The authority of civil society or the state is no more legitimate than the authority of property. Humans must consciously organize their lives in accordance with their desires and instincts, unfettered by the arbitrary restraints of tradition. Tradition finds virtue in discipline and self-denial; against these, Reich argued, the revolution "must set the principle of happiness and abundance on earth."[24] Reich was fully convinced that a free society could be based only on the satisfaction of humans' instinctual needs. Socialism could be based only on a faith in people to self-regulate their activity.

Reich's analysis provided an opportunity for socialists to expand their criticism of bourgeois society and deal with its pervasive repressiveness. Economic problems are not the only ones which trouble people, nor is economic dependency the only or even most significant conservative force in people's lives. Repression of erotic desires, family ties, the very structure of the family and identification with other symbols of authority all serve as buttresses of the status quo. The problems these buttresses produce are thus very political ones and must be treated as such. They are political in that, as Reich went to great lengths to demonstrate, they are grounded in the social forces which characterize the production of commodities in market societies. They also are political insofar as they determine the individual's acceptance of certain political ideologies and his rejection of others. The antecedents of class consciousness could be found in the way individuals dealt with these problems.

Reich's expanded critique of capitalist culture builds from many psychoanalytic formulations and models. Freud elaborated a theory of the fragmentation of the personality and the introjection of social authority. Reich interpreted these psychological processes as consequences of social processes. The fragmentation of the personality is conditioned by the fragmentation of experiences within the alienated social roles formed by capitalist relationships. The authority introjected is the authority expressed within those social relationships. From this perspective Reich was able to examine how deeply class relationships exert themselves in everyday life. Engels earlier had examined the relationship between class structure and the institution which dominates personal life, the family.[25] Reich added to this an analysis of the role of the family in repressing sexual needs and the role of sexual repression in adapting individuals to the existing society.

Unfortunately, socialist leaders have tended to be leery of psychological theories which, they have felt, invert the relationship between being and consciousness. Reich went to great lengths to demonstrate that this was not necessarily so. In fact, he claimed that by failing to recognize the psychological stimulants of human behavior, socialists were acting like mechanistic materialists who ". . . left the praxis of the subjective factor to the idealist."[26] Reich maintained that this praxis could not be understood by sociology alone. Sociology could explain only rational human consciousness and activity, that is, those compatible with the living conditions of those who hold them. Therefore, although sociology can explain the existence of class consciousness, it cannot explain its absence. To understand why most individuals irrationally cling to beliefs which facilitate their own exploitation and repression we must know more about what goes on within people, the processes by which beliefs are formed and held. "The point is," Reich suggested, "that every social order produces in the masses of its members that structure which it needs to achieve its aims."[27]

Marx himself was fully aware that the intrusion of society into the innermost regions of the individual has been one of the most powerful buttresses of the status quo. This was made obvious to him by the Protestant Reformation. Luther, Marx claimed, "shattered the faith in authority by restoring the authority of faith. . . . He liberated the body from its chains because he fettered the heart with chains." Henceforth, man needed to struggle not against the "priest outside himself" but against "his own internal priest, against his own priestly nature."[28]

However, without a depth psychology, Marx lacked a means for understanding the concept of the "internal priest." Consequently, a very basic problem in the materialist conception of history has been to explain the acceptance by a majority of people of ideas which conflict with their class interests. This was the basic problem of Reich's political psychology. "It is a problem, in short, of comprehending the nature of the psychological structure of the masses and its relation to the economic basis from which it derives."[29]

The questions raised by Reich and the Sex-Pol movement are fundamental to an understanding of working-class consciousness. His was the most serious attempt by any socialists to explain the psychological mediations in the process of the social conditioning of consciousness. He developed a psychological theory of ideology to complement the sociological one. He did this not by eclectically drawing from two traditions but by making explicit the unconscious sources of ideological thought and the social factors which condition unconsciousness. As we shall see in Part II, social determinants already were incorporated into Freudian psychoanalysis, but only abstractly and ideologically. In Part III, we return to Reich's political psychology and consider his synthesis of Marx and Freud in greater detail.

SUMMARY AND CONCLUSIONS

Marxists have imputed to the working class the consciousness necessary to transform society. This consciousness should develop from the social position of workers and out of their struggles against capitalist exploitation and hegemony. Yet when these struggles take the form of struggles between factions of workers and factions of capital, the struggles of particularly oppressed or exploited groups, or even more comprehensive movements for economic, political, or social reform, what may develop is a conflict rather than class consciousness.

The emergence of the working class as the hegemonic social force is contingent upon its comprehending that a qualitative improvement in the conditions of working-class life requires a fundamental transformation of social relationships. Yet the lives of most workers are bound by the immediacy of capitalist society. Thus, an organized leadership must act as a mediation and catalyst in the development of class consciousness. Although socialists have formed political parties to institutionalize this imputed consciousness, a progressive social movement must be based on the participation of large numbers of workers. A party cannot act as the agent of the class, for, as such, it becomes another reified institution abstracted from the structure of social relationships which takes on an ideological significance over and above the activity of workers. Class consciousness must be developed in a class rather than in an elite.

An organized leadership can act effectively to develop class consciousness only if it understands working-class life and recognizes the antecedents of class consciousness in the workers' own understanding of their conditions. Yet workers' awareness may be an ideological lack of awareness of the effects of social relationships on their lives. Socially conditioned psychological processes further obscure their awareness.

Reich attempted to utilize psychoanalytic theory to provide an explanation of those psychological factors and their connection with social relationships and activity. In Part II of this study I examine Freud's psychology of consciousness and unconsciousness and evaluate Freud's own attempt to apply psychoanalytic theory in the examination of social problems. This will set the stage for a more detailed consideration of Reich's theories and politics in Part III.

NOTES

[1] Robert C. Tucker (ed.), *The Marx-Engels Reader* (New York: W.W. Norton & Co., 1972), especially pp. 127–157 (The German Ideology), and *Economic and Philosophic Manuscripts*, trans. T. B. Bottomore, contained in Erich Fromm, *Marx's Concept of Man* (New York: Frederick Unger Publishing Co., 1961), especially pp. 119–123, 132, 136–137, 140–150.

[2] Lukacs, *History and Class Consciousness*, trans. Rodney Livingstone (Cambridge: MIT Press, 1971), pp. 83–209; Mannheim, *Ideology and Utopia*, trans. Louis Wirth and Edward Shils (New York: Harcourt, Brace & World, 1936), pp. 112–113, 118–123.

[3] Clymer, "Conservatives Share Liberal Views," *New York Times*, January 22, 1978, Sec 1, p. 1.

[4] Tucker (ed.), op. cit., p. 346 (Manifesto of the Communist Party).

[5] Giddens, *The Class Structure of the Advanced Societies* (New York: Harper and Row, 1973), pp. 112–113. Although I find this distinction by Giddens useful, his theory of class and class structures, as well as the conditions required for the emergence of class consciousness, are different from that being developed here. Although we both are interested in the lack of militancy of the working class, Giddens' explanation for this is fundamentally different from my own. Giddens does not explain the situation as a consequence of the strength and effectiveness of bourgeois hegemony but attributes it to a fundamental change in class structure. Gidden develops a neo-Weberian theory of class which incorporates "market capacities" but fails to consider the fragmentation of work and social roles, and the alienation of the function of control, as discussed in the previous chapter. Although the worker as a producer has little say in the process of production and, as a consumer, is manipulated to participate in the market in ways which most effectively actualize surplus value, Giddens fails to deal with the structure of social relations which gives continuity to the process of capitalist production. Rather, he sees the more-visible changes in lifestyle as indicative of change in social structure. For him, "pure capitalism" exists in early industrial and post-feudal societies, where traditional institutions and relationships are being undermined. Contemporary societies are "neo-capitalist" (p. 164).

[6] See the citation from Marx, "Letter to F. Bolte, November 3, 1871", Montgomary, *Beyond Equality*, (New York: Alfred A Knopf, 1967), p. 168.

[7] Lenin cites Engles in Christman (ed.), *Essential Works*, (New York: Barton Books, 1966), p. 252 (Imperialism: The Highest Stage of Capitalism).

[8] Ibid., pp. 177–270.

[9] Aronowitz, *False Promises* (New York: McGraw-Hill Book Co., 1973), pp. 53–54, 236; and Dubofsky, *Industrialism and the American Workers, 1865–1920* (Carlington Heights, Illinois: AHM Publishing Corp., 1975), pp. 53–54. Dubofsky also describes how the militancy of workers and their organizations increased as a result of an increased demand for labor during World War I (Dubofsky, op. cit., pp. 111–112). Empirical evidence supporting this position can be found in David Montgomary "The 'New Unionism' and the Transformation of Workers' Consciousness in America," *Journal of Social History*, vol. 7 (summer 1974), 512–513.

[10] Aronowitz, op. cit., p. 140; and Dubofsky, op. cit., p. 133. Frances Fox Pivan and Richard A. Cloward seem to have a different point of view in *Regulating the Poor: The Functions of Public Welfare* (New York: Random House, 1971). These authors suggest that workers militantly react to economic crises and that those groups most affected by crises react the most militantly. However, they also describe how the movement for public-works projects and welfare programs during the depression became fragmented from the workers' movement and subsequently lost its effectiveness (pp. 106–114). Furthermore, they offer an interesting counter-example to the impoverishment thesis: the lack of militancy among poor Southern whites dislocated in the 1960s. In explaining this lack of militancy, they argue that the dislocation of a sector of workers is not a sufficient cause for their radicalization. Workers' militancy is developed through *precipitous* dislocation and the *concentration* of the dislocated in a new locality (pp. 212–214). By adding the variables of speed of dislocation and concentration of relocation, they seem to be suggesting that a community of the dislocated must be formed before the dislocated can constitute themselves as a militant social force.

[11] Lukacs, op. cit., p. 305.

[12] See ibid., p. 310.

[13] Examples of disciplined crowd activity can be found in Thompson, "Patrician Society, Plebian Culture," *Journal of Social History*, vol. 7 (Summer 1974), 402; and James, "Colonialism and the National Liberation in Africa: The Gold Coast Revolution" in Miller and Aya (eds.) *National Liberation: Revolution in the Third World* (New York: The Free Press, 1971), pp. 115–118, 131, 133–134, James argues that Michelet's description of the French Revolution as a revolution led by the masses is applicable to the national liberation movement in Ghana. The ability of the crowd to formulate a political program is described in Uldricks, "The 'Crowd' in the Russian Revolution: Towards a Reassessment of the Nature of Revolutionary Leadership," *Politics and Society*, vol. 4 (1973–1974), 412. (Uldricks also cites the activity of the French crowd as a precedent.)

However, both James and Uldricks stressed the role of leadership in organizing the movements. Uldricks emphasized the ability of the Bolsheviks to organize the wave of radicalism (Uldricks, op. cit., p. 412); James, the leadership of Nkrumah and the constituent assembly in implementing the policy of positive action (James, op. cit., pp. 117, 120, 127–132).

[14] Tucker (ed.), op. cit., p. 346.

[15] Christman (ed.), op. cit., pp. 74–75 (What is to Be Done).

[16] Lukacs, op. cit., p. 41.

[17] Christman (ed.), op. cit., p. 75 (What is to Be Done).

[18] Tucker (ed.), op. cit., p. 405 (Circular Letter to Bebel, et. al.).

[19] Cattier, *The Life and Work of Wilhelm Reich,* trans. Chislaine Boulanger (New York: Horizon Press, 1971), pp. 78–80, 88–89, 150–163; and Reich and Teschitz, *Selected Sex-Pol Essays: 1934–1937* (London: Socialist Reproduction, 1973), pp. 41–42, 48–51 (History of the Sex-Pol Movement).

[20] Reich *Sex-Pol Essays 1929–34,* ed. Lee Baxandall, trans. Anna Bostock, Tom Dubose, and Lee Baxandall (New York: Random House, 1972), p. 289 (What is Class Consciousness?).

[21] Ibid., p. 339.

[22] Ibid., p. 357.

[23] Ibid., p. 356.

[24] Ibid., p. 292.

[25] Engels, *The Origin of the Family, Private Property and the State,* ed. Eleanor Burke Leacock (New York: International Publishers, 1972), Chapter 2.

[26] Reich, *Sex-Pol,* p. 284 (Class Consciousness). For a summary of criticism of Reich and psychology by socialist leaders, see Reich and Teschitz (eds.), op. cit. pp. 72–106 (Toward a Critical Analysis of Communist Policy in Germany, and Objections to Mass Psychology). A major goal of Reich's work was to show how depth psychology can help us to develop a materialist explanation of ideology. See especially *Sex-Pol,* pp. 3–74 (Dialectical Materialism and Psycho-Analysis), and the chapter "Ideology As a Material Force," Reich, *The Mass Psychology of Fascism,* trans. Vincent R. Carfagno (New York: Farrar, Straus and Giroux, 1970).

[27] Reich, *Mass Psychology,* p. 23.

[28] Tucker (ed.), op. cit., p. 19 (Contribution to the Critique of Hegel's Philosophy of Right: Introduction).

[29] Reich, *Mass Psychology,* p. 14.

II

FREUD: CONSCIOUSNESS AND UNCONSCIOUSNESS

We are not reformers it is true; we are merely observers; but we cannot avoid observing with critical eyes, and have found it impossible to give our support to conventional sexual morality or to approve highly of the means by which society attempts to arrange the practical problems of sexuality in life. We can demonstrate with ease that what the world calls its code of morals demands more sacrifices than it is worth, and that its behavior is neither dictated by honesty nor instituted with wisdom.

Sigmund Freud, *A General Introduction to Psychoanalysis*

But how ungrateful, how short-sighted after all, to strive for the abolition of culture! What would then remain would be the state of nature and that is far harder to endure. . . . Indeed, it is the principal task of culture, its real raison d' etre, to defend us against nature.

Sigmund Freud, *The Future of An Illusion*

4

UNCONSCIOUSNESS AND THE PSYCHOLOGY OF PARTIAL CONSCIOUSNESS

IN this chapter and the next, I will establish the basis and the limits for the formulation of a psychoanalytically informed political psychology. I will begin by describing Freud's practice of reconstructing latent thoughts and processes through an analysis of the free associations of conscious thought. His methods and theories allowed him to pursue these latent thoughts to social experiences that "preformed and deformed the subject."[1] By directing attention toward the experiential antecedents of subjectivity, Freud developed a perspective on human actions and their motivations. Freud's perspective can be utilized to examine the association between human consciousness and social relationships.

Freud's major contribution to our understanding of consciousness was his exploration of the unconscious. He was extremely hopeful that his work on the unconscious would open new roads for those intellectual fields concerned with the development of human beings and their societies.[2] Yet to utilize Freud's theory of the unconscious, we must avoid what Paul Roazen has characterized as "the mistaken shortcut of focusing solely on Freud's social thought, exclusive of the concern of clinical psychoanalysis."[3] In this chapter, I will provide a somewhat technical summary of Freud's descriptions of unconscious processes and their relationship to conscious thought. In Chapter 5, I will make explicit the shortcomings of Freud's own attempts to generate a social theory from his exploration of the psyche.

In the first section of this chapter, I will discuss the evidence with which Freud supported his positing of the unconscious. But the existence of the unconscious is only the point of departure for psychoanalytic inquiry. In the second section, I will describe the metapsychological models that Freud formulated to reconstruct the processes and content of the unconscious and the relationship between unconsciousness and consciousness. As we shall see, these models cannot be understood as closed systems or a solipsistic theory of consciousness. In psychoanalytic theory, psychic processes are constituted by social relationships and conditions. In the third section I will consider the process of psychological maturation and the role of social influences in it. The chapter will conclude with an evaluation of the critical potential of psychoanalytic theory.

EVIDENCE OF THE UNCONSCIOUS:
ERRORS, DREAMS, SYMPTOMS

Freud claimed that his assumption of the existence of the unconscious is both legitimate and necessary. It is legitimate because it demands nothing more than the application to ourselves of the method by which we make intelligible the acts and utterances of others, by inferring the existence in them of a consciousness similar to our own. It is necessary because

> The data of consciousness are exceedingly defective; both in healthy and in sick persons mental acts are often in process which can be explained only by presupposing other acts, of which consciousness yields no evidence.[4]

Mental acts which cannot be explained without looking beyond consciousness include the verbal, written, perceptual, and recollective errors of every discourse; the dreams we all have but remember with varying consistency; and the obsessions of those inflicted with neurotic disorders. Of course these acts were known to be common occurrences long before Freud, but is was not until his development of psychoanalytic theory that they were constituted as evidence of an unconsciousness.

In a series of lectures introducing psychoanalysis to a group of medical students, Freud proceeded from an examination of those events which are most commonly experienced (errors) to those which provide the most basic support for psychoanalytic theory (dreams and symptoms).[5] In that work, Freud was concerned with demonstrating the continuity of the mental processes underlying these different types of events and to reveal, beneath all three, the working of the unconscious.

In terms of supporting the theory of the unconscious, this last step is the crucial one. For ". . . unlike the poets and story-tellers to whom he always gave credit for their recognition of the unconscious, Freud could not believe in the unconscious, he had to know it."[6] Yet the unconscious is something that we cannot come to know directly. We only can approach it through its manifestations. Freud's claim to knowledge of the unconscious was based on the ability of his theories to make conscious thoughts and behavior intelligible by explaining them as manifestations of unconscious mental activity.[7]

The psychoanalytic method attempts to make intelligible a seemingly arbitrary occurrence by examining why the particular occurrence happens when it does. To categorize an occurrence as a dream, obsession, or slip of the tongue, the common procedure of Freud's time, when these were being considered at all, is not to explain it. Freud argued that an understanding of errors, dreams, and symptoms required not only an examination of the content of the event, but the inference of certain pyschic processes.

For example, any error may be explained as a "functional disturbance." That is, we may claim that errors are made when an individual "(1) . . . is tired or unwell, (2) when he is excited or (3) when his attention is concentrated on something else." This does not make the content of the error intelligible by attributing to it a meaning or sense. When Freud speaks of the meaning of an error, he means ". . . nothing else but the intention which it serves and its place in a mental sequence." Thus we can ask why, for instance, did the President of the Austrian parliament once begin a session by saying, "Gentlemen, I declare a quorum present and herewith declare the session *closed*." Of course, the error may be attributed to functional disturbances and the exact wording considered insignificant. However, if we know that "He expects no good result from the session and would be glad to be able to disperse forthwith" we may be inclined to see the error as an attempt to avoid the meeting, even if the President never intended to make his desire known, or indeed, even if he was unwilling to admit it to himself.[8]

A willingness to consider the latter interpretation described above enables us to consider the phenomena of "slips of the tongue" in a new light. In the exaple given before, Freud sees not the formation of one but of two different intentions in the statement. In the president's remark, the unconscious desire to avoid the meeting had excluded the conscious intention to open it. In another type of error the exclusion is less complete, and one intended word or idea only succeeds in distorting or modifying another, resulting in seemingly senseless utterances.[9] In all cases one of the competing meanings is always manifest but the other(s) need not be. The latent meaning may be known only indirectly, through a theory of mental processes which occur without the awareness of the subject. Of course Freud has not yet "proved" the existence of these processes, but, on the basis of the evidence, Freud believed that the existence of the phenomena was probable enough to warrant the pursuit of an explanation in this direction.[10]

Although Freud began his introductory lectures with an examination of errors, his own work proceeded differently. His theory of the existence of an unconscious emerged not from the study of errors but from the clinical discovery that the symptoms of nervous patients had meaning. When the patients mentioned their dreams while speaking of their symptoms, Freud suspected that dreams too had meaning.[11] The theory of the unconscious was a tremendous advance in the treatment of these patients, and this was taken as its strongest support.

However, in attempting to construct a proof of his theory, Freud considered it wiser to begin with a demonstration of the effects of the unconscious in the acts of all people, not just those with psychological disorders. Whereas the study of neurosis enabled him to explore and describe more fully unconscious processes, the study of errors and dreams allowed him to claim that these processes were a prevalent component of human mental activity. Since the unconscious is manifest in conscious thoughts and actions, a general theory of consciousness (or a more specific theory of political consciousness) must be concerned with the unconscious as well. But the discussion of errors is hardly sufficient for the assumption of the prevalence of unconsciousness, nor does it reveal much about its operations. Therefore we must follow Freud into the realm of dreams and symptoms.

In studying dreams, Freud felt he was treading on thin ice. Their association with mystics and visionaries hardly made dreams a matter for serious scientific investigation. But Freud believed that one need not be a mystic to suggest that dreams had a meaning. He explained them as ". . . the mode of reaction of the mind to stimuli acting upon it during sleep."[12] Since sleep is a withdrawal from the outer world, and the avoidance of stimuli, the stimuli of dreams must arise from within the individual himself. These internal stimuli can be mental as well as physical. It is the former which psychoanalysis emphasizes.

From an examination of dreams (his own and those of his patients), Freud was led to the hypothesis that these internal stimuli are wishes so powerful that they must be expressed, but so potentially disturbing that they must be disguised and distorted if sleep is to continue. The distortion, as in the case of errors, is the compromise between two conflicting intentions, one of which the subject need not be aware. Indeed dreams function to keep the dreamer unaware of certain intentions, thus protecting sleep.

The dream is an utterance which the dreamer himself does not understand. Actually, he ". . . really does know the meaning of his dream but he does not know that he knows it."[13] That is, whereas the intentions underlying the dream are his own, at least one intention exists in his mind only latently. These latent intentions are what Freud called the latent dream. He contrasted the latent dream with its disguised expression in the manifest dream. The manifest dream is a censored and distorted version of the latent dream. Freud called the processes through which the distortion is accomplished the dream work.[14] Psychoanalysis attempts to demolish the dream work by recovering the latent dream from the manifest dream. The latent is recovered from the manifest by the method of "free association."

Free association is employed because it is extremely difficult to understand a dream until the dreamer has given what information he can about it. Thus he is asked to say what comes to his mind about any given element in a dream. It is the patient's associations and not the translation of symbols that allows the analyst to attribute a meaning to the dream. Actually, the meaning of the dream is nothing more than the dream's meaning for the dreamer.[15] But it is a meaning that the dreamer can become aware of only by following his associations without resistance. In this regard, the skill of the analyst is crucial.[16]

Psychoanalysis makes the same assumptions about and applies the same method to the study of neuroses as it does to the study of dreams. Both have a meaning for the subject of which he can be made aware by following his associations. Both express an ungratified impulse of which the subject lacks awareness: the dream as a wish-fulfillment and the symptom as a substitute satisfaction. Yet whereas psychoanalysis does not attempt to stop dreaming, it does attempt to cure the pathology which produces symptoms. Since the distortion of the symptom (as of the dream) is a result of the repression of its meaning from the consciousness of the subject, the therapy proceeds by attempting to transform something unconcious into something conscious.[17] The analyst's ability to do this, with the acknowledgement of the subject, can be taken as the strongest evidence in support of the existence of the unconscious.

Thus far we have spoken of the unconscious only descriptively, as thoughts or emotions of which the subject is unaware, that is, as thoughts which are latent within the psyche. Such a conception is only the point of departure for the psychoanalytic study of unconsciousness. Freud referred to his systematic psychology of the psychical processes beyond consciousness as his metapsychology. In the following section, I will discuss the relationship between consciousness and unconsciousness as Freud formulated it in his metapsychological models.

FREUD'S METAPSYCHOLOGICAL MODELS

Freud utilized four models to describe unconscious processes and their relationship to consciousness: the topographic, dynamic, structural, and economic. Actually Freud was not satisfied with a simple topography which could be used merely to categorize conscious and unconscious thoughts and emotions. He formulated his model of psychic dynamics to explain why a thought was conscious or unconscious. This model described how the psyche protected itself, through the dynamics of repression and defense, from the conflict that might occur from the awareness of a thought or an impulse. But the ideational content of the impulse and the mechanisms of repression and defense could not be distinguished topographically, since each may exist unconsciously. To detect in consciousness the expressions of the unconscious conflict between impulses and defense mechanisms, Freud subsequently formulated his structural model. This was a model of psychic agencies which represented the needs of the individual, the social demands he encounters, and his internalization of those demands. Furthermore, Freud maintained that the manifestations in consciousness of the energy of psychic impulses and unconscious emotions could not be understood in the same terms used to explain the dynamics of thought. He conceptualized his economic model to explain the movements and manifestations of psychic energy.

In this section I will discuss Freud's dynamic, structural and economic models.

THE DYNAMICS OF UNCONSCIOUSNESS

Pursuing the association from dreams or symptoms, the analyst is led to memories or feelings which apparently were present in the patient's psyche but of which he was not aware. These may be traced to the previous day's experience or as far back as early infancy. Through analysis we learn that memories of infancy play a much more fundamental role in dream formation. The more recent memories provide material for the specific ways in which the infantile memories are expressed.[18] However, in the analysis of symptoms we learn that unconscious memories of adult life, when sufficiently traumatic and of similar content as infantile memories, can play this fundamental role. Furthermore, analysis reveals that the contemporary residues and infantile memory traces (or adult equivalents) are not unconscious in the same way. To pursue this, we must begin to speak differently of the unconscious than we have.

The analysis of dreams and symptoms showed that the unconscious is neither a passive receptacle nor a depository of faded memories; it is constantly striving toward conscious expression. Some thoughts can be expressed with little difficulty; others can only be expressed through a long and difficult process, if at all. When we descriptively refer to both these types as unconscious, we lose this important distinction. Accordingly, the first prerequisite of a dynamic viewpoint is the introduction of a new category which will allow us to differentiate the two. Henceforth, we will refer to the thoughts of which we are at least temporarily unaware as preconscious. We will retain the term unconsciousness only for those that are deeply hidden.[19] With the introduction of "preconsciousness" we complicate the relationship between consciousness and unconsciousness. Both unconsciousness and preconsciousness are latent. Yet preconscious thoughts can be expressed in consciousness directly; unconscious thoughts, only in a distorted and censored way.

We cannot become conscious of censored thoughts under ordinary circumstances. "We call them then repressed." Repression prevents the expression of an unconscious idea through the ordinary medium of language. Consequently an unconscious idea must be disguised before it can be expressed. However, connecting the idea of the thing with the idea of the word is not, ". . . identical with actually becoming conscious but only with the potentiality of this; it is therefore characteristic of the system pcs [preconsciousness] and of that only."[20]

The dynamic model does not deny that there is a censorship operating between consciousness and preconsciousness. It claims only that the censorship operating between preconsciousness and unconsciousness is more fundamental. The displacement of the main barrier in the categorization of mental entities from activity-latency to preconscious-unconscious is summarized by the formula CS, PCS/UCS.[21]

As he developed his dynamic model, Freud came to consider the processes of the system UCS to be the oldest and most fundamental mental processes. He believed they were ". . . the residue of a phase of development in which they were the only kind of mental processes." These "primary processes" strive towards gaining pleasure and draw back from (repress) an operation which might arouse unpleasantness. Our nocturnal dreams, which express but avoid confronting our most painful thoughts, while serving as fantasy substitutes for our deepest yearnings, are remnants of this pleasure-unpleasure principle and proof of its power. So too, are our waking tendencies to shut out painful impressions.[22]

The pleasure principle dominates the mental life of the infant. However, its reign is short-lived. During an early stage in its development, the infant is

> . . . impressed by the fact that some sources of excitation, which he will later recognize as his own bodily organs, can provide him with sensations at any moment, whereas other sources evade him from time to time—among them what he desires most of all, his mother's breast—and only reappear as a result of his screaming for help.[23]

Henceforth, the pleasure principle must take into account the conditions of external reality; it becomes modified by the demands of the external world. "A momentary pleasure, uncertain in its results, is given up, but only in order to gain in the new way an assured pleasure coming later."[24] The reality principle tempers the pleasure principle.

Our impulses in pursuit of pleasure and the avoidance of pain form the nucleus of the unconscious. These impulses are understood not physiologically but psychologically. An instinct is "the psychic representative of a continually flowing inner source of stimulation. . . ." It is not the continually flowing inner stimulation itself. A somatic source of stimulation can be active in the psyche only when represented by an idea. It is, in the words of Ives Hendrick, ". . . a biological need experienced mentally as emotion, and impelling the organism to tension-releasing behavior." Since a somatic source of stimulation can be active in the psyche only when represented by an idea, the concept "impulse" or "instinct" signifies the boundary between the psychic and the physical. When we speak of a repressed instinctual impulse, Freud maintained, "We can mean only an instinctual impulse the ideational presentation of which is unconscious. . . ."[25]

The primal instincts are those which could not be resolved further in respect to their somatic sources as manifest in psychic activity. At first Freud distinguished two types of primal instincts:

self-preservation instincts and sexual instincts.[26] The former are manifested as hunger, thirst, and the need for physical security; the latter, are the libido or sexual appetite. The self-preservation instincts have to be satisfied directly and almost immediately, whereas libidinal impulses can be repressed into unconsciousness, inhibited in their aim, and satisfied with certain approximations to satisfaction. Another essential distinction between these two groups of instincts is that the self-preservation instincts are dependent for their satisfaction on objects external to the individual; the sexual instincts can be satisfied, albeit perversely in Freud's view, by the individual himself. So, while the reality principle asserts itself directly and immediately into the domain of self-preservation, its modification of the sexual impulses are less drastic.

The distinctions between self-preservation and sexual instincts have several implications. First, since self-preservation cannot be repressed as easily and in as many ways as sexuality, psychoanalysis as a method is better suited for investigations of libido and its effects.[27] Second, again given the demanding and practical nature of satisfying self-preservation instincts, the individual is forced to submit them more readily to the psychic processes which evaluate his perceptions of reality. Conversely sexual instincts can be more easily preserved from such processes. However, if the self-preservation instincts come into conflict with sexuality, the latter may be repressed in favor of self-preservation.

Identifying the process of repression and defense enabled the psychoanalysts to penetrate the full depths of human unconsciousness. The unconscious contains not only impulses, feelings, and ideas which have been rejected from consciousness but also the processes through which the unawareness of these elements is established and maintained. Freud's psychic dynamics enabled him to examine these elements and processes despite the patients' lack of awareness of them. But even with his dynamic displacement of the main psychic barrier, Freud's psychoanalytic investigations pointed to processes that could not be adequately described with topographic categories. He formulated his model of psychic structures to explain the complex processes by which repressed elements were distorted before being expressed in consciousness.

PSYCHIC STRUCTURES

The processes of repression and defense are the means by which the unconscious and preconscious, and preconscious and conscious, are separated yet connected. These processes, especially when amplified to include the process of testing reality, may function either consciously or unconsciously. Hence rather than describing them as a property of a topographical system, Freud came to see them as "a coherent organization of mental processes" which he called the ego.[28]

That which is repressed, the impulses which comprise the core of the unconscious, forms a mental region alien to the ego. Freud, following Nietzsche, used the German impersonal pronoun *Es* to refer to this region. Es is ordinarily translated as "it" but in the psychoanalytic context is translated as *id*. The id is a part of the self which seems alien to the self; it is the dark inaccesible part of our personality which knows neither logic nor negation, and in which contrary impulses exist comfortably together.[29] Like the ego the id is not a place but the residue of psychic processes. In contrast to the ego, the id lacks a coherent organization.

Initially the entire psyche is id. The ego breaks off in subservience to the reality principle and comes to represent the external world to the id. The reality principle asserts itself as soon as the infant is impressed with the fact that he cannot satisfy all his needs and desires by himself. For Freud the discrete self (the ego) begins to emerge at that moment in which the absence of the objects of the infant's needs leads it to differentiate itself from the outer world.[30] This process of differentiation includes the process of psychically adjusting to the frustration that the pleasure-seeking impulses, because of their object-directness, necessarily encounter. That is, the child must abandon those objects of his libidinal impulses which are tabooed or otherwise socially restricted. Yet these objects may be abandoned only partially. The object relationship, rather than being completely repudiated, may be displaced by an identification with the abandoned object. That is, abandoned objects may be incorporated within the ego as ego ideals.[31] The consequence of this is twofold. On the one hand, the impulse may be redirected toward the ego ideal and the individual seeks to fulfill its demands. On the other, the ego ideal may forbid the expression of certain impulses. In other words, ego ideals may condition the individual by either encouraging or discouraging behavior.

The demands of the ego ideals become a source of severe psychic conflict. The ego ideals are associated with the moralistic restriction of pleasure-seeking impulses. The infant is not capable of living up to these demands. Motivated primarily by the threat of the loss of parental love and protection, the behavior of the amoral infant is limited not by ethical or theological conceptions of right and wrong but by his consideration of the potential consequences for self-preservation of his activity. Accordingly, the strictly self-interested ego of the helpless infant is not a very reliable agent of social control and hence not a satisfactory means to test reality in the interest of self-preservation. The adjustment of the infant to the demands of the outer world is accomplished instead through a further organization of psychic processes whereby a part of the ego sets itself over the rest of the ego and acts as the agent of the ego ideals. This is done through the superego the function of which is to watch the real ego and measure it by the standards of its ideals.[32] This psychic process, like the others, usually operates beyond the individual's awareness.

The superego is what many observers, including value theorists and theologians, understand intuitively as the conscience. It is responsible for the sense of guilt connected with any prohibited act or thought. Freud's description of the superego, however, strips the conscience of its mystical and metaphysical qualities and firmly grounds it in the situation within which the infant develops.

In the discussion of the unconscious I began with the topographical point of view in which psychic content is merely conscious or unconscious but quickly moved to the dynamics of CS,PCS/UCS in which psychic content takes form as impulses, their representations, and the processes of repression. By theoretically establishing the details of a dynamic topography, Freud could describe more fully the unconscious impulses behind slips of the tongue, or manifest dream traces, or neurotic symptoms. Yet the conflict between erotic impulses and processes of repression could not be understood simply as a conflict between consciousness and unconsciousness. It was necessary to introduce psychic structures (id, ego, and superego) which organize our impulses and repressive processes. Freud formulated the structural model in the 1920s, and by that time psychoanalytic theory was already well developed. The structural model is important not for the additional categories it contributes to psychoanalytic theory but for its capacity to guide our understanding of how the incessant flows of impulses and repression can somehow constitute a psychological individual.[33] The relationship between the structural and dynamic model was diagrammed by Freud in the figure below.[34]

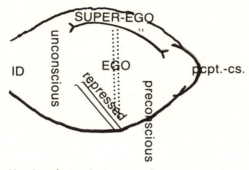

SOURCE: *New Introductory Lectures,* p. 78.

Freud's dynamic model emphasizes the effects of repressed ideas on conscious thought. The structural model focuses on the conflict between the primary impulses and the social and psychic forces which oppose and modify them. Just as unconscious ideas strive for conscious expression, but achieve only a partial or distorted expression, so too do psychic energies and emotions strive for release, but achieve only a partial or modified release. Freud's relentless pursuit of psychic processes demanded more than a psychology of ideas. To describe more precisely the effects of impulsive energy and unconscious emotions on conscious thought, Freud formulated his economic model.

PSYCHIC ECONOMICS

Psychic representations may exist as feelings as well as ideas. When these feelings express a strong inner need, they may become a source of energy. The economic point of view is concerned with that which is represented in feelings without passing into ideas. Paul Ricoeur has called this the nonspoken, nonspeaking, "the unnameable at the root of speech."[35] Freud investigated this continuous and persistant source of energy with an analogy of charge and discharge.

Psychic energy can be directed and redirected onto objects and internal psychic processes. The economic model focuses on the flow of energy, within and between consciousness and unconsciousness. This flow is directed by the ego. In the interest of avoiding a painful conflict with the outer world, the ego may repress the impulse's drive toward discharge or it may redirect the drive toward a safer form of release or gratification.

This model of psychic energy is drawn from physics, but analogy implies differences as well as similarities. The distinction between mental and physical energetics is maintained and psychoanalysis investigates the former. Psychic energy cannot be understood as "pure" or "bare" energy (waves or particles which flow in abstraction from human needs and desires) but only "forces in search of meaning."[36] This meaning is found in the aim and objects with which the impulses are associated.

The economic model describes the impulses which serve the pleasure principle. The aim of these impulses is to maintain stimulation since "painful feelings are connected with an increase and pleasurable feelings with a decrease in stimulation."[37] But without a means of measuring the charge and discharge of the impulse, the psychoanalyst can understand this aim only indirectly, through the objects to which it affixes itself. The charging of an object with energy is called cathexis. Through cathexis, an otherwise repressed impulse may remain psychically active.[38] That is, even while the association of the impulse with an inaccessible object has been repressed, the impulse may continue to strive toward other, external objects. These new cathected objects need not be connected directly with the original aim of the impulse; ideas and symbols, as well as people may become the object of libidinal cathexis.

Libidinal energy is not expended over a straightforward course for its discharge. There are social obstacles and internal tendencies which oppose the primary processes of the impulses. Various functions of the ego and superego strive to prevent the discharge of the impulse in order to prevent a conflict which might arise from the impulse's attempt to gain satisfaction. These opposing influences may bring about dramatic changes (vicissitudes) in the impulses themselves. In his clinical practice Freud discerned set patterns of instinctual vicissitudes which he attempted to categorize in his metapsychology: reversal of the aim into its opposite, turning round of the energy upon the subject, repression, and sublimation. The first two are closely related. The third is the one most extensively treated in Freud's work. The last is the one most closely connected with social activity. Sublimation is also the vicissitude most difficult to analyze.

Reversal can be achieved in two distinct ways: "a change from active to passive and a reversal of the content." The latter mode is observed only in the single instance of the change of love into hate. Actually, the attitudes of love and hate are not primary characteristics of the relationships of instincts to their objects but secondary characteristics which result from the modification of the impulse by the ego. Freud argued that "hate relations are derived not from sexual life, but from the struggle of the ego for self-preservation and self-maintenance."[39] Examples of the change from an active to passive aim of the object are pairs of opposites such as sadism-masochism and voyeurism-exhibitionism. Here the active aim to punish or to look at is transformed into the passive aim to be punished or to be looked at. This change of aim coincides with a change of object which brings us to the second vicissitude. For example, masochism is sadism *turned around* upon the subject's own ego. But this coincidence does not imply an identity. The reversal of an instinct and the turning around of an instinct are interconnected yet distinct processes. In one the aim of the instinct is transformed; in the other, the subject of the instinct becomes its object (through an intermediary).

Alongside the reversed and turned-around impulse there always exists the earlier, active, other-directed impulse. This complicates the circuitry of the charge-discharge model, for now an impulse originating from the id may be directed toward either an object (object libido) or stored through an ego cathexis (ego libido). The latter corresponds to the condition of narcissism, which Freud considered to be a primary process of the pleasure principle since the ego was originally undifferentiated from the id. The active, other-directed instinct has left self-satisfaction behind, while the passive, turned-around instinct holds fast to the narcissistic object. The reversed and turned-around instincts "are dependent upon the narcissistic organization of the libido and bear the stamp of that phase."[40]

In his paper on "Instincts and Their Vicissitudes" Freud does not consider either repression or sublimation. The reasons for these omissions seem to be different for the two cases. Sublimation, as we shall see, is probably the most complicated and least understood of the vicissitudes. Freud never achieved a systematic presentation of its operation. Repression, however, was treated systematically in a short paper which was published immediately after his paper on instinctual vicissitudes.[41]

The discovery of repression in the clinical situation was a milestone in the development of psychoanalytic thought. Freud considered the theory of repression to be not only one of the most original components of psychoanalysis, but "the cornerstone on which the whole structure of psychoanalysis rests. It is the most essential part of it. . . ."[42]

We previously have seen the importance of repression in connection with the dynamic model. Stated in economic terms, repression consists of the withdrawal of impulsive energy from a conscious or preconscious ideational representation. The representation of the impulse then remains inactive (without cathexis) or receives cathexis from the unconscious. But since the impulse and the idea always are striving toward consciousness, repression must be renewed constantly. The preconscious guards itself against the intrusion of the unconscious by anticathexis, using energy withdrawn from the representation of the impulse for its repression.[43]

The purpose of repression is to avoid the painful conflict which could result from the impulse being satisfied through a particular object. However, since the energy of the impulse will continue to cause psychic stimulation, the repression may succeed against the ideational element yet still result in feelings of discomfort, anxiety, or even pain. Repression prevents excitations from attaining their ends and consequently drives them off into other paths until they express themselves as symptoms or other substitutes. However, neither of these expressions are caused by the repression itself but by its partial nature. That is, symptoms and substitutes express the return of the repressed.[44]

Sublimation, in contrast to repression, allows a potentially dangerous level of psychic energy to be utilized and discharged in other spheres. In sublimation, both the aim and the object of the instinct are changed, and the energy is spent in a socially valued way. Sublimation retains the main purpose of eros, unity and binding, but is a milder form of satisfaction than that sought by the pleasure principle. Sublimation is the process by which impulsive energy is placed in the service of cultural achievement.[45]

Now that we have discussed the four vicissitudes we still do not know why and when a particular one will operate instead of another. If asked why not, Freud probably would reply that there is a multiplicity of causes or an overdetermination, and that our knowledge is much too limited to predict the occurrence of a particular vicissitude.[46] But in the clinical situation the trained psychoanalyst could demonstrate that a particular vicissitude happened, and reconstruct the circumstances that effected it. Again, psychoanalysis validates itself by making conscious the unconscious.

There is, however, another aspect to overdetermination which Freud, influenced as he was by a mechanistic model of science, did not make explicit. In the psyche, interpenetration seems more crucial than causality. Events, ideas, processes interact and affect one another. A phenomenon can react upon the very conditions which brought it forth. For example, the instincts are the foundation of the psyche, the base upon which the complicated superstructure of psychic life rests. Yet the instincts themselves can be changed drastically by the elements of the psyche which have developed in reaction to them and the frustrations imposed by the social environment.

The influence of the social environment on the psyche can be seen most clearly by comparing the vicissitudes of sublimation and repression. Freud recognized that an understanding of the process of avoiding conflict by repressing from consciousness the aim and object of the impulse required an understanding of the social conditions which frustrated the impulse. He maintained that repression was necessary for the redirection of libidinal energy into social activity. Accordingly, repression is closely associated with sublimation, since the more libidinal energy can be sublimated, the less it needs to be repressed.

Freud characterized sublimation as "an especially conspicuous feature of cultural development; it is what makes it possible for higher psychical activities, scientific, artistic, or ideological, to play such an important part in civilized life."[47] But, if he stressed the beneficial social consequences of sublimation, he failed to consider whether social antecedents were necessary for the occurrence of this process. Instead, he explained the capacity to sublimate in terms of internal psychic factors. (This will be developed in Chapter 5).

Freud, however, emphasized the sociological antecedents of repression. He contended that the concept of repression imposes upon the psychoanalyst

> . . . The task of investigating the development of the relation of the neurotic and of mankind in general to reality and of bringing the psychological significance of the real outer world into the structure of our theory.[48]

In other words, Freud's pursuit of the unconscious antecedents of consciousness brought him to a point where it became necessary for him to consider the experiential antecedents of consciousness. The psychic models presented in this section allow us to reconstruct the experiences which the individual has repressed from awareness but which continue to exert an influence on his thought and behavior. Yet these models allow us to see in consciousness much more than the simple reflection of social experience. Experiences also are represented in consciousness through the unconscious processes they initiate, encourage, or support. In short, Freud's models describe a socially conditioned unconsciousness. Through the processes of the unconscious, social conditions are internalized. But once internalized, they are appropriated. Since the individual does not recognize these processes as a source of his thoughts or behavior, their influences may not be appropriate to the individual's present situation. That is, the distortion and redirection of impulses may proceed long after there is a need for them. In the next section, I discuss the social and psychological implications of this.

REPRESSION AND THE PSYCHOLOGICAL SIGNIFICANCE OF THE OUTER WORLD

Freud believed that what is appropriate in one stage of development becomes inappropriate in another. The fixation at past stages and the regression to them are essential characteristics of psychopathology. Normality is a realistic appraisal of one's current life situation and relationships. The reenactment in adult relationships of infantile patterns of relationships reveals a pathological lack of development.

Freud's psychology has often been accused of an excessive emphasis on pathological processes.[49] Yet Freud's analysis of the processes underlying errors, dreams, and symptoms revealed the similarities between normal and pathological phenomena. The difference between normality and abnormality is one of degree, "the tendencies in the one are but an exaggerated form of the tendencies in the other."[50]

If Freud tended to concentrate on the exaggerated tendencies it was not only because they were easier to observe. Psychoanalysis is first and foremost a clinical theory for the treatment of psychopathology. Since my primary concern is with the political-psychological significance of psychoanalytic theory, I have sought to describe mainly the most general, that is, "normal," psychic processes. However, we can now gain a richer insight into the interaction of social reality and the psyche by contrasting normal and pathological psychic development.

In this section I first discuss how infantile patterns are established and preserved in the unconscious, and then contrast psychic health and pathology as appropriate and inappropriate responses to particular situations.

THE ESTABLISHMENT AND PRESERVATION OF INFANTILE PATTERNS OF RELATIONSHIPS

Very early in the infant's development, the instinct for self-preservation leads to a modification of libidinal impulses. The infant's first erotic objects manifest this. The person at whom infantile libidinal strivings are directed, the mother, is the same person responsible for satisfying the self-preservation of the infant. The culmination of childhood sexuality, the Oedipus complex, is the situation in which the child is forced to abandon this attachment.

Overcoming the Oedipus complex prepares the child for the demands of social life and results in the introjection of morality via the superego. It is in childhood that each individual's pattern of interaction with the environment is first formed. An understanding of the development of childhood sexuality is required for an understanding of the sources of not only adult sexuality, but also of the individual's attitude toward the authority he confronts.

The sexuality of childhood has little in common with the sexuality of adulthood. Rather, it is the experience from which adult sexuality and the mature psyche are developed. The individual develops through a series of stages, during each of which the individual seeks pleasure from a particular bodily organ or erogenous zone. Freud considered the satisfaction that is derived from these erogenous zones to be sexual because they were aimed at the attainment of pleasure and release of tension. In doing so Freud challenged the generally recognized association of sexuality and procreation and the correlate of that association, the belief that sexuality emerged with puberty.

The stages of childhood sexuality discerned by Freud are the oral, anal, and phallic stages. The sexual impulses of these stages can be objectless or autoerotic. That is, the child, by his own efforts, can obtain sufficient pleasure in the erogenous zone corresponding to each of these phases. But the influences of his environment exert themselves even then, and the child comes to seek satisfaction through objects in his environment.

The environment exerts itself most powerfully in the realm of self-preservation. The interaction between the self-preservation and sexual impulses causes the individual to choose particular sexual objects. The child obtains nourishment through the act of sucking. The desire to suck, however, becomes independent of the taking of nourishment. It becomes the first partial impulse, "pleasure-sucking." Accordingly, "sucking for nourishment becomes the point of departure from which the whole sexual life develops, the unattainable prototype of every later sexual satisfaction, to which, in times of need, phantasy often reverts."[51]

The desire to suck is directed toward the source of nourishment, most notably the mother's breast. However, the child learns that he can satisfy this desire, in a way, with parts of his own body, such as his thumb. Pleasure-sucking and the taking of nourishment are then differentiated and the autoerotic nature of the sexual impulses becomes manifest.

What occurs in the case of sucking also occurs in connection with the organs associated with other vital processes. Freud observed that:

> ... infants experience pleasure in the evacuation of urine and the contents of the bowels, and that they very soon endeavor to contrive these actions so that the accompanying excitation of the membranes in these erogenous zones may secure them the maximum possible gratification.[52]

The appearance of teeth decreases the association between sucking and nourishment. The strengthening of the muscular apparatus yields an increased control of the sphincter muscle. As a result of these physiological developments the child's sexual life passes into the anal stage.[53]

The child now discovers that he can hold back his feces to the point that their passage will produce an irritating yet pleasurable sensation in the mucous membrane. The association of pleasure and pain in this stage led Freud to characterize it as the sadistic-anal phase. The masturbatory excitation produced by the retention and excretion of feces leads the child to perceive them as extentions of his own body and gifts he can bestow upon those for whom he cares. It is only through the "toilet-training" efforts of his parents that the child begins to develop "civilized" attitudes toward his feces and learns to coordinate retention and excretion with the wishes of others. "In this way, he is required to exchange pleasure for value in the eyes of others."[54]

The abandonment of anal eroticism leads the child to a phase of sexual activity that has much in common with that of adults, the phallic stage. In this stage, the dominant erogenous zones are the penis and clitoris, and the child's pleasure-seeking now takes the form of genital masturbation.[55]

In the phallic phase the mental and social aspects of sexuality become apparent. Sexual activity is characterized by such practices as "choice of object, distinguishing of particular persons with affection, even decision in favor of one sex or another, and jealousy. . . ." Since the relationships of the family focus the child's emotional ties on the mother, the mother is again adopted as the erotic object in this stage. But rather than the mother's breast, it is the mother herself that is the object of the impulse. Furthermore, the mother has become the object not only of organ pleasure, but of an emotional impulse as well. The child in the phallic stage seeks an external object of satisfaction despite the fact that he may have "only very vague notions as to what constitutes satisfying erotic intercourse. Indeed the boy may not know that women do not possess a penis and the girl may not know that men have one."[56]

The acquisition of this knowledge is a crucial step in the development of the dynamics of the sexual impulse. The perception of the difference between the male and the female genitals makes the threat of castration plausible to the infant. Henceforth the boy must learn to identify with his father but must not aspire to be *too* much like his father in regard to his mother. The girl must learn to identify with her mother and to transfer her emotional attachments to her father.[57]

The repression of the desire for the mother is not, however, its annihilation. The child's attitudes towards and relations with his parents are marked by ambivalence. Alongside his identification with his father the boy retains a hostility based on "a wish to get rid of his father in order to take his place with his mother."[58] The girl blames her mother for her own lack of the means to sexually possess her mother, and develops a hostility toward her former erotic object. She aspires to take her mother's place with her father and receive from him a substitute for the penis: a baby. The situation is complicated by an original bisexuality in children and the fact that boys and girls, take, in varying degrees, both parents as the objects of affection.[59]

The resolution of the oedipus complex is culturally defined as successful when the boy identifies with his father and represses his desire for his mother, or when the girl transfers her attachment from mother to father. However, there are other possible resolutions of the oedipus complex. The boy may take the father as love object and identify with his mother. The girl may abandon her father as an erotic object and identify with him instead. Juliet Mitchell observed that, "At the dissolution of the oedipus complex, all four possibilities will be present with varying degrees of strength (that is, both parents as objects, both parents taken in identification)." The importance of the existence of these possibilities goes beyond sexual development and object choice. Since the ego develops by incorporating the renounced erotic objects, the incorporation of an inappropriate ego ideal, such as the parent of the opposite sex, affects the very development of the ego and its capacity to test reality.[60]

The renounced objects also are incorporated as the agents of repression. The superego is formed when the prohibitions are maintained by an internal authority. That is, to avoid the conflict which results from his attempts to satisfy his libido, the very authority which forbids satisfaction is introjected into the child. This prolonged identification with his parent is an ego defense by which the child obtains a sense of his own power as equal to that of the threatening authority. But it also forces the child to surrender a part of his own interest. "The enemy he feared on the outside reappears within."[61]

The resolution of the oedipus complex is thus the crucial event in the development of the individual's attitudes toward authority. It ends in the establishment of the superego, which can function in support of any formidable authority. Indeed as the individual grows older and becomes more independent from his parents, their power over him decreases. The superego may function in support of such authority figures as, in various stages of life, educators, religious leaders, and representatives of the state. Furthermore, in the course of its development, the superego departs from the original model of the parents and becomes more and more impersonal.[62] Yet even as the authority confronting the individual becomes increasingly abstract, his identification with it forces the adult, like the child, to surrender a part of his own self-interest.

With the internalization of the prohibition of the incestuous desire for the parent, and with the identification with the parent of the same sex, the oedipus complex is resolved. A measure of the success to which the individual achieves this is the extent to which, after a period of sexual latency extending to puberty, the individual directs erotic impulses toward more socially acceptable objects. The more the sexual objects of the adult are associated with the oedipal objects, the more they will conjure up the latent fear of the threats against infantile sexuality. This becomes manifest in the erotic life of the adult as anxiety.[63] In ordinary circumstances, the individual can become aware of these unconscious memory traces only through the interpretation of their distorted expression in dreams and neurotic symptoms.

The unconscious memory traces of infancy that are expressed in dreams and symptoms need not have been events that occurred in reality. Traumas of the mind can have as powerful effects as traumas of real life. It is hard to distinguish the two on the basis of their unconscious memory traces or their distorted and censored conscious expressions. Since we return in our dreams to the infantile state of psychic development, with its incestuous object choices and fantasy relationships, Freud's analyses of dreams led him to the conclusion that "*the unconscious is the infantile mental life.*"[64]

If the unconscious is the infantile mental life, then psychological fixations at and regressions to infantile psychic processes are an exaggerated expression of the processes occurring in all of us. Accordingly, an examination of these pathological processes should help us to understand the average or "normal" psyche. In the following section I will contrast the processes of pathological response and normal adjustment to the current conditions of one's life. In doing so, I hope to specify the psychoanalytic conception of the psychological significance of the outer world.

PATHOLOGY AND ADJUSTMENT

The healthy adult psyche is characterized by the ability to exist within its given environment without withdrawing into fantasy, as well as the ability to enter into appropriate sexual and emotional relationships. Neither the neurotic nor psychotic can evaluate and confront his environment as it is. Sexual perversions, that is the seeking of sexual satisfaction *exclusively* through aims and objects which are not associated with genital sexuality, preclude the establishment of mature, erotic attachment to another person. Therefore, they too were considered by Freud to be pathological.[65]

The psychoanalytic investigation of mental disorders reveals them to be characterized by "almost incredible independence and lack of susceptibility to influence on the part of the unconscious." Freud understood these disorders as the manifestations of conflicting intentionalities, one conscious, the other not. Since the intentions never confront each other directly, the conflict can never have a final outcome. In contrast normal conflict is when the competing impulses operate in the same topographical system.[66]

Pathological conflict is evident in the condition of anxiety. Anxiety is an excessive or exaggerated state of fear. As a reaction to a real, external situation, fear may be a rationally motivated expression of the instinct for self-preservation. Fear helps to direct the individual's attention toward potentially dangerous objects. Fear can produce a readiness to cope with danger which will allow the individual to act appropriately.

Anxiety may prepare an individual to cope with danger. But in its excessive state it can paralyze every action in the face of that danger. Freud used the term anxiety to refer to the subjective condition exclusive of the object. Its antecedents are found within the subject rather than in the situation. Anxiety is a manifestation of the present situation being unconsciously associated with infantile experiences and thus activating infantile fears.[67]

The relative strength of infantile memory traces determines the extent to which anxiety functions to produce either a readiness to deal with danger or paralysis in the face of danger. If the traumatic experience, which generates the anxiety, is limited to a signal or warning of imminent danger, the individual's reaction ". . . can adapt itself to the new situation of danger and can proceed in flight or defense." If the psychic repetition of the trauma overwhelms the individual, ". . . the total reaction may consist in no more than a generation of anxiety, in which case the effective state becomes paralyzing and will be inexpedient for present purposes."[68]

In this latter condition of anxiety, "neurotic" anxiety, the individual is overwhelmed by his own libidinal impulses but does not recognize this to be so. Childhood experiences have taught the individual the dangers of unbinding these impulses. Anxiety in the adult expresses a fixation on or regression to the attitudes provoked by the infantile situation. In infancy repressions arise directly from traumas, that is, from situations of danger that are represented in mental experience by "a state of highly tense excitation, which is felt as unpleasure and which one is not able to master by discharging it."[69] These traumatic moments cannot be explained by applying the normal rules of the pleasure principle. The affective element of the repressed impulses is discharged as anxiety.

Yet, although anxiety is dependent upon the repressed impulses for its energy, we cannot say that repression causes anxiety. When the ego associates a libidinal demand with a potential danger, anxiety is awakened as a signal of an earlier situation of danger and of the need to bring about the repression of the impulse. So while anxiety has its source in the libido, it also signifies the flight of the ego from its libido. Psychoneurosis is a result of the ego losing its capacity to confront the libido.[70]

There is a significant development when the ego, attempting to defend itself against the libido, perceives the libido as an external danger which is threatening it. The process whereby an internal stimulus is perceived as external and defended against as such is called projection. The process of projection is crucial in the formulation of neurotic phobias and paranoiac states.[71]

Projection, however, is not limited to pathological states. Just as we all introject social prohibitions and moral dicta, so, too, we all project onto the environment the inner impulses against which the introjected norms were directed. This fundamentally affects the way in which we consciously constitute ourselves and our life world. A situation in which a pleasure-seeking yet self-preserving organism confronts a repressive social environment is perceived as a situation in which a moral, self-sacrificing individual confronts an immutably tempting and hostile world.

Through the processes of projection and introjection, in healthy as well as pathological cases, the fundamental conflict between the individual and a repressive social environment is further removed from the consciousness of the individual. The individual confuses

internal and external stimuli, and behavior is based on a consciousness which is distorted by unconsciousness.

Unconscious processes may preclude a rational response by the
individual to a given situation. They may remain relatively autonomous and resistant to external influences. Yet we cannot understand irrational behavior exclusively in terms of psychological
processes. Freud observed that there are cases in which ". . . the
solution of a conflict by neurosis is the one most harmless and
most tolerable socially." That is, the individual's health may be
sacrificed to a real, unavoidable suffering, a suffering grounded
in the social rather than psychological conditions of one's life. In
such cases, the "flight into illness may be justified fully." In other
cases, psychoanalytic treatment may remain completely ineffective
as long as the everyday circumstances of the patient's life remain
the same.[72]

Cases such as these clearly demonstrate that the patients' symptomology is grounded in his life world. Different mental disorders
may have symptoms which are typical to them, but the symptom's
meaning for the patient can be understood only through the
patient's experiences. For example, agoraphobia is the fear of
spaces. The spaces feared, however, might be closed rooms, or
wide open squares, or long roads, or narrow or wide streets, or so
on. The form taken by the symptom is determined by experiences
peculiar to the patient, in conjunction with his psychological
disposition.[73]

To say that psychopathology cannot be understood without
reference to the social situation is to imply that psychological
health likewise cannot be understood abstractly. Thus it seems that
Hartmann was correct in claiming that, from the study of neurosis,
the main focus of psychoanalytic interest turned to the entire
complexity of the individual's relationships with others. Of all
these relationships Freud emphasized, of course, the child's relationships with parents. Nevertheless, the entire social structure is
expressed in symptomology. The same neurosis will have different
implications and different symptoms for people living in different
social and economic situations. What is important is how and to
what degree a social structure brings to the surface, provokes, or
reinforces certain instinctual tendencies and sublimations, and

how it facilitates the solution of psychic conflicts by participation in the given social reality.[74]

For example, Freud argued that participation in the institutions of either totemism or religion may facilitate the solution of psychic conflict. Freud conceived of religion as a universal neurosis and proclaimed that, "the true believer is in a high degree protected against the danger of certain neurotic afflictions; by accepting the universal neurosis, he is spared the task of forming a personal neurosis." In totemism Freud saw the same unconscious introjection of social prohibitions that characterizes obsessional neuroses, only now it assumed a socially defined form. This is an essential difference despite the similarities of the processes and effects for "taboo is not a neurosis but a social institution."[75]

In these attempts to compare symptoms with social institutions, Freud transformed his criteria of mental health from one of appropriateness to one of adaptation. That is, he considered health only in terms of how well individuals adjusted to the demands of the social structure, and the effects those demands had on them. The major difference between health and illness is a practical one: "how far the individual remains capable of a sufficient degree of capacity for enjoyment and active achievement in life."[76] Of course, participation in social institutions does not diminish these capacities. Consequently, it does not matter whether social institutions reinforce the conditions of unconscious conflicts, as long as they alleviate the symptomatic consequences of those conflicts.

Yet the unconscious has not been made conscious and a great potential for eruption may remain. Individuals may be "normal" in a statistical sense, but the average need not be healthy. The problem is that in Freud's concept of mental health, people are not considered as subjects, as creators of their social environment. In such circumstances the individual may have no alternative to developing a neurosis, or he may avoid neurosis by participation in social institutions. In either case, he confronts his social situation as an immutable presence.

This is why we began from Freud's psychology of the psyche rather than his formulations on the relationship between the individual and society. Freud's analysis of the unconscious revealed the extent to which the individual was preconditioned by the institutions of society. It can be used to explain the way in which individuals develop their awareness of their social interests. However, Freud failed to appreciate the significance of the fact that social institutions may require a level of repression beyond that necessary for social interactions, that people may be responding appropriately when they resist the degree of repression demanded of them.

Having precluded these possibilities, Freud could not develop the critical insights of psychoanalysis. In his social theory, his description of repression became an apology for the existing level of repression. In the next chapter I will show how this resulted from certain ideological presumptions, rather than the models, concepts, or hypotheses of psychoanalysis.

CONCLUSION: UNCONSCIOUSNESS AND SOCIAL REALITY IN THE METAPSYCHOLOGY

Freud's metapsychology describes a psychic system which operates in accordance with internal laws and processes, but which is dependent on external stimuli for its specific contents and particular development. The metapsychology conceives of an individual who not only confronts his environment but incorporates it as well. The modification of the pleasure principle into the reality principle results from this incorporation. So too, do the structures which organize our impulses and psychic processes.

Modification first occurs in the realm of the self-preservation impulses. But while infantile autoeroticism allows the sexual impulses to be more resistant to the demands of reality, their interaction with the self-preservation impulses leads to the dominance of the reality principle even in this realm. Through the reality principle the environment is incorporated into the amorphous energy deriving from and operating within the organism, the impulses. An impulse asserts its presence in consciousness in one of two ways: either in its successful discharge through an object or the manifestations of the lack of discharge. The process of object selection and its economic success depend upon the demands of the ego operating in accordance with the reality principle.

If the satisfaction of the impulse through a particular object could bring about an unpleasurable conflict with the individual's social environment (such as, the oedipal situation), the ego may repress the awareness of the object as an object of the impulse. If no suitable replacement is found, the individual may withdraw from reality into fantasy but not without serious psychic repercussions in the form of dreams, neurotic symptoms, or the formulation of other substitutes. If the individual can displace the impulse onto another object or if he can rest content with certain approximations to satisfaction (as in sublimation), the original object of the striving may be repressed without serious consequences. But this clearly is a function of the alternatives made available to the individual by his environment. Social considerations bring about not only the repression but the particular consequences of the repression.

Psychic structures are differentiated as a result of the infant's relationship with his parents. The ego's differentiation from the id results from the infant's need for criteria to decide how his feelings for his parents can be expressed most effectively in his relationships with them. The abandonment of his parents as erotic objects can lead to an identification with them. The infantile ego develops through these identifications. The superego is differentiated from the ego as an internal substitute for the prohibiting agent. Although the ego ideals and authority figures may change in the course of the individual's life, the structure of these relationships is determined by the parent-child relationship.

The Freudian system, with its stress on the role of object relations and ego ideals in the formation of the psyche, incorporates the study of intersubjectivity into the study of psychology. The relationships which Freud emphasized were the relationships between the individual and the immediate representatives of authority in his life. As long as these infantile relationships are preserved in the unconsciousness of the adult, the infantile condition of helplessness is preserved as an unconscious feeling of helplessness. Social experience conditions psychic development, but the psyche, via its relatively autonomous internal processes, appropriates these experiences. Past experience, as distorted and preserved in the unconscious, conditions the experiences of the present.

According to psychoanalytic theory, actions and thoughts which are expressed manifest conflicting intentionalities, one or more of which may be repressed from entering consciousness directly. We cannot predict what the outcome of a psychic conflict will be because psychic events are determined both in the sense of a multiplicity of causes and in the sense of the continual interaction and development of the impulses and the processes of discharge and repression. But we can reconstruct the conditions which cause a particular conscious manifestation and make it more intelligible to ourselves.

Psychoanalysis explains consciousness in terms of its unconscious components. Ricoeur claimed that this is achieved "only when we posit instinct as the fundamental concept with everything else being understood as a vicissitude of instincts."[77] The vicissitudes result from the demands of the reality (within which the instinctual impulses strive for satisfaction) in conjunction with the processes by which psychopathogies develop or are avoided. The conditioning of experiences (or perhaps it is more precise to say the conditioning of the perceptions of experiences) can result in an unrealistic or atemporal response to a particular situation. It is probable that an individual will satisfy an impulse directly if he is allowed to and if he has not internalized its prohibition. But even if the individual can discharge his impulses the object he adopts will be influenced by social conditions.

Although Freud formulated a psychological method which incorporated the effects of social conditions on psychic development, he failed to appreciate the historical specificity of those social factors. This failure had two consequences for Freud's thought. First, Freud came to understand the psychological consequences of the conflict between the pleasure-seeking impulses of the individual and the repression of those impulses demanded by social life as an unalterable characteristic of the human psyche. Second, Freud was led to conceive of the social environment as an immutable presence.

In the next chapter, I will examine both of these tendencies.

NOTES

[1] Jacoby, *Social Amnesia* (Boston: Beacon Press, 1975), p. 79.

[2] Freud, *A General Introduction to Psychoanalysis*, trans. by Joan Riviere (New York: Washington Square Press, 1964), p. 26.

³ Roazen, *Freud: Political and Social Thought* (New York: Alfred A. Knopf, 1970), p. 21.

⁴ Freud, *General Psychological Theory*, ed. Phillip Reiff (New York: Macmillan Publishing Co., 1973), pp. 116–117, 119–120 (The Unconscious).

⁵ These lectures were published as *General Introduction*. Freud began these lectures by making explicit the skepticism he expected these students to express toward his new psychological approach (see pp. 21–25). The lectures were arranged to allay their skepticism.

⁶ Mitchell, *Psychoanalysis and Feminism* (New York: Random House, Pantheon Books, 1974), p. 6.

⁷ According to Theodore Mischel, psychoanalysis fulfills the criteria of explanation:

> with respect to (a) the way conduct is explained, not in terms of causes, but in terms of considerations ('reasons') which make what was done intelligible, given the agent's beliefs, etc., and (b) the fact that something may be my reason for acting even though I do not suspect it but "discover" that this is what it must have been.

See "Concerning Rational Behavior and Psychoanalytic Explanation" [Wolheim (ed), *Freud: A Collection of Critical Essays*, (New York: Anchor Books, 1974), p. 331.]

⁸ *General Introduction*, pp. 32, 44, 36–37; Freud offers many such examples in Lectures 2 to 4 and refers us to his book, *The Psychopathology of Everyday Life*, for others. However, for the sake of continuity in summarizing the general outline of his theories, my citing of examples will be minimal.

⁹ Freud, *General Introduction*, p. 46. An example of this second type is a young man who speaks of "insorting" an unknown lady. Freud claims that this reveals a conscious intention to "escort" her and an intention to "insult" her of which the speaker was not aware or intended not to express.

¹⁰ Science in its catechism has but few apodictic percepts; it consists mainly of statements which it has developed to varying degrees of probability. The capacity to be content with these approximations to certainty and the ability to carry on constructive work despite the lack of final confirmation are actually a mark of the scientific habit of mind (ibid., pp. 54–55).

¹¹ Ibid., p. 87.

¹² Ibid., p. 93; see also pp. 88–91.

¹³ Ibid., p. 106.

¹⁴ The three main processes of the dream work are (1) condensation, (2) displacement, and (3) transformation of thoughts to visual images. See ibid., Lecture 11. Symbolism is also a means through which dream distortion is achieved, see p. 158.

[15] See ibid., p. 196; and Weiss, "Meaning and Dream Interpretation," in Wolheim (ed.), op. cit., p. 64. In this article Weiss argues that Freud claims to be doing too much in dream interpretation. Weiss claims that the manifest dream is not being interpreted but rather used as a means to reveal thoughts of which the patient ordinarily lacks awareness. Of course, this accepts the existence of an unconsciousness and suggests that there is some connection between unconsciousness and dreams. What is questioned is whether the method of free association can be construed as the reversal of the mechanistic process of the dream work transforming the latent dream into the manifest dream. Thus the objection is not directed toward the evidence posited in support of the unconscious, but against a claim made about a particular technique of psychotherapy. As such, it is beyond the scope of this chapter.

[16] In therapy the patient at times seems to refuse or to be unable to associate freely. Freud states that in this situation:

We realize that the work of dream interpretation is encountering opposition by a resistance which expresses itself in this very form of critical objections. This resistance is independent of the theoretical conviction of the dreamer . . . (T)he associations which people wish to suppress in this way prove without exception to be the most decisive for the discovery of the unconscious thought (*General Introduction*, p. 122.).

It is the task of the analyst to guide the associations in this difficult direction.

[17] Ibid., p. 291.

[18] Ibid., p. 238.

[19] Freud, *General Psychological Theory*, p. 52 (A Note on the Unconscious in Psychoanalysis).

[20] Ibid., p. 148 (The Unconscious); and *General Introduction*, p. 306.

[21] Ricoeur, *Freud and Philosophy* (New Haven: Yale University Press, 1970), p. 392. The symbols CS, PCS, UCS refer to the systems consciousness, preconsciousness, unconsciousness, respectively. I emphasize that these symbols are used only when speaking of psychic systems, and are not meant to describe the status of ideas. This systematization of the psyche is made possible only by a dynamic theory of psychic activity and the interaction between latent and active thoughts.

This model, however, applies only to ideas, not to emotions. The latter are either perceived as feelings (the final expression of the process of discharge) or they exist as unconscious affects. *General Psychological Theory*, p. 127 (The Unconscious). See also *The Standard Edition of the Complete Psychological Works of Sigmund Freud*, vol. XIX (London: Hogarth Press, 1961), p. 13 (The Ego and the Id). In the text, I consider this further in regard to the economic model.

[22] Freud, *General Psychological Theory*, p. 22 (Formulations Regarding the Two Principles in Mental Functioning).

[23] Freud, *Civilization and Its Discontents*, ed. and trans. James Strachey (New York: W. W. Norton & Co., 1961), p. 14.

[24] *General Psychological Theory*, p. 26 (Two Principles in Mental Functioning).

[25] Freud, *Three Contributions to the Theory of Sex*, trans. A. A. Brill (New York: E. P. Dutton & Co., 1962), p. 30; Hendrick, "Instinct and Ego During Infancy," *The Psychoanalytic Quarterly, vol. II* (1924), 40; and *General Psychological Theory*, p. 126 (The Unconscious).

[26] See for example *General Psychological Theory*, p. 89 (Instincts and Their Vicissitudes). Freud later posited a death instinct as a primary instinct. See for example, ibid., p. 183 (The Libido Theory). I discuss why I do not accept the latter hypothesis in the section on *Thanatos* in Chapter 5.

[27] Ibid., p. 180 (The Libido Theory).

[28] *Standard Edition*, vol. XIX, p. 17 (The Ego and the Id). See also *General Psychological Theory*, p. 136 (The Unconscious). In this earlier work Freud associates reality testing with PCS(CS).

[29] Freud, *New Introductory Lectures on Psychoanalysis*, trans. and ed. James Strachey (New York: W. W. Norton & Co., 1965), pp. 72, 74.

[30] Mitchell, op. cit., p. 384.

[31] *Standard Edition*, vol. 19, p. 29 (The Ego and the Id).

[32] *Civilization and Its Discontents*, pp. 71–72; *General Psychological Theory*, p. 75 (On Narcissism: An Introduction); and *New Introductory Lectures*, p. 65.

[33] See Roazen, op. cit., p. 74.

[34] The first time Freud presents this diagram the superego is not presented. *Standard Edition*, vol. 19, p. 24 (The Ego and the Id), and Freud explicitly rejects any attempt to localize it (p. 36). Also, acoustic perception is represented separately.

[35] *Civilization and Its Discontents*, p. 19; and Ricoeur, op. cit., p. 454.

[36] Ricoeur, op. cit., p. 151; see also Marshall, "Freud's Psychology of Language," in Wolheim (ed.), op. cit., p. 362.

[37] Freud, *General Psychological Theory*, p. 86 (Instincts and Their Vicissitudes).

[38] *General Psychological Theory*, p. 109 (The Repressed). See also *Three Contributions*, p. 75.

[39] *General Psychological Theory*, p. 101 (Instincts and Their Vicissitudes). See pp. 91, 97, 101–102.

[40] Ibid., p. 96; see pp. 91–98. See *General Psychological Theory*, p. 65 (On Narcissism); and *Standard Edition*, vol. 19, p. 65 (Editor's Introduction to Ego and Id).

[41] "Repression" and "Instincts and Their Vicissitudes" were part of a five-paper set written in 1915 and which have come to be known as the papers on metapsychology. (See the editor's note in *Standard Edition*, vol. 14, p. 105.)

[42] *Standard Edition*, vol. 14, pp. 15–16 (On the History of the Psycho-Analytic Movement).

[43] *General Psychological Theory*, pp. 129–230 (The Unconscious).

[44] Ibid., p. 111 (Repression).

[45] *Three Contributions*, p. 94; *Standard Edition*, vol. 19, p. 45 (The Ego and the Id); and *General Psychological Theory*, p. 181 (The Libido Theory).

[46] Freud says that psychoanalysis first discovered that psychic acts and structures are "overdetermined," that is, "have two or more simultaneous determinants." *Totem and Taboo*, ed. James Strachey (New York: W. W. Norton & Co., 1950), p. 100.

[47] *Civilization and Its Discontents*, p. 44.

[48] *General Psychological Theory*, p. 21 (Two Principles of Mental Functioning).

[49] Examples of Freud's critics include the following: Roazen says that Freud understood the process of self-deception but ignored that of self-healing (Roazen, op. cit., p. 233); Hartman sees the need for the development of a general psychological theory ("ego theory") to offset the "narrow clinical concept" of analysis which limits it to the understanding and therapy of neurosis (Hartman, op. cit., p. 11); Erich Fromm attributes the shortcomings of Freud's characterology, even while praising its developmental and antirelativistic aspects, to the fact that Freud was mainly concerned with the neurotic character and devoted little attention to the mature (or genital) character. *Man for Himself* (Greenwich, Conn.: Fawcett Publications, 1947), p. 45.

[50] Osborn, *Freud and Marx* (New York: Equinox Co-Operative Press, 1937), p. 64.

[51] *General Introduction*, p. 323.

[52] Ibid., p. 324.

[53] *New Introductory Lectures*, p. 98.

[54] *General Introduction*, p. 324. See also pp. 336–337; and *New Introductory Lectures*, pp. 98–102.

[55] See *General Introduction*, pp. 334–335. The phallic stage is so called to differentiate it from post-pubescent genital sexuality (Freud, *New Introductory Lectures*, p. 99).

[56] *General Introduction*, p. 335; and *Standard Edition*, vol. 19, pp. 141–177 (The Dissolution of the Oedipus Complex).

[57] *Standard Edition*, vol. 19, pp. 176, 34 (The Dissolution of the Oedipus Complex and The Ego and the Id); and *New Introductory Lectures*, p. 129.

[58] *Standard Edition*, vol. 19, p. 32 (The Ego and the Id).

[59] *New Introductory Lectures*, op. cit., pp. 124, 128 (The Ego and the Id); and *Group Psychology and the Analysis of the Ego*, trans. and ed. James Strachey (New York: Liveright Publishing Corp., 1967), pp. 37–42; and *Standard Edition*, vol. 19, p. 33 (The Ego and the Id).

[60] Mitchell, op. cit., p. 70–71.

[61] Thompson, "Identification with the Enemy and Loss of the Sense of Self," *The Psychoanalytic Quarterly*, vol. 9 (1940), 37.

[62] *New Introductory Lectures*, p. 64.

[63] Ibid., p. 86. Initially Freud saw anxiety as the result of libidinal repression; anxiety was dammed-up libido. But further clinical evidence led him to reformulate this. Anxiety came to be seen as the result of the subject finding himself in a situation which activates the unconscious fears of the oedipal situation, especially the fear of castration. Anxiety triggers the ego mechanism of repression against the impulse whose satisfaction will bring about the feared situation (pp. 86, 89–90). This will be discussed further in the section on "Health, Pathology, and the Unconscious," in this chapter.

[64] *General Introduction*, p. 221. (Emphasis in original.) See also *New Introductory Lectures*, p. 120.

[65] Although the problem of evaluating reality is more acute in the case of psychosis than neurosis, both involve the confusion of reality and fantasy. The psychotic attempts to replace the real external world with his fantasy construction; the neurotic exaggerates particular aspects of the real world. Freud, *General Psychological Theory*, p. 206 (The Loss of Reality in Neurosis). Freud refers to neurosis as the negative of perversion (*Three Contributions*, pp. 29, 94). Both serve the economic function of binding anxiety. Both are expressions of the perseverance of infantile psychic activity. Furthermore, both involve a regression of the libido to a partial stage. In the perversion, a regressed ego does not oppose the libidinal regression. In the neurosis, the ego, which has developed beyond the regressed libido, institutes a repression against the partial impulse (*General Introduction*, pp. 360–361).

[66] *General Psychological Theory*, p. 141 (The Unconscious); and *General Introduction*, p. 440.

[67] In pathological cases the association may be with the fantastic yet traumatic fears of the oedipal situation, indicating that the oedipus complex has not been successfully overcome. In almost all individuals, anxiety exists as the residue of the experience of birth (*General Introduction*, pp. 403–404).

[68] *New Introductory Lectures*, p. 82. Actually, Freud revised his theory of anxiety between the *General Introduction*, and *New Introductory Lectures*. The revised theory is first presented in *Inhibitions, Symptoms, and Anxiety*, (see *Standard Edition*, vol. 20). The discussion of anxiety in the text is consistent with the revised theory.

[69] *New Introductory Lectures*, p. 93; see also p. 89.

[70] Freud distinguishes psychoneurosis from actual neurosis in *General Introduction*, pp. 394–395. The former may express the mental consequences of a sexual disturbance. They may also come about as the result of some other occurrence which weakens the ego vis-á-vis the libido, such as loss of fortune or severe illness. The latter represents the direct somatic consequences of sexual disturbances such as coitus interruptus or abstinence. The psychoanalytic study of neurosis concentrates on psychoneurosis.

The ego strives to bind anxiety for, as we have seen, anxiety can paralyze the individual's actions. But the binding of anxiety in symptoms is hardly an effective response to this. A great amount of energy is expended both in the symptom and in combating it. This may result in a very serious impoverishment in available mental energy, thus disabling the individual for important tasks of life (*General Introduction*, op. cit., p. 367).

[71] See ibid., pp. 405–416; and Freud, *General Psychological Theory*, p. 32 (On the Mechanism of Paranoia).

[72] *General Introduction*, pp. 390, 467.

[73] Ibid, pp. 282, 287.

[74] Hartmann, "Psychoanalysis and Sociology," *Psychoanalysis Today*, ed. Sandor Lorand (New York: International University Press, 1944), pp. 331–332. It is significant that this emphasis of social structure is by a leading "ego-psychologist" primarily concerned with therapeutic rather than sociopolitical problems.

[75] Freud, *The Future of an Illusion*, trans. W. D. Robson-Scott (New York: Doubleday & Co., nd.), p. 79; and Freud, *Totem and Taboo*, p. 71.

[76] Freud, *General Introduction*, p. 465.

[77] Ricoeur, op. cit., p. 122.

5

IDEOLOGY IN FREUD'S SOCIAL
AND POLITICAL THOUGHT

THE attempt to employ psychoanalysis in social and political
research is not particularly novel or esoteric. Political theory
traditionally has been characterized by an expansiveness of concern
and comprehensiveness of inquiry. Furthermore, one could hardly
find "a more recurrent problem in political theory than the concept
of human nature."[1]

There is good reason that so much attention has been paid to
the problem of human nature in the history of Western political
thought. The more we known about the potentialities and limitations of human activity, the more rationally we can discuss the
possibility of alternative social and political structures. However,
most of the traditional theories of human nature were based on
little more than historically ungrounded speculations and normative assertions. We need a more specific psychology of human
needs and motivations if we are to pursue the problem of alternative social structures.

In contrast to traditional political theory, the concept of human
nature that emerges from psychoanalytic theory is based on the
analysis of conscious free associations and the reconstruction of
unconsciousness in the clinical situation. Freud enabled us to
understand human consciousness and behavior in terms of the
interaction between the needs of the individual and the demands
of the environment within which those needs are satisfied. He
described how the articulation of human needs is socially conditioned, especially as the infant first confronts society through the
family.

The problem is that the confrontation between the individual and society is for Freud everywhere the same. He conceived of society not as a historically evolving structure of social relationships, but as a universal structure of authority. For example, Freud's social psychology presupposes an instinctual structure which must be repressed in the interest of civilization. Groups can be formed only when individuals internalize a common authority. In other words, repression and internalization are essential for social interaction. Furthermore, Freud sought to discover the primeval cause of the conflict between individual and social interests, the psychological reason for this historically recurrent conflict. Having formulated the problem as a psychological one, Freud explained the history of this conflict in terms that he developed to explain the history of the individual's relationship with authority. History becomes just so many manifestations of the return of the repressed as we compulsively struggle to overthrow and then restore the authority of the father.

The assumptions involved in Freud's understanding of the psychology of social interaction, and his understanding of historical processes, transformed the critical insights of psychoanalysis into an ideological justification of the status quo. In this chapter, I will outline Freud's social psychology and historiography and make explicit the assumptions which underlie each.

SOCIAL PSYCHOLOGY

Freud saw a strong continuity between the psychoanalytic investigation of an individual and the investigation of the psychological antecedents and consequences of social interactions. This continuity was a result of the fact that individual psychology must consider the individual's relationships with others. The distinction between the relationships considered in social psychology and individual psychology revolves around the closeness of the individuals to one another and the number of individuals involved. Whereas individual psychology emphasizes the individual's relationships with his parents, siblings, lovers, friends, and other significant acquaintances, social psychology investigates the influence on the individual by large numbers of people, with whom he is somehow connected, but who otherwise may be strangers. Thus social psychology is concerned with the individual as a member of a race, nation, caste, profession, institution, a more temporarily organized group, or, as Freud seems to have overlooked, as a member of a class.[2]

In these interactions, the individual must renounce or modify some of his own needs in the interest of civilization. He must adjust to the patterns of interaction which define the group. In this discussion of Freud's social psychology I will consider, first, the relationship between civilization and instincts and then, the psychological structures of social interaction.

CULTURE AND THE INSTINCTS: THE PRIMORDIAL CONFLICT

By "culture" or "civilization" Freud meant "all those respects in which human life has raised itself above animal conditions." This includes the institutions and relationships which structure social interaction. It also includes the symbolic, theoretical, and technical realms of existence.[3]

Freud was concerned not as much with the effects of particular political, social, or economic institutions as with the effects of civilization per se. According to Freud, civilization developed under the pressure of the struggle for existence, a struggle which required sacrifices in the pursuit of instinctual satisfaction. As each individual repeats the sacrifices by overcoming the oedipus complex, the culture is recreated within him.[4]

Yet the instincts which are repressed in exchange for acceptance into a culture are the same instincts that bind the individual to his fellows, "For the sexual function is the only function of a living organism which extends beyond the individual and secures its connection with its species."[5] Although there may be a greater advantage from establishing relationships by work in common, erotic relationships are a stronger basis for interpersonal ties because of the exceptionally high degree of pleasure they involve. Besides, according to Freudian libidinal economics, the energy of the ego instincts is narcissistic libido which has been directed away from external objects. This narcissistic libido can be redirected, through a process similar to but not identical with sublimation, toward fellow workers in an aim-inhibited way. Freud claimed that these aim-inhibited ties were stronger than the ties arising from the necessity of social labor.[6]

For aim-inhibited libidinal relationships to be established, the restriction of sexual life is required. Repressive morality dams up erotic energy in aim-inhibited work relationships. The social repression of human sexuality was ultimately motivated by economics. However, it was the economics of scarcity rather than the economics of a particular social structure which Freud considered to be responsible.[7]

Freud observed that every culture was based on compulsory labor and instinctual renunciation. Culture was therefore a source of human suffering and the object of much hostility. Freud considered this unavoidable, since culture was based on "the external primordial struggle for existence."[8] Necessity is a harsh task-master. The mature individual must resign himself to this. Although scarcity, as a condition rooted in the technological level and the social relationships of the productive forces, could be overcome through human activity, it did not seem likely to Freud that this would be accomplished. Rather, he conceptualized scarcity as a mythical, immutable force: *ananke.*

With the mythologizing of scarcity as Ananke, repression becomes essential for the maintenance of human existence at a current level of civilization. Significantly, this mythologizing occurred at the time that Freud posited the struggle between the life and death instincts, *Eros* and *Thanatos*, as the fundamental instinctual conflict. If there was an instinct for aggression, death and destruction, then the conflict between the instincts and culture was irreconcilable. Thanatos had to be repressed or at least modified and socially directed for the maintenance of civilization.

Before considering Freud's hypotheses on the relationship between social activity and the repression of Eros, we will consider his conceptualization of thanatos, the death instinct.

Thanatos. While Freud was emphasizing the duality and interaction between the self-preservation and sexual impulses, he explicitly stated that this distinction between groups of instincts was only a hypothesis, an "auxiliary construction to be retained only so long as it proves useful. . . ."[9] Though the evidence gathered in psychoanalytic research supported this hypothesis, the psychoanalytic system could stand without it.

As his psychoanalytic work progressed, however, Freud found it increasingly difficult to fit the clinical facts to his hypothesis. Freud began to see the libido as the source of all instinctual energy. The economic theory of narcissism revealed that the ego instincts themselves had a libidinal component. What were once called ego instincts (self-preservation) and libinal instincts were subsequently both considered to be of a libidinal nature. What distinguished them was that the libidinal instincts were object-directed and the ego instincts were self-directed, or narcissistic libido.

With the libidinization of the self-preservation instincts, the libido became closely associated with Eros, "the preserver of all things." However, Freud believed he had discerned another type of ego instinct, which, given the underdevelopment of his ego psychology, was still strange to him.[10] They manifested themselves less clearly than the sensual and self-preservation instincts, and so could be understood only theoretically. Even then, an understanding of them required a revision of some of the most basic principles of psychoanalysis.

In the course of his clinical work, Freud observed many instances of patients displaying a compulsion to repeat unpleasurable experiences. Although many of these instances could be explained in terms of the reality principle or "the process by which repression turns a possibility of pleasure into a source of unpleasure . . . ," a great deal more could not be. Freud identified this compulsion to repeat experiences, which could not possibly be sources of pleasure, as an instinct more basic than the life-preserving impulses of self-preservation and sexuality, an instinct which displayed an urge in organic life to restore an earlier state of things. Since the earliest state of matter is inorganic, this is an instinct which strives to annihilate the existence of the organism; that is, it is a death instinct. But death is an aim which "the living organism has been forced to abandon under the pressure of external disturbing forces. . . ." Nevertheless, this impulse remains active through an unconscious cathexis.[11]

Freud responded to clinical difficulties which resulted from the compulsion to repeat by conceiving of the compulsion as an instinct. He attributed the long-term resistance to therapy (and thus to health and the potential for happiness) exhibited by some patients to an innate characteristic rather than to problems of technique. Once he posited this new death instinct he had to make it credible. This required first fitting it into the body of psychoanalytic theory and then revealing its manifestation in the life and consciousness of the individual.

Fitting the death instinct into the body of psychoanalytic thought required explaining how it could be more basic than the pleasure principle. It thus became necessary to separate the pleasure principle from the principle of constancy. The latter is the more accurate title of the economic principle of minimizing excitement. The pleasure principle can no longer be reduced to it. Henceforth, we must make a qualitative as well as quantitative distinction between pleasure and pain. Sexual excitement may involve a pleasurable *increase* of tension, at least when the potential for discharge is present.[12]

The principle of constancy or the Nirvana principle has as its aim the minimization of stimuli, and strives to bring about an inorganic state. But in the living organism the Nivarna principle interacts with the libido. This interaction results in a modification of the Nivarna principle: the pleasure principle. The pleasure principle now is conceived as a secondary, rather than primary process.

In order for the pleasure principle, and its socially imposed modification, the reality principle, to assert their dominance, the impulses associated with them must be bound before being discharged. In the free state, the aim of the impulses is the annihilation of excitation; in the secondary, bound state, it is the pleasurable discharge of tension.[13]

The modification of the Nirvana principle to the pleasure principle was brought about by "the life instincts, the libido, which has thus wrested a place for itself alongside the death instinct in regulating the processes of life."[14] The life instincts, too, are conservative in that they are peculiarly resistant to external influences and preserve life for a comparatively long period. But they also are responsible for the "progress" and "higher" development of life. Freud likened human life to a journey in which the one group of impulses causes the individual to rush toward the final aim as swiftly as possible; the other jerks him back at a certain point. He starts anew and prolongs the journey. Life moves toward death but only at its own pace and in its own fashion.[15]

Freud utilized biological and historical evidence in support of his theory of the death instinct. Freud himself admitted that the biological case was not that strong. The evidence showed coexisting trends to immortality and death in higher organisms, and biologists disagreed on how to interpret it.[16] Furthermore, there is a problem in using biological evidence to support this psychological hypothesis. The evidence of a natural movement to death in organic matter need not imply the aim or intention of death in these organisms. Inorganic matter may display the same tendency to deterioration, but we do not attribute a corresponding impulse to it. A biological proof of the death instinct would require replacing a theory of intentionality with a teleology.

Freud seemed to admit that biology did not prove the existence of the death instinct. Rather, he concluded that biological facts did not contradict the hypothesis. He realized that his own method required that he give examples of its manifestations. The first example he gave was taken from the clinical situation, the recognition of a sadistic component in the sexual instinct.[17] However, to accept this as a manifestation of the death instinct we must be willing to assume that the death instinct is only to be found in fusion with life instincts. We also must assume that the death instinct, under the influence of narcissistic libido, has been turned around from the ego to an object.

Once we are willing to make these assumptions all instances of externally directed aggression and destruction can be taken as manifestations of the death instinct. Since history is full of such instances, Freud can claim that history, along with the conditions of sadism and masochism, supported his hypothesis. In addition, Freud argued that the outward expression of this instinct cannot proceed unimpeded. When the energy of this impulse is not being used in self-destruction or aggression, it is taken over by the superego and used to repress the aggression of the ego. This results in a sense of guilt which expresses itself as a need for punishment.[18] In other words, the self-destructive impulse is directed outward and then internalized. Its energy is used to repress itself. With the introduction of the death instinct, the harsh superego, the compulsive features of which the psychoanalyst once attempted to cure, becomes necessary to check our innate destructiveness. It is the aggressiveness of the ego turned around on itself.

This is a crucial revision of the metapsychology. Repression and the distortion of impulsive strivings are no longer conceived as resulting primarily from a conflict between the organism, which seeks instinctual gratifications, and its social environment. Rather, they are derived from a conflict between libidinal impulses of both a sexual and self-preserving nature, which seek discharge through external objects, and a more primal psychological function that strives for the annihilation of all stimuli. The basic conflict now is carried out entirely within the individual's psyche.

The evidence for the existence of the death instinct is not convincing. Freud himself stressed the "often far-fetched speculation" involved in this hypothesis.[19] In its defense he cited its ability to explain anomalous clinical data. This ability can be countered by two other arguments. First, the facts which are explained also can be explained by a less-drastic revision of the metapsychology. Second, the social consequences of the acceptance of such a tentative hypothesis are extreme. I will consider each of these points in turn.

Freud believed that the inference of a death instinct explained more adequately the existence of certain symptoms and conditions, most notably the condition of masochism. Originally Freud conceived of masochism, the extreme expression of the desire for self-punishment and nihilistic peace, as a secondary drive. The masochist redirects an aggressive tendency against himself. However it is not the pain but an accompanying erogenous excitement which is enjoyed. With the death instinct, masochism becomes a primary drive; "it is the suffering itself that matters."[20]

Emphasizing the conflict between instincts and environment, Reich, as Freud originally did, explained masochism as a secondary drive. Yet even in his original formulation Freud misunderstood its dynamics. The masochist, Reich argued, sought not pain or punishment, but sexual pleasure. However the masochist could not pursue pleasure without being overwhelmed by a sense of guilt and the fear of punishment. The self-inflicted punishment is milder than the expected punishment and intended to be a substitute for it. "Thus it represents a special kind of defense against punishment and anxiety."[21]

His analysis of masochism led Reich to conclude that the longing for peace, death, nothingness is nothing more than "the manifestation of complete resignation, a retreat from a reality which has become solely unpleasurable, into nothingness."[22] The death instinct thus is retained as a psychological tendency of individuals in a repressive world, but it is rejected as an attempt to explain psychological phenomena with a biological theory supported by sociohistorical evidence. The death instinct is reinterpreted as a secondary manifestation of the fundamental conflict between the pleasure-seeking organism and its environment. In terms of instinctual conflict, destructiveness is the result of the need to repress sexual impulses in the interest of self-preservation.

Freud's formulation of the death instinct pressumed a repressive social order. Reich's reformulation suggested that the Nirvana principle operates as a tendency to restore an inorganic state of existence only in the context of an intolerably repressive social situation. That is, it aims, not at the annihilation of life, but at the restoration of a less tension-ridden state of existence. As such even before modification it may have a great deal in common with the pleasure principle. If the aim of the death instinct, as Herbert Marcuse has stated,

> . . . is not the termination of life but of pain—the absence of tension—then paradoxically in terms of the instinct, the conflict between life and death is the more reduced, the closer life approximates the state of gratification. Pleasure principle and Nirvana principle then converge. At the same time, Eros, freed from surplus repression, would be strengthened, and the strengthened Eros would, as it were, absorb the objective of the death instinct. . . . As suffering and want recede, the Nirvana principle may become reconciled with the reality principle.[23]

The hypothesis of a death instinct obscures the fact that the psychological processes which most forcefully oppose the sexual instincts "are moral inhibitions imposed by the outer world, by society."[24] Reich claimed that, although psychoanalytic theory broke new ground in exploring the social antecedents of psychological pain and suffering, the new theory of instincts impeded further investigation of these antecedents.[25] Reich's and Marcuse's reformulations of the death instinct make possible an examination of the ways in which the social environment can be made more tolerable to the pleasure-seeking organism. All things equal, this would make it a more useful hypothesis for social research.

Yet the conflict between the instincts and culture that Freud posited cannot be dismissed by reformulating his hypothesis of the death instinct. If the death instinct is derived from the social frustration of libidinal impulses, then the conflict between human impulses and civilization has only been displaced, not reconciled. Instead of an innate aggressiveness, aggression and destruction are manifestations of repressed libido. Let us now consider Freud's argument that the condition of scarcity (Ananke) requires the repression of pleasure-seeking activity in the interest of social life.

Ananke and the Repression of Eros. Before positing the death instinct, Freud observed that the prevailing morality demanded more sacrifices than it was worth. Although he considered himself to be an observer rather than a reformer, he claimed that he "could not avoid observing with critical eyes" and could not support conventional sexual morality.[26] In his paper on "Civilized Sexual Morality and Modern Nervous Disorders" he claimed that the prevailing morality might not even accomplish its primary goal. Whereas its function is to redirect sexual energy toward cultural achievements, it often results in neuroses which make the individual's adjustment to the demands of civilization more difficult. Furthermore, while the sublimation of sexual energy is necessary for intellectual activity, there seemed to be a point beyond which the repression of sexuality is counterproductive to this end. For example, Freud attributed what he perceived as a socially conditioned intellectual inferiority of women to the excessive repression imposed on them. He also claimed that sexual abstinence usually produced "well-behaved weaklings" who were lost in the great mass. Since all cultural institutions were closely interconnected, the repression they demanded and the effects of that repression could not be alleviated without regard to the entire social structure.[27]

Freud developed these critical insights while examining the

position of the individual within society. However, in his social theory, his defense of the individual was countered by the needs of culture. Cultural repression was required for the production of the products necessary for self-preservation. Cultural achievements alleviated the suffering derived from the merciless forces of nature and our own physiologies. While the necessity of culture was responsible for the frustration of libido, certain realms of culture, such as professional work and art, allowed for displacing the libido and shifting instinctual aims so that they would not come up against the frustration of the world.[28]

The suffering caused by civilized morality, either through repression or the unconscious sense of guilt associated with transgressions, was justified in terms of Ananke (scarcity), Thanatos, and cultural achievement. Work is required to overcome scarcity. Repression is required to limit our pleasure-seeking activity and control our aggression. The achievements of art, science, philosophy, and such are milder satisfactions which, as displacements of our necessarily repressed primal instincts, are made possible by the existing level of culture.

As we have seen in connection with instinctual vicissitudes, sublimation is the process by which impulsive energy is placed in the service of cultural achievement, particularly the alleviation of the condition of scarcity. Freud claimed that sublimation is accessible only to a few people. He suggested that sublimation required a psychological constitution which was predisposed to this vicissitude and which could be satisfied in its mild way. Freud saw this constitution as being prevalent among artists and professionals. Yet "the great majority of people only work under the stress of necessity, and this natural human aversion to work raises most difficult social problems."[29]

Eros, no less than Thanatos, is in conflict with civilization. Although productive activity is necessary for the preservation of human life within the condition of scarcity, the pleasure-seeking organism had a natural aversion to work. Since Freud was concerned with culture per se rather than with the characteristics of a particular culture, he never considered the actual conditions of most people's employment. Freud assumed that if the average worker, in contrast to the artist and professional, was unable to find sublimated satisfaction is his work, it was because the average worker was unable to be satisfied in this milder form. The actual conditions of work which differentiate the activities of the two groups, the privileged position of professionals and artists in regard to other workers, the greater control they may have over the process and product of their labor, a less-extensive division of their work, are not even considered by Freud. If the great majority cannot find satisfaction in their work, it is because their psychological dispositions preclude it.

The fact that professionals and artists are more prone to sublimate through their work may be due not to their predispositions, but the social conditions of their work. The more control the individual has over his job, the more opportunity he may have to sublimate libidinal energy through it. The "natural human aversion" to work may be little more than a human response to alienated, exploitative labor; the social problems may arise from the organization of work itself.

Having precluded this critical perspective on the problem, Freud was concerned instead with the processes through which the fundamental conflict between human impulses and apparent social necessity were psychologically mediated. The majority must be coerced to work. Presumably, they are not involved in the cultural achievements of human history. For culture to be maintained, the mass had to be led; this was a precondition of human society. Freud's social psychology sought to explain the psychological processes by which the masses came to repress their antisocial impulses and to internalize the demands of their culture.

In his consideration of the psychological traits of the masses Freud hardly considered the role of the existing social structure in developing those traits. So, although Freud in his analysis of the psychology of group dynamics provided critical insights, he left them abstract and ahistorical. The mass became a transhistorical entity; history, a recurring pattern; political activity, a vicious cycle. As we shall now see, in Freud's group psychology, psychoanalytic theory became a justification of social hierarchy.

THE PSYCHOLOGY OF GROUP DYNAMICS

Freud's psychology of the masses was based on an elitist ideology that attracted him to a middle class, authoritarian, school of thought. Indeed, even his use of the term "mass" displayed the ideological underpinnings of his social psychology. The German word *massen* emerged from an elitist, conservative, even reactionary school of thought. His explicit use of a spokesman for this school, Le Bon, reflected an authoritarian strain in Freud which existed alongside his great defense of the individual against repressive society. Le Bon's *The Crowd* was an intractably hostile critique which was very popular among the French middle class and which marked the culmination of a new political psychology. Freud used Le Bon to sum up his own position, citing verbatim entire passages from his work.[30]

According to Freud group life may be able to raise its members' morality in the form of unselfishness and devotion to an ideal, but it can do this only after it had broken down their individual inhibitions and stirred up their cruel, brutal, and destructive instincts. These are then brought under control by the power of suggestion, especially, the suggestion of leaders.[31] The group has a potential for altruistic as well as extremely destructive conduct.

Yet, although the ethical conduct of a group may rise above that of an individual (who is always primarily motivated by self-interest), the intellectual capacity of a group is always below that of an individual. The cultural accomplishments of the group (such as language, arts and crafts, folksongs, and folklore) notwithstanding, Freud saw the mass as lazy and unintelligent. Thought in the group is characterized by simplicity. The group demands illusion. It has difficulty distinguishing between what is real and what is not. The individual loses the capacity for criticism and is affected much more strongly by emotional appeal than by rational argument. The group needs a leader to manipulate it and readily submits to his authority.[32]

One forfeits his distinctiveness and allows himself to be influenced by suggestion only because he feels a need to be in harmony with the other members of the group rather than in opposition to them.[33] But beneath the susceptibility to suggestion in the group Freud discerned the role of libidinal ties in binding the group.

Group psychology is characterized by the individual establishing libidinal, emotional ties in two directions: with the leader on one hand and the other group members on the other. "Love for oneself knows only one barrier—love for others, love for objects."[34]

The group effectively limits the individual's narcissism and increases his tolerance toward his fellows by producing an emotional, aim-inhibited bond with them which binds them beyond the point necessary for profit or even survival. Yet, although the influence of suggestion is exercised not only by the leader but also by every individual on every other individual, the key to Freudian group psychology is not the individual's relationship with one another but the relationship of each with the leader. Freud examined two highly organized, lasting, and artificial groups—the Catholic Church and the army—to show why this is so.

These groups are held together by the illusion of a leader who loves all the members equally (Jesus in the Church, the commander-in-chief in the army). Since all are loved equally all have an equal share in his love. Their mutual emotional investment and dependence on the leader led to the development of ties among the members similar to sibling ties.[35]

If in the Oedipus complex we distinguish identification with a parent from the choice of the parent as an erotic object, so we must make the same distinction in regard to the relationship between the group leader and each of the members. Identification is the earliest emotional tie with another, being possible before any sexual object choice has been made. "Identification endeavors to mould a person's own ego after the fashion of the one that has been taken as a model." The introjection of the object into the ego as an ego ideal is the basis of Freudian group psychology. Freud defines a primary group as, "a number of individuals who have put one and the same object in the place of their ego ideal and have consequently identified themselves with one another in their ego."[36]

The group substitutes regressive identification for libidinal relationships with objects. The authority submitted to as a consequence of this identification usually is, a personal one. However, a common tendency, leading idea, or common hatred against a particular group or institution may take the place of a leader or be the basis of the leader's position.[37] Identification produces a narcissistic satisfaction which counteracts the individual's hostility toward a restricting authority.

Freud concluded that humans can live together in groups only when they identify with a common leader. Although the demand for equality was an essential feature of the process of identification in groups, it applied only to the members and not the leader. If a contract for equality was implied in society, it was a contract from which the leader was exempt. In this crucial respect Freud's view of society was similar to Hobbes'. The leader had little obligation to the led, other than to lead them effectively.[38]

This similarity between Freud and Hobbes is related to a similar conception of human nature. From Hobbes through Freud, as Erich Fromm has noted, there is a line of Western political thought which stresses an unalterable contradiction between human nature and society.[39] Human nature is seen as persisting through history and unalterable; it is aggressive and insecure, and this requires strict authority to control. Freud, as a more modern liberal than Hobbes, considered this a defense not of an absolute sovereign but of the authority of culture, which offered a double-edged protection against the frightening conditions of a state of nature. On the one hand, cultural achievements and advances protect us against the brute force of nature; on the other, cultural prohibitions and restraints regulate social relationships and protect us from the aggression of others.

Yet Freud's description of an aggressive, "natural man" was based, as have been all such descriptions, on observations of civilized man. As socialists have long argued, traits such as aggressiveness and greed are essential for success in a competitive market society. Thus history, rather than nature, may be responsible for these traits. History was a consolation that even Le Bon offered in his diatribe on human irrationality. Yet Freud did not follow Le Bon in seeing the modern mass as a product of industrial, urban societies. While Freud's social psychology was a "psychology of being ruled," for him the ruled had no history, only a psychology.[40]

Freud failed to consider the role of social structure in shaping group interaction. Thus although some of his insights might have been valid as description, they failed to get to the root of the problem. The social structure itself may be the major source of the psychological traits which appear to make it necessary. Through its rewarding of competitiveness and its moralistic repression of pleasure-seeking activity, the social structure may bring to the fore the aggressive aspects of the individu·'l's personality. Cultural activity may allow for the release of repressed erotic impulses through sublimated activity and aim-inhibited relationships. But it also, as Freud himself observed, demands more repression than is necessary for human social life and leads to the damming-up of more psychic energy than could be effectively released. The substitution of the group ideal, as embodied in the leader, reduces the individual's resistance to others and weakens the ability of the ego to perceive and test reality. The perceptions and evaluations of the group ideal are substituted for the faculty of conscience as a code of ethics critical of one's self and society. The individual seeks authority because his own ego has not been allowed to develop.

Overlooking the effects of the social structure on the psyche led Freud to offer psychological explanations for socio-historical problems. He explained the irrationality prevalent in groups as a regression to the psychic level of primitive, prehistoric man. Beneath the surface of civilized man he saw the remnants of this archaic heritage. Like Hobbes and the other liberal theorists on social contract, he sought to reconstruct this prehistoric state by revealing transhistoric absolutes of human nature. He then used this reconstructed state to argue against the feasibility of a qualitatively less repressive culture. In the following section, I will argue that Freud's resignation and conservativeness toward social problems resulted from this method of transhistorical generalization rather than from any of the metapsychological models or assumptions of psychoanalysis.

FREUD'S HISTORIOGRAPHY

In the history of the species, Freud asserted, "something happened similar to the events in the life of the individual." The species, too, suffered an early trauma which, although defended against and forgotten, left permanent traces in the psyche. After a long period of latency there was a partial return of the repressed material creating phenomena "similar in structure and tendency to neurotic symptoms."[41]

The phenomena Freud had in mind was religion. Freud saw monotheistic religion as a return of the repressed, a restitution of the authority of a harsh, primeval father. He constructed a fantastic prehistory to explain the development of religion in terms of the Oedipus complex. Like the individual, the species, in its primitive past, had to overcome a similar situation. Indeed Freud perceived a direct analogy between the development of culture and the individual psyche. Like the oedipal infant, primitive man was subject to a repressive paternal authority, which he rebelled against and then internalized. This primeval situation was the model for the infantile situation.

In this section, I will examine first the analogy between the development of the species (phylogeny) and the individual (ontogeny) as Freud perceived it. Then I will discuss the way in which his social theory is marred by the attempt to explain socio-historical processes in terms of the psychic processes of the individual.

PHYLOGENY AND ONTOGENY

Freud believed that the critical cultural transformation occurred between an assumed, prehistoric, precultural period, and the emergence of civilization. Although very much concerned with the evolution of culture, he did not seem to find the transformations of social structures or the differences between cultures to be very significant. So-called primitive cultures are themselves "as old as civilized races," and their present conditions have likewise distorted and modified the primeval past.[42] To reveal man's true nature, we must go back to a time before culture. We reconstruct a prehistorical state of human existence, and then base our analysis of human potentiality and possible social structures on this reconstruction.

Freud, following Darwin, hypothesized a state in which primitive man lived in a horde ruled by a brutally strict father.[43] This primal horde was structured like the oedipal family, only its prohibitions were much harsher. The male children were forced to repress not only their infantile longing for their mother but also their erotic feelings for all the women. The father appropriated the women of the horde for himself. If a male child excited his father's jealousy, he was killed, castrated, or expelled from the horde.

After wandering about, he might have procured a wife. A few might even have succeeded in establishing their own hordes and instituting similar prohibitions. The luckiest of the brothers usually was the youngest, who was in the position to replace the father after his death.

The brothers who were driven out and who married exogenously lived in small communities. Some cultural advance, such as a new weapon, led the brothers to realize that together they could do what individually they could not: overpower the severe father and end the patriarchal horde. "Cannibal savages as they were, it goes without saying that they devoured their victim as well as killing him."[44] By consuming his flesh, they completed their identification with the violent father who doubtless had been the feared and envied model of each.

After the primal patricide, the affection which the brothers also felt for the murdered father reasserted itself. Remorse and a sense of guilt was felt by the group. After struggling among themselves for the right to succeed the father, they came to see this struggle as futile and dangerous. They each agreed to renounce their claim if the other would do likewise. The war of all against all was averted by a social contract. They all gave up their claim to the women of the clan and thus the clan became exogenous. This aggravated the guilt and remorse over the patricide, for now they were renouncing the goal of the crime. Consequently, the authority of the father was restored and the crime repudiated and repressed through the deification of a father surrogate. This occurred first through the totemic system with its prohibitions and rituals. Religion emerged when the worshipped being was humanized.

The primal murder was thus the beginning of social organization, moral restrictions, and religion. Society was based on complicity in the common crime. The restoration of the father's authority climaxed in the dominance of authority—religious or secular—in social life. "The leader of the group is still the dreaded primal father. . . . The primal father is the group ideal which governs the ego in place of the ego ideal."[45]

If the primal horde is the model for all group dynamics, then group psychology must be as old as individual psychology. The strict primal father, by prohibiting the direct satisfaction of erotic impulses, forced his sons into aim-inhibited, emotional ties with him and with one another. "He forced them, so to speak, into group psychology."[46] Yet he, alone, was exempt from the emotional ties of the group. He, alone, had an individual psychology.

The patriarchal family marks a return of the repressed memory of the primal father. "And yet the new family was only a shadow of the old one; there were a number of fathers and each one was limited by the rights of the others." It was perhaps in the context of the family that some individual sought to free himself from the group and take the father's part by the only means feasible—in his imagination. He formulated the ego ideal of the mythical hero who by himself slew the monstrous father. The heroic myth "is the step by which the individual emerges from group psychology."[47]

The individual does in fantasy what the brothers did in reality. Beneath the Oedipus complex of the individual is the Oedipus complex of the species. The basic theoretical construct of Freud's social theory is the analogy between the individual and society, between the psychological and the historical. This analogy is asserted as axiomatic. Ontogeny recapitulates phylogeny. Just as embryonic development summarized evolution, so too, the first few years of childhood summarized the development from the Stone Age to civilization.[48]

The primitive and the child survive in our memory as representatives of the past. The primeval takes its place alongside the infantile as determinants of psychic states and human behavior. Primal memories are a phylogenetic possession. Through these memories, the individual inherits the experiences of past ages.[49] Accordingly, the Oedipus complex is not the result of a particular family arrangement in a particular social structure but a phylogenetic inheritance. The consequent formation of the superego and submission to authority are likewise universals of human existence.

These assertions are the basis of Freud's conservative conclusions on the possibility of a qualitatively different human future. Their force depends upon the acceptance of Freud's construction of human prehistory. Yet, like the death instinct, the evidence in support of this prehistory is far from convincing. Although Freud himself emphasized its hypothetical nature, he was convinced that it had great explanatory value; that the analogy between phylogeny and ontogeny expressed at least a literary truth of human nature.[50] Humans need authority and readily submit to it. However, humans are essentially ambivalent to that authority. This abivalency leads them to rebel against it, only to be overwhelmed by guilt and, eventually, a resurgence of repressed memories of the primal father and the crime of the brothers. People compulsively seek strict leaders to replace the father who was treated so brutally. By emphasizing the primal reasons for the individual's need to be led, Freud precluded the possibility of a cooperative, nonhierarchical social structure. Hence the truth of his analogy is not as much literary as ideological. As Reiff explained:

> Freud's well-known pessimism as a social thinker must be approached in terms of his model of recurrent time, as against the openness of a qualitatively different future. There is nothing qualitatively different beyond this life and this way of life. . . . The content of human rationality is to face up to the comfortless world as it was, is, and will be.[51]

For Freud humans are historical objects but not historical subjects. We are a product of historical development and even a factor in it. But we are not capable of taking control of our historical development and redirecting it. The patterns of our social life have been established in our primeval past and permanently embedded in our psyches. All subsequent history has been a manifestation of this. As Reiff noted, in Freud's analogical system, public, social events were only the points at which private, psychological mechanisms revealed themselves. Freud's social theory was self-consciously dependent on the translation of the public into the private. Psychological mechanisms informed and defined the social process.[52]

Freud's translation of the public into the private and his psychological explanation of social processes is the subject of the next section.

SOCIAL PROCESSES AND PSYCHOLOGICAL EXPLANATION

While psychoanalytic theory introduced social determinants into the innermost recesses of the psyche, the analogy between phylogeny and ontogeny devalued the social context within which psychological processes operate. That is, although psychoanalytic theory developed a model to examine the effects of social and historical factors on human consciousness, Freud conceptualized these factors ahistorically. For example, Freud posited ananke as a given of human existence. In doing so, he hardly differentiated the scarcity of the present from the scarcity of the past. He paid scant attention to the ways in which technological progress allows us to overcome scarcity, while the social relationships of production maintain it. These relationships are the result of the way the given society organizes the human interaction essential for the production of life's necessities. Yet Freud viewed the suffering which results from social relationships as no less inevitable than the suffering which comes from our own bodies or the merciless forces of nature.[53]

Freud found it "remarkable that, little as men are able to exist in isolation, they should yet feel as a heavy burden the sacrifices that culture expects of them in order that a communal existence may be possible."[54] Critical theorists have suggested that it is the excessive demands of a class society rather than the intrinsic demands of human existence to which men and women are reacting. Freud hardly considered the existence of what has been called surplus repression or its effects on the human psyche.[55] His insight that certain social classes may develop a hostility toward civilization if they are required to sacrifice more than other classes which reap more of the benefits was not incorporated fully into his social psychology.[56] Indeed, it is difficult to see how it could have been given Freud's pessimistic views on the industriousness of working people and the lack of historical referents in his conceptualizations of such conditions of human existence as scarcity and aggression. He had to conclude that all cultures were based on repression which evoked the hostility of the individual who then became an enemy of his culture.

Freud blamed the individual for his hostility toward civilization. Freud saw this hostility as the result of the individual's immaturity, his failure to accept the demand of the reality principle. But, since he never considered the content of the reality principle, Freud's explanation of the individual's hostility toward civilization was inadequate. He failed to consider that the individual's resistance to the reality principle may be rationally motivated. Society indeed may demand greater sacrifices of one person than of another, who might be enjoying more of its privileges.

Freud asked whether a reconciliation between individual needs and cultural requirements could be achieved by the restructuring of society, but it does not seem likely that Freud considered such a restructuring to be possible. The social relationships of the family, state, and society are regulations made by ourselves for our mutual protection and benefit. Yet we have been unable to avoid the suffering that derives from this source. Freud takes this historical failure as a sign of the impossibility of the task, as a manifestation of a piece of our unconquerable nature.[57]

If civilization emerges from socially necessary activity rather than from a primeval, mythical situation, then the interest of the individual and the community come into irreconcilable conflict only as a result of the individual defending his own particular interest against the social demands he confronts. These demands are reproduced by his own activity but have acquired a power over and above him. A certain amount of conflict between the individual and the community, and of human suffering derived from this source may be necessitated by the demands of self-preservation. But the suffering and conflict derived from the current division of labor and commodity production is greater than this. In the relationships of commodity production human needs and the development of human potential are subsumed in the processes of capital accumulation and the production of surplus value.

The failure of working people to recognize that things could be different results from the ideological hegemony of the ruling class. In the Marxian conception, ideologies are explained as a misunderstanding of social life, a false consciousness. They are not an accidental or arbitrary misunderstanding but a misunderstanding in the interest of the privileged class. The dominance of an ideology expressed by a ruling class is a precondition for the dominance of the ruling class itself. For workers, ideology opposes the development of the consciousness necessary to structure social relationships according to their own interests.

Freud did not believe that ideologies could be understood in exclusively economic terms. "Mankind never lives entirely in the present. The past, the tradition of the race and of the people, lives on in the ideologies of the superego, and yields only slowly to the influences of the present." Operating through the superego past conditions exert a powerful influence in human life, "independently of economic conditions."[58]

Freud was right to suggest that ideologies may be based on the conditions of the past. But this is not incompatible with the view that ideologies emerge in association with class interests. Rather, Freud's position underscored the role of psychic processes in mediating the development of human consciousness. Ideologies function to impede people from developing an awareness of their role in social processes and an awareness of their own potential. Aspects of past ideologies may be retained as long as they function to confuse people about social processes.

The acceptance of the existing level of social repression as necessary at one time might have been based on reason, but now it is based on ideology. As Habermas noted, if technical progress opens up the objective possibility of reducing socially necessary repression below the level of institutionally demanded repression, the utopian content of technical progress can be freed from its fusion with the ideological components of culture that have been fashioned to legitimize authority. This utopian content can be converted into a critique of power structures that have become obsolete. The more the power of technical control is extended and the pressure of reality correspondingly decreased, the weaker become the prohibitions of instincts compelled by the systems of self-preservation. However, as long as technology is administered by a social class, "then class specific privations and denials are linked to general ones."[59]

As we have seen, Freud was not unaware of the existence of unnecessary repression. He noted that in social psychology,

> The critical question is whether and to what extent one can succeed, first, in diminishing the burden of the instinctual sacrifices imposed on men; secondly, in reconciling them to those that must necessarily remain, and thirdly, in compensating them for these.[60]

Without forming a concept of class in capitalist society, Freud could not consider these questions seriously. His analysis remained abstract and ahistorical. For Freud class struggle was reducible to a manifestation of the primeval struggle between hordes.[61] In his conception of recurrent time and compulsive repetition of the primeval past, the critical insights of psychoanalytic theory were lost. The task of drawing them out and utilizing them in a critical political psychology was left for others.

CONCLUSION: FREUD AND POLITICAL THEORY

Freud's social theory was influenced greatly by ideological assumption. Freud observed a pervasive aggresiveness and destructiveness in human behavior and attributed it to our instinctual nature. He observed a hostility on the part of the individual toward culture and posited an irreconcilable conflict between the interests of the individual and of society. In Freudian social psychology this conflict is mitigated only by an introjection of the cultural ego ideal at the expense of the development of the individual's own ego functions. The individual's antisocial nature is constrained by the power of suggestion in his aim-inhibited relationship with the leader. For Freud, as for Hobbes, the leader is the source of group cohesiveness.

Having described the antisocial tendencies of human nature, Freud, like the liberal theorists on social contract before him, attempted to reconstruct a primeval state of nature in which human nature could be seen more clearly since it was less constrained socially. According to Freud humans in this natural state lived in primal hordes characterized by strict patriarchal authority. The members of the horde had a contradictory reaction to the patriarch. The brothers revolted against the strict authority of the father and killed him. Following this, they were overcome by a sense of guilt and remorse which led them to reinstitute the authority of the father in a symbolic form, to bring about the return of the repressed.

Consequently, human civilization requires the exercise of patriarchal authority on both the ontogenetic and phylogenetic level. The patriarchal family marks the return of the repressed memory of the primal father. The resolution of the Oedipus complex through the internalization of patriarchal authority is an ontogenetic prerequisite for human culture. The primal horde is Freud's model for all group dynamics. Individuals may revolt against the authority of the leader or the cultural ego ideal, but they are doomed to reenact the primal pattern. Political activity cannot alter the hierarchical nature of civilization. The resurgence of repressed memories and experiences always will result in a reinstitution of patriarchal authority.

Consequently we must look beyond Freud's social treatises (such as *Totem and Taboo, Group Psychology and the Analysis of the Ego, Civilization and Its Discontents*) to ascertain Freud's contribution to political theory. Freud spoke to the right questions. What is the basis of human communities and the causes of their dissolution? What is the nature of authority and its function in our lives? Why are our instincts frustrated and what effect does this frustration have on human psychology? And ultimately, what is the basis of the conflict between the individual and society and how can it be reconciled?[62]

These are radical questions which require us to get to the root of socio-historical processes. The psychoanalytic investigation into the lack of human freedom in an unfree society, as Theodore Adorno observed, resembled the historical materialist critique of society blindly influenced by its economic forces. But under Freud's deadly medical gaze, the lack of personal freedom becomes petrified as an anthropological constant.[63] Confronted with this unalterably repressive social environment, psychoanalysis became both a defense "of the private man defending himself against public encroachment . . ." and a defense of the necessity of culture to defend itself against the antisocial tendencies of the individual. It dealt with this conflict by undercutting the problem of social constraints while emphasizing "the theme of the anti-political individual seeking his self-perfection in a context as far from the communal as possible."[64]

The failure of people to accept the "fundamental" conditions of human existence was seen by Freud as a psychological problem. Civilization required the modification of the individual's instinctual structure. The public interest was opposed to the private interest. In Freudianism, the individual must accept this and get on with the tasks of life. But the class analysis of society has shown that the conflict between the public and private interest, to a large extent, results from the contradiction of class interests. "Society" demands greater sacrifices from some classes while granting greater privileges to others. For people to accept this is for them to accept repression and exploitation which might be and have been challenged by political action. The discontent of the exploited in a class society is rational; it need not be explained in terms of unconscious processes (although the form of expression of this discontent might be). What is less understandable is the widespread acceptance of the class structure and its ideological justifications.

The Marxist theory of ideology stressed the socioeconomic determinants of ideological thought. Engels wrote that "ideology is a process accomplished by the so-called thinker consciously, indeed, but with a false unconsciousness. The real motives impelling him remain unknown to him."[65] Engels reconginzed that this was so. Freud showed how and why it was so.

The socioeconomic determinants explained the social rather personal sources of ideologies, "the way these notions come about."[66] Psychoanalysis is concerned with the internal processes of self-deceptive consciousness. Even if he saw no possibility of overcoming this condition, Freud's investigation of distorted human consciousness teaches us a great deal about human beings as they really are in the present society. Freud revealed the unconscious determinants of our perception of reality and the reasons for and processes by which we may psychically escape from reality. These processes are of critical importance for, as Reuben Osborn states,

> If the Marxist desires to get the workers to grips with reality, to teach him that he can change it by his own efforts, he must combat those mental tendencies by which the worker seeks to escape from the world of reality.[67]

Utilizing the psychoanalytic theory of partial consciousness, ideological consciousness can be understood in terms of the original instinctual dispositions of humans in interaction with the social environment. This is why critical theorists have seen in the psychoanalytic method a potential to reconstruct social determinants through an analysis of subjectivity. For example, Reich's and

Marcuse's reformulations of the death instinct were themselves based on psychoanalytic models and Freud's own earlier hypotheses. Marcuse emphasized that Freud's concepts have a social as well as psychic content.[68]

Our understanding of the process of the social conditioning of consciousness certainly can be enhanced by those aspects of the Freudian system which enable us to understand the interpenetration of the human psyche and its social environment. Yet we must avoid the ideological assumptions and psychological explanations of social processes which pervaded Freud's social and political thought. A critical revision of these assumptions and explanations, like Reich's and Marcuse's revisions of the death instinct, is necessary.

Reich made the first and still most systematic attempt to revise Freud's theories along these lines. The behavior that Freud explained in terms of human nature, Reich explained in terms of second nature or a socially conditioned character structure. In the next part of this study, I will consider the extent to which Reich's theory of character structure systematically incorporated historically specific social influences into psychoanalytic theory and revealed the psychological processes which influence the social conditioning of consciousness.

NOTES

[1] Roazen, *Freud: Political and Social Thought* (New York: Alfred A. Knopf, 1970), p. 3.

[2] Freud, *Group Psychology and the Analysis of the Ego*, trans. and ed. James Strachey. The International Psychoanalytical Library, no. 6 (New York: Liveright Publishing Corp., 1967), pp. 1-2.

[3] Freud, *The Future of an Illusion*, trans. W. D. Robson-Scott (New York: Doubleday & Co., n.d.), p. 3.

[4] Freud, *A General Introduction to Psychoanalysis*, trans. Joan Riviere (New York: Washington Square Press, 1964), p. 27.

[5] Ibid., p. 420.

[6] Freud, *Civilization and Its Discontents*, trans. and ed. James Strachey (New York: W. W. Norton & Co., 1961), pp. 49–50, 69; and Freud, *General Psychological Theory*, ed. Phillip Reiff (New York: Macmillan Publishing Co., 1974), p. 183 (The Libido Theory).

[7] Freud, *Civilization and Its Discontents*, p. 56; and *General Introduction*, p. 32.

[8] *General Introduction*, p. 321. See also *Future of an Illusion*, p. 11.

[9] *General Psychological Theory*, pp. 89–90 (Instincts and Their Vicissitudes).

[10] Freud, *Beyond the Pleasure Principle*, trans. James Strachey (New York: Liveright Publishing Corp., 1961), pp. 46–47.

[11] Ibid., pp. 30, 51–55.

[12] *General Psychological Theory*, p. 191 (The Economic Problem of Masochism).

[13] *Beyond the Pleasure Principle*, p. 56.

[14] *General Psychological Theory*, p. 191 (The Economic Problem of Masochism).

[15] *Beyond the Pleasure Principle*, pp. 22–25.

[16] Ibid., pp. 39–41.

[17] Ibid., pp. 43, 47.

[18] *Civilization and Its Discontents*, p. 70.

[19] *Beyond the Pleasure Principle*, p. 18.

[20] Compare Freud's formulations in *General Psychological Theory*, p. 93 (Instincts and Their Vicissitudes); and pp. 196–197 (The Economic Problem of Masochism).

[21] Reich, *Character Analysis*, 3d ed., trans. Vincent R. Carfagno (New York: Simon & Schuster, 1976), p. 266.

[22] Ibid., p. 308.

[23] Marcuse, *Eros and Civilization: A Philosophical Inquiry into Freud* (Boston: Beacon Press, 1974), p. 235.

[24] Reich, op. cit., p. 310.

[25] Ibid., p. 257.

[26] *General Introduction*, p. 441.

[27] *The Standard Edition of the Complete Psychological Works of Sigmund Freud*, vol. 9, ed. James Strachey (London: Hogarth Press, 1962), pp. 198–199, 202 (Civilized Sexual Morality and Modern Nervous Disorders).

[28] *Civilization and Its Discontents*, p. 44.

[29] Ibid., p. 27.

[30] Reiff, "Psychology and Politics: The Freudian Connection," *World Politics*, vol. 7 (January 1955), 297; and Reiff, "The Origin of Freud's Political Psychology," *Journal of the History of Ideas*, vol. 17 (April 1956), 236, 242. See also Freud, *Group Psychology*, pp. 5–8.

[31] *Group Psychology*, p. 11.

[32] *Future of an Illusion*, p. 7; and *Group Psychology*, p. 12.

[33] *Group Psychology*, p. 24.

[34] Ibid., p. 34. See also p. 27.

[35] Ibid., p. 26.

[36] Ibid., p. 38; 48.

[37] Ibid., p. 32.

[38] See ibid., p. 53; and Hobbes, *Leviathan: On the Matter, Forme, and Power of a Commonwealth Ecclesiastical and Civil*, ed. Michael Oakeshott (New York: Collier Books, 1972), p. 135.

[39] Fromm, *The Sane Society* (New York: Holt, Reinhart, & Winston, 1955), p. 74.

[40] Reiff, "The Origins of Freud's Political Psychology," pp. 240, 248.

[41] Freud, *Moses and Monotheism*, trans. Katherine Jones (New York: Random House, 1937), pp. 102–107.

[42] *Totem and Taboo*, ed. James Strachey (New York: W. W. Norton & Co., 1950), p. 102n.

[43] Ibid., p. 125. The following discussion of the primal horde is drawn from this work, pp. 125–126, 140–146; and *Moses and Monotheism*, pp. 102–107.

[44] *Totem and Taboo*, p. 142.

[45] *Group Psychology*, p. 59.

[46] Ibid., p. 56.

[47] Ibid., pp. 67, 68.

[48] Reiff, "History, Psychoanalysis, and the Social Sciences," *Ethics*, vol. 63 (1952–53), 107; and Reiff, "The Authority of the Past: Sickness and Society in Freud's Thought," *Social Research*, vol. 2 (Winter 1954), 431.

Freud also drew a parallel between the development of civilization itself and the development of the individual. The individual phases of narcissism, object-choice, and mature adjustment to reality, corresponded to the cultural phases of totemism, religion, and science. The last stage of each sequence is seen as the end of a process, beyond which no development is possible (*Totem and Taboo*, p. 90).

[49] *General Introduction*, p. 380.

[50] *Group Psychology*, p. 54.

[51] Reiff, "The Authority of the Past," p. 449.

[52] Reiff, "History, Psychoanalysis, and the Social Sciences," p. 109.

[53] *Civilization and Its Discontents*, p. 24.

[54] *Future of an Illusion*, p. 4.

[55] This term is used by Marcuse to differentiate the repression which results from a particular structure of social relationships over and beyond that necessary for social activity. Marcuse, op. cit., p. 35.

[56] *Future of an Illusion*, p. 18.

[57] *Civilization and Its Discontents*, pp. 43, 33.

[58] *New Introductory Lectures*, trans. and ed. James Strachey (New York: W. W. Norton & Co., 1965), p. 670.

[59] Habermas, *Knowledge and Human Interest* (Boston: Beacon Press, 1971), p. 281.

[60] *Future of an Illusion*, p. 6.

[61] *New Introductory Lectures*, p. 177.

[62] Reiff, "Psychology and Politics," pp. 297, 305.

[63] Adorno, "Sociology and Psychology," *New Left Review*, no. 47 (November-December 1967), 83.

[64] Reiff, *Freud: The Mind of the Moralist* (New York: Anchor Books, 1961), pp. 278, 280.

[65] Selsam and Martel (eds.), *Reader in Marxist Philosophy*, (New York: International Publishers, 1963), p. 214 (Engels' letter to Mehring, 1893).

[66] Ibid., p. 215.

[67] Osborn, *Freud and Marx* (New York: Equinox Co-Operative Press, 1937), p. 81.

[68] Marcuse, op. cit., p. 197.

III

REICH: CHARACTER STRUCTURE AND SOCIAL STRUCTURE

"What is society's interest in sexual repression?" No answer was provided by the established sociology, except for the stereotypical "Civilization requires morality." Finally a study of Marx and Engels produced a store of insight into the functions of material existence. It came as a shock, at first, to waken to the fact that one might pass through high school and university without ever being told of Marx and Engels. Soon one understood why.

Wilhelm Reich, "The Imposition of Sexual Morality"

Sex-economic sociology was born from the effort to harmonize Freud's depth psychology with Marx's economic theory. Instinctual and socio-economic processes determine human existence. But we have to reject eclectic attempts to combine 'instinct' and 'economy' arbitrarily. . . . Psychoanalysis is the mother, sociology the father of sex-economy. But a child is more than the sum total of his parents. He is a new, independent living creature; he is the seed of the future.

Wilhelm Reich, *The Mass Psychology of Fascism*

6

CHARACTER STRUCTURE, IDEOLOGY, AND THE INTERNALIZATION OF SOCIAL RELATIONSHIPS

FREUD'S great contribution was to develop the concepts and techniques which theorists have applied to try to reveal the influence of social forces on the individual psyche. Yet Freud himself failed to recognize the historical nature of the relationship between, on the one hand, the development of our civilization and, on the other, the repression and distortion of human needs and desires. As we have seen in the preceding chapter, his social theory was based on the ideological presupposition that manifest behavior reflected certain universals of human nature which have been retained throughout history. Thus Freud could conclude that the conflict between the demands of civilization and the needs of the individual was inevitable and that the mature individual would be able to accept the limitations that are imposed on his activity. Many of Freud's followers became even more conformist in their theory and therapy. Lacking a critical perspective on the relationship between the individual and society, many psychoanalysts focused their research on the therapeutic aim of psychic accommodation to social conditions. Reich's early work was the first attempt to develop a critical perspective on Freud; it remains the most significant.[1]

Reich argued that Freud's work was an invaluable contribution to the study of human consciousness. While Marxian theory explored the conditioning of consciousness by social factors, it could not explain how this takes place, "what happens in man's brain in this process."[2] Consequently it was more adequate for explaining beliefs and activities that were consistent with one's social position than those which were not. Since psychoanalysis revealed the irrational forces which underlie conscious thought, Reich believed that it was essential for understanding beliefs and activities that were inconsistent with the interests of one's social class.

Reich emphasized four findings of psychoanalysis which could be used to explain how social factors conditioned conscious thought. First, consciousness is conditioned by unconscious processes that are not accessible to conscious control. Second, the small child develops a lively sexuality that has nothing to do with procreation. Third, the child's sexual activity is repressed by the fear of punishment. Though the repression withdraws his sexuality from the influence of consciousness, repression also intensifies sexuality's force. This intensification is manifested in various disturbances of the mind. Finally, the moral code which inhibits instinctual gratification is derived from the suppression of childhood sexuality.[3] Reich claimed that

> Just as Marxism was sociologically the expression of man becoming conscious of the laws of economics and the exploitation of a majority by a minority, so psychoanalysis is the expression of man becoming conscious of the social repression of sex. Such is the principle social meaning of Freudian psychoanalysis.[4]

Freud originally distinguished two main groups of instincts, which could not be reduced further in psychological terms. These are the self-preservation instincts and the sexual instincts. Whereas the self-preservation instincts have to be satisfied directly, the sexual instincts can also be satisfied indirectly. Reich observed that the frustration of the self-preservation instincts leads to rebelliousness, while the repression of sexuality leads to an unconscious inhibition of rebelliousness.[5] The repression of sexuality results in a psychological structure which submits to rather than resists the social restraints imposed upon it. This psychological structure mediates the process of the conditioning of consciousness by social conditions, so that even the self-preservation instincts can subsequently be influenced. In contrast, the psychology implicit in the traditional Marxian theory of class consciousness assumes a more

immediate relationship between the frustration of the self-preservation instincts and its manifestations in consciousness.

Freud revealed how the psychic structure of the individual
develops in conformity with the social order. Yet, although Freud
ably described the psychology of the fragmented psyche and
partial consciousness, he considered them to be necessary consequences of the instinctual repression required by human civilization. By legitimizing the repression of instinctual pleasure seeking
in the interest of social interaction, Freud obscured the critical
potential of psychoanalytic theory. Reich sought to demonstrate
that it was not social interaction in general which is being preserved
by the socially demanded repression but the exploitative relationships of a class society. The psychic structure that Freud described
is native to a particular form of social organization.

In response to Freud's conformist views, Reich suggested that
political psychology seek "to determine, as completely as possible,
the myriad intermediate links in the transforming of the 'material
basis' into the 'ideologic superstructure.' "[6] This requires analyses
of both the immediate and mediated effects of social conditions
on our impulses and psychic processes. As we shall see in the
following section of this chapter, this analysis led Reich to the
conclusion that the process of psychological development described
by Freud is nothing more than the process by which the social
structure is psychologically reproduced within the individual as a
corresponding character structure and that this process of reproduction takes place within a specific institutional setting. In the
second section, I will be concerned with the institution which Reich
saw as the first and most important organ for the reproduction of
the social order, the nuclear family. Drawing from Engels and
Freud, Reich's analysis of the family made the connection between
psychoanalytic and Marxian theory more explicit. Finally, in the
third section, I will consider Reich's theory of character structure
as a psychological supplement to the Marxian theory of ideology.
I will discuss Reich's application of his theory of character structure
to explain the psychological mediations underlying, on the one
hand, the working class's acceptance of the dominant ideologies
and, on the other, the class differential in the development of
character structure. The chapter will conclude with a discussion

of the relationship in Reich's work between sexual repression and political psychology.

I emphasize that my presentation of Reich's theories in this chapter focuses exclusively on his early works in psychoanalysis and political psychology. Reich's later work in orgonology in many ways negated the insights of his earlier work and revealed the susceptibility of the earlier work to mechanistic inferences. In a way, orgonology was a logical extension of Reich's relentless pursuit of the physiological source of libido. The problems involved in utilizing Reich's physiological conception of libido will be made explicit in chapters seven and eight. In Chapter 7, I argue that Reich contradicted the theory behind character analysis when he characterized libido as a natural, atemporal energy. I go back to Freud and ahead to Marcuse to reconstruct Reich's libido theory in a way compatible with the theory of character structure. In Chapter 8, I relate developments in Reich's thoughts to changes in his involvement in active political movements and draw out some of the practical implications of his political psychology. (It is ironic that as Reich's political commitment decreases, some of the controversy surrounding his work increases.[7])

THE PSYCHOLOGICAL REPRODUCTION OF THE SOCIAL STRUCTURE

Reich's psychology emphasized the historical flexibility of the instincts and the social specificity of the frustrations they encounter. The reality principle, the concept with which Freud refers to all limitations and social necessities which diminish fundamental needs or defer their satisfaction, may require varying types and degrees of modification of the pleasure principle. Accordingly social conditions impinge upon and transform human impulses and needs before these impulses and needs can be socially expressed.[8]

Reich contended that the limitations imposed by the reality principle upon the human organism in its attempts to discharge tension are greater than those necessary for social existence or the development of human culture; they are necessary only for the maintenance of a class society. Rigorously conceived, the reality principle embodies the demands of the existing society with its specific institutions and social relationships. To conceive it as the demands of "society" or "reality" in general or as an absolute, is to lapse into abstraction. In a society in which the owners of capital accumulate surplus value produced or actualized through surplus and detailed labor, the reality principle must reflect the contradiction between the needs of the workers and material interests of capital. The reality principle and the consequent psychic modification is an essential component of capitalist hegemony. Reich claimed that the reality principle of the capitalist era imposed "upon the proletarian a maximum limitation of his needs."[9] Economic exploitation and authoritarian institutions interact to effect a severe frustration of material and sexual needs and desires. The result is widespread anxiety, pain, and psychic conflict.

The idea that psychic processes function to avoid painful conflict with the outer world is basic to psychoanalytic theory. Reich believed that what remained to be explained was the way in which the individual characteristically absorbed and diffused anxiety and filtered disturbing internal and external stimuli. Reich referred to these characteristic processes as the individual's character structure. Reich argued that character structure develops as a response to the demands and prohibitions confronted by the individual and constitutes the individual's general pattern of responses to internal and external dangers.

The primary concern of the following discussion of Reich's work on human character will be to make explicit its implications for social and political theory.[10] First I will consider how social repression creates the need for psychic repression, which in turn inhibits conflict with repressive social conditions. Then I will compare Reich's theories on character development with Eric Fromm's, which seems to emphasize the psychological impact of social conditions more than Reich's. However, as the comparison will show, Reich's theory grasps more fundamentally the relationship between social and psychological influences.

THE SOCIAL CONDITIONING OF CHARACTER

Reich developed his theory of character structure through clinical practice. As a clinician, Reich emphasized problems of technique: How could the analyst best effect a cure for the psychological disturbances which troubled the individual. In 1922, at Reich's suggestion and with Freud's enthusiastic approval, a psychoanalytic "technical seminar" for the study of therapeutic problems was established. Reich was to lead this seminar from 1924 to 1930. In the course of this seminar he began to develop his theories on the psychological function of the orgasm and character analysis. Also in 1924 Reich formally introduced the concept of orgastic potency.[11] These ideas marked the beginning of Reich's work on the human capacity for sexual self-regulation. His conceptualization of mental health as the ability to overcome repression and to establish a social life based on the satisfaction of instincts contrasted sharply with Freud's adaptationist criterion. Even as a clinician, Reich stressed the importance of social conditions in the formation of psychic structures and processes.

In his work on character structure, Reich attempted to make the psychoanalytic theory of neuroses more systematic. In psychoanalytic theory, anxiety stemming from sexual stasis is manifested in and absorbed by neurotic symptoms. The person's resistances prevent him from becoming conscious of the causes of the anxiety. Very often the resistances also block awareness of the anxiety as anxiety. The resistance is made up of the repressed libidinal impulse and an ego defense which represses it. Both the impulse and the defense operate unconsciously. Reich reached the conclusion that the economic function of absorbing anxiety is not a function of isolated symptoms and resistances but of the character of the individual's entire pattern of interacting with his environment. Hence underlying pathologies can be expressed in character traits no less than in symptoms.

The person's character begins to develop as soon as he attempts to adjust in infancy to the demands of his environment. Reich dissected character into three levels. The most obvious is that of personality, the conscious sense of self that we present in our social interactions. Personality is the most rational and cultivated level of character and the area on which cognitive psychologists and social scientists focus. Reich saw personality as a mask which can be dropped to expose the second layer of character, which is comprised of all the "cruel, sadistic, lascivious, rapacious, and envious impulses" that led Freud to posit a primary death instinct. However, Reich argued that these antisocial impulses are secondary drives, perverted expressions of more fundamental drives, the expression of which is repressed. These fundamental or primary drives constitute the third level of character which Reich called the biological core. "In this core, under favorable social conditions, man is an essentially honest, industrious, cooperative, loving, and if motivated, rationally hating animal."[12]

Character structure represents "an armoring against the stimuli of the outer world and the repressed inner drives. The external form of this armoring, however, is always historically determined." Although this "character armor" is essentially formed in infancy and early childhood, the ego continues to mold character throughout life. Since the ego represents the more-or-less conscious sense of self that the individual forms in the context of a specific social structure, character is conditioned by the existing social institutions. Character structure "represents an expression of the person's entire past" and "is the congealed sociological process of a given epoch." Reich claimed that, "every social organization produces those character structures which it needs to exist."[13] This is not to suggest that social institutions explicitly aim at producing a particular character or are even invariably successful in accomplishing this, but only that the infant's ego always develops character in response to the prevailing social order and its prohibitions.

The specific structure of the individual's character is a result of the opposition of an aggregate of repressed drives which are directed toward the outer world and an aggregate of defense forces which maintain the repression. "The two formed a functional unity within the person's specific character."[14] What is to be repressed and how severely is always socially determined. The conflict between the primary drives and the organism's environment produces the antisocial drives that Reich situated in the second character layer.

Reich's theory of character structure is a theory of psychological development and the social expression of physiological impulses. The cooperative and otherwise positive potential of the inner core of character can only be realized in "favorable social conditions." Reich's formulation of character structure, in opposition to Freud's formulation of the psyche, suggests that there need not be a severe conflict between the needs of the individual and the demands of civilization; the latter rather than the former might require modification. For Reich, as for Marx, human nature "is no abstraction in each single individual . . . it is the ensemble of social relations."[15] Indeed, Reich developed the implications of Marx's insight. Through the reality principle the structure of social relationships fundamentally transforms human needs and impulses. These transformed needs and impulses become active elements in the individual's character. The contradiction which Freud observed is not inherent in human existence. It is a contradiction between the socially distorted secondary drives and the social structure which produces them.

Reich carefully differentiated several character types on the basis of the infantile conditions of impulse frustration.[16] These are important clinical distinctions. In terms of political psychology however, the crucial distinction is that between the genital character and the neurotic character. The genital character binds anxiety through genital sexuality and sublimation; the neurotic, through symptoms and reaction formations. Reich compared these two ways of binding anxiety as follows:

> What strikes us about these phenomena is that the reaction formation is spasmodic and compulsive, whereas the sublimation flows freely. In the latter case, the id, in harmony with the ego and ego-ideal, seems to have a direct contact with reality; in the former case, all achievements seem to be imposed upon a rebelling id by a strict superego.[17]

The harmony of the genital character referred to by Reich is by no means free of tension. The sexually healthy person still may experience tension, but he or she will avoid the severe conflict that results when an internalized compulsive morality confronts the pleasure-seeking strivings of the organism. Stasis anxiety, which results from the repressive self-restriction of the primary impulses, may be avoided. But real anxiety, which results from the inevitable clash between a pleasure-seeking organism and a repressive social order, cannot be; "the more real anxiety is avoided, the stronger stasis anxiety becomes, and vice versa."[18] The healthy character, because it is in contact with its environment, realizes it must resist its environment's repressive demands; the pathological character avoids at all costs conflict with its environment. Consequently it is overwhelmed by its own internal conflicts.

The sound libido of the genital character can provide the individual with the capacity for self-regulation. The gratification of primary drives allows the genital character to minimize the expression of antisocial secondary drives. Its capacity for the orgastic discharge of libidinal tensions makes it capable of sublimating energy in socially constructive uses.

The potential of the human organism for self-regulation is the central theme of the theory of character structure. Socially responsible people will not tolerate authoritarian institutions and excessive regulation of life. Yet some social regulation is necessary, although it inhibits social responsibility, for the socially distorted secondary drives must be regulated in the interest of social interaction. More fundamental than the contradiction between the individual and his civilization is a historical cycle of social repression—psychological repression. Social repression results in psychological processes which reproduce and reinforce the need for social repression. But the cycle need not be a vicious one. The way out, according to Reich, is to change the social conditions which demand the excessive repression:

> To the extent that society makes possible the gratification of needs and the transformation of the corresponding human structures, the moral regulation of social life will fall away. The final decision lies not in the sphere of psychology but in the sphere of the sociological processes.[19]

Reich's conception of character structure is a critical description of human psychology as it has been formed through the history of a particular society. For Reich social processes and psychological processes are interpenetrating components of the process of human development. Social repression results in the formation of antisocial secondary drives. Once produced, these secondary drives become deeply ingrained in the individual's character and hence must be regulated socially. Yet social regulation may exacerbate the problem and may make necessary more regulation in the future. The potential for self-regulation, stunted by social repression, can be actualized through collective activity aimed at abolishing the source of social repression.

Reich's theory of character structure is meant to describe the conditioning of character through the interaction between basic needs and social relationships. Like Freud, Reich defined mental health as an appropriate response to social conditions. In contrast to Freud, Reich sharply distinguished appropriateness from adaptation. Furthermore Reich could not follow Freud in seeing as inevitable the conflict between the impulse and social institutions. Reich believed very strongly that the antisocial expressions of instincts results from their repression and that the instincts can become socialized under less-repressive institutions.

In a well-known work on social character Erich Fromm, arguing against Freud and implicitly Fromm's own earlier theory on character, claimed that we must move beyond the categories of the libido theory to describe more adequately the connections between character and social relationships. Utilizing such terms as productive, hoarding, receptive, exploitative, and marketing orientations, Fromm appeared to be presenting a characterology which developed the psychological insights implicit to Marx's writings.[20] Fromm explained character types in terms of market relationships. In contrast, Reich traced the development of character to the institutions and authority figures confronted in childhood and examined the processes through which the individual internalizes the authority of a class society long before participating in the relationships of commodity production and exchange. Rather than grounding character directly in class relationships, Reich examined the extent to which capitalist social hegemony affected the individual's psychological development. Furthermore, Reich's exploration of the social and psychological processes through which character develops was concerned with more than categorizing character types. Reich sought to make explicit the psychological and social sources of repression in order to raise the possibility of overcoming repression. By comparing Reich's characterology with Fromm's, I will make these aspects of Reich's theory of character more explicit.

CHARACTER AND SOCIAL RELATIONSHIPS:
REICH AND FROMM

Fromm differentiated character types on the basis of their orientation toward social production. He differentiated the productive character from various types of unproductive characters and claimed that

> The whole personality of the average individual is molded by the way people relate to each other, and it is determined by the socio-economic and political structure of society to such an extent that, in principle, one can infer from the analysis of one individual the totality of the social structure in which he lives.
>
> The receptive orientation is often to be found in societies in which the right of one group to exploit another is firmly established. Since the exploited group has no power to change or any idea of changing its situation, it will tend to look up to its masters as to its providers, as to those from whom one receives everything life can give.[21]

Although this passage seems to be a straightforward attempt to describe the effects of capitalist social relationships on psychological orientations, it nevertheless reveals succinctly the most fundamental problem of Fromm's position. That is, Fromm fails to distinguish the surface layer of personality from the deeper character layers. In a class society, the totality of social structure can be inferred from the analysis of one individual only by analyzing the deeply rooted contradictions within the individual as manifestations of the contradictions of the social order. In Reich's categorization of libidinal types, social contradictions are mediated through unconsciousness before being expressed in consciousness; in Fromm's categorization of productive types, social contradictions are expressed more immediately in consciousness.

For example, Fromm's description of the "receptive orientation" fails to differentiate the actual helplessness of the exploited class from the psychological "feelings of helplessness which prevent it from engaging in meaningful collective action." As Theodor Adorno has claimed, actual helplessness "might be expected to prompt resistance to the social system rather than further assimilation to it," whereas feelings of helplessness are associated with the psychological inability of individuals to "experience or confront

their helplessness."[22] This feeling of helplessness can be understood as an active defense against social responsibility. Workers
socially produce the products necessary for life; they do not receive
them from an outside source. Yet they evade the responsibility
that control over the process of production would entail. As in
neurotic symptoms such as anxiety, this evasion is a futile effort
to avoid pain by avoiding conflict with a repressive environment.
Reich explained the fundamental role of the social frustration of
libidinal impulses in producing this type of defense. The passivity
of the working class does not result directly from its exploitation.
Rather, passivity is a defense against the frustration of basic
impulses, a frustration which occurs when the impulses are expressed within exploitative social relationships.

In addition, Fromm bemoans the fact that psychoanalytic
thought has been so little concerned with the healthy human
character or the productive orientation.[23] Yet Fromm's description
of the productive orientation suggests the same behavior in social
interaction as Reich's self-regulating character. For example, both
the self-regulating and productive individual can relate meaning-
fully to other persons as more than mere objects for the gratification of his needs. He can participate without coercion in life-
supporting social activity when the social relationships of the labor
process do not fragment his role and alienate him from control of
the process. The difference is that Fromm conceived of the healthy
character in terms of ethical ideals; Reich conceived of it as the
potential of a pleasure-seeking yet self-preserving organism within
the context of "favorable social conditions." However, within a
repressive and exploitative social structure, this self-regulating
potential is extremely difficult if not impossible to actualize. Social
repression brings about the psychic processes which distort and
transform human needs. The potential for self-regulation can be
achieved only when the individual becomes conscious of these
psychic processes and resists the repressive social conditions which
underlie them. In Reichian theory, the way the individual relates
to the world is a function of his libidinal organization. Yet the
libido develops only in the context of the institutions and relationships which define society. It is only by maintaining a dichotomy
between libido and social relations that Fromm can claim that "the

character system can be considered the human substitute for the instinctive apparatus of the animal." Character is no substitute for the instincts. Rather, as Reich has shown, it is the outgrowth of the necessary interaction between primary drives (self-preservation and the release of tension) and the outer world.

While the primary impulses require participation in social relationships for their satisfaction, the institutional structure of these relationships conditions the impulses themselves, thereby modifying or distorting them. By forming relationships, we act as the agents of the social process. But we become objects of the very same process when we confront these relationships as institutions beyond our control. These reified institutions then reproduce themselves within us by molding corresponding psychic structures.

Fromm may have described a more direct relationship between consciousness and social position than Reich, but in doing so he lost much of the richness of both psychoanalytic and Marxian modes of explanation. This richness is preserved in Reich's theory of character which attempts both to make the unconscious conscious and to suggest how change in character can result from social activity. To accomplish these aims, Reich emphasized the psychic mediations involved in the development of a character structure.

Yet Reich did not emphasize the psychic mediations at the expense of the social antecedents of character structure. He sought to make explicit the institutional framework within which character develops. The most effective institution for the molding of the prevailing character structures was, for Reich, the nuclear family. In the family the social structure reproduces itself within the child, leaving him susceptible to later influences by an authoritarian social system. In his analysis of family relationships, Reich sought to make the connection between psychoanalytic and critical Marxist theory more explicit. Reich's analysis of the family is the subject of the following section.

THE NUCLEAR FAMILY AND THE INTERNALIZATION OF SOCIAL AUTHORITY

Reich saw the family as the institution through which the complementary social processes of economic and social repression interacted and mediated one another.[24] For this reason the family has been a concern of both psychoanalytic and Marxian research. Freud examined the role played by family relationships in the transmission of social values. Engels was concerned with the connection between family relationships and the social forces of production. In Reich's analysis, the family is at once an economic unit, a transmitter of social ideologies, and an agent in the development of a submissive character structure. Let us consider each in turn.

In his classic study of the family, Engels, even while describing the decline of the family as a mode of social production, refers to the family as the basic economic unit of capitalist society.[25] The division of labor between the sexes places the man and woman in an asymetrical economic relationship and effects the position of each on the labor market. The man's task generally is considered to be to earn a living and to support his family. According to Engels, "that in itself gives him a position of supremacy without any need for special legal titles and privileges." In contrast, the wife is charged with the private service of household management and, to the extent that she performs this service, is unable to participate fully in the labor market and unable, therefore, to earn wages. She can participate in the process of social production and earn independently only to the detriment of her domestic function. Engels claimed that "The modern individual family is founded on the open or concealed domestic slavery of the wife, and modern society is a mass composed of these individual families as its molecules."[26]

Reich, like Engels, recognized the exploitation of women within the nuclear family. He described the connection between the domestic and social division of labor. The family as a social institution directly supported the dominant social relationships of a class society. Although the wife provided comfort for her husband, the main beneficiary of the domestic exploitation of women was the employing class:

> The women's economic dependence on the man and the lower value placed on her participation in the productive process transforms marriage into a protective institution for her, even though she is doubly exploited in this "protective set-up." Not only is she the sexual

object of her husband and the birth apparatus of the state, but her unpaid work in the household indirectly raises the profits of the employer. For the man can produce surplus value at current low wages only if a certain amount of work is taken off his shoulders at home.[27]

Reich's analysis of the economic significance of the family assumed a society with a rigid domestic division of labor. In fact, he assumed that the division of labor is more rigid in regard to the division of domestic chores between the sexes than in regard to the exclusion of women from the labor market. Both Reich and Engels observed that in working-class families it is not at all uncommon for the wife to perform wage work as well as her domestic chores. Yet her job is generally of secondary importance. Engels claimed that she participates in social production only as "proletarian wife." Reich observed that the working woman continues to perform "additional, unpaid work to keep her house in order."[28]

Here we begin to confront a contradiction between the woman's domestic and social positions. While women's position in the household continues to be subordinate, women are being increasingly integrated into the work force. Yet, whether or not the woman makes a significant contribution to the financial support of the household, the man continues to assume the position of authority that Engels attributed to his role in the process of social production, a role which made him the major provider. Accordingly, the persistence of domestic roles cannot be explained entirely in terms of economic dependency; the nuclear family persists ideologically even while its economic determinants are changing. Nevertheless even as an ideological rather than economic arrangement, the family reinforces class relationships. That is, Reich argued that the family had an ideological as well as economic function.

The ideological function of the family is experienced by its members as feelings of family responsibility. For example, the man, as head of the household, is held to his job not only by economic necessity. If he lost his job, the hardship caused might be alleviated by having his wife and children enter the labor market, at least temporarily. The fear of losing a job is also the fear of the stigma of having failed in his responsibility as family provider. Thus the wage earner accepts the conditions of employment imposed by the employer and represses the anger provoked by his exploitation. This ideologically reconciles the worker to his subordinate position in the labor market. The woman, also reconciled ideologically by family responsibility, continues to serve as the domestic servant of the household.[29]

Reich claimed that what is being served by the domestic arrangement is not as much the economic interests of the family members as the structure of capitalist relationships. The family is that social institution through which a compliant working class, necessary for the maintenance of capitalist production, is reproduced both biologically and ideologically. In this regard the domestic division of labor reinforces capitalist ideological hegemony and its repression of social criticism. The patriarchal nuclear family breeds conservatism by ideologically reconciling its members to capitalist relationships and repressing the articulation of anger and frustration in the interest of family responsibility.

Reich added to Engels' analysis of the economic interrelationship of the social and domestic divisions of labor a description of their ideological interrelationship. For Reich the family is the factory for the reproduction of social ideologies and the germ cell of political reaction. The parents, who are ideologically reconciled to the existing social order, communicate their reconciliation and acceptance to their off-spring.[30] But the family's ideological role is neither exclusively nor primarily a matter of conscious thought. Reich believed that the ideological hegemony of the exploiting class requires a particular character structure among the exploited, for conscious reconciliation is too susceptible to conscious criticism. In Reich's analysis the nuclear family was the major agency for reproducing social ideologies by molding a compatible character structure.

The influence of the family on character development is to condition its members to submit to social authority. The family performs this function by providing an effective framework for the lifelong repression of sexuality. The repression of sexuality results in the association of unconscious feelings of guilt with sexual desires. Consequently, sexuality is inhibited by ego conflicts and the increasing inability of the ego to resist sexual prohibitions. This same psychological disposition is the basis of mass acceptance of class authority and exploitation. From the very time that the child surrenders a part of his own interest by assimilating internally the external authority he so fears, the individual is predisposed to submit to and internalize the authority he confronts.[31]

Reich analyzed the role of the family in the repression of sexuality through three major stages of the individual's life: childhood, adolescence, and adulthood. By outlining this process of repressing sexuality, the role of the family in conditioning character will be made evident.

In psychoanalytic theory, the family is the setting within which the child learns to introject and identify with the authority figures upon whom he depends for his well-being. The relationships of the nuclear family are the child's most immediate social interactions. The structure of the nuclear family and its effects on the child's sexual and hence psychological development brings about that crucial situation—the Oedipus complex and its mode of dissolution—by which the child is initiated into the culture within which he will live. In the process of resolving the Oedipus complex and internalizing the oedipal prohibitions, the general pattern for the individual's reaction to authority is established. Reich claimed that

> Translated into the language of sociology, Freud's central thesis concerning the importance of the oedipus complex in the development of the individual means precisely that social being determines that development. The child's instincts and disposition—empty molds ready to receive their social contents—go through the social processes of relationships with father, mother, and teacher, and only then acquire their final form and content.[32]

Reich sought to make Freud's theory more specific by examining the interconnections between the patriarchal structure of authority in the family and the class structure of authority in society. He claimed that the fact that "an oedipus complex occurs at all must be ascribed to the socially determined structure of the family."[33] Reich found support for his historical understanding of the Oedipus complex in the anthropology of Bronislaw Malinowski. Malinowski's work on the Trobriand Islanders convinced Reich that the social repression of the incest desire need not lead to neurotic formations if direct erotic gratification were a real possibility. Furthermore, since the relationship between parent and child defined by the family structure is different for the Trobrianders and ourselves, the way in which the incest desire was repressed would also be different with qualitatively different consequences. Reich interpreted Malinowski as saying "that the oedipus complex is a sociologically conditioned fact which changes its form with the structure of society."[34] For Reich, the obvious conclusion of Malinowski's work was that the nuclear family is the primary cause of the neurotic disturbances which are so pervasive in modern societies.

Reich's views contrast sharply with Freud's. For Freud, as his choice of mythic terms suggested, the Oedipus complex was a "universal event of childhood."[35] For Reich it was a product of the patriarchal nuclear family, which was itself historically conditioned and the methods of child-rearing peculiar to it. What was important to Reich was not just the development and repression within the nuclear family of the sensuous and tender feelings of the child for the parent, but the additional repression of alternative means of satisfaction. If the child is allowed to interact erotically with his playmates, Reich argued, the repression of the oedipal feelings would not be so damaging. The child's simultaneously contrived isolation within the nuclear family and forced repression of libidinal drives directed toward family members are what make the effects of the oedipal situation so severe. "A child who might be raised from the third year on in the company of other children, uninfluenced by ties to his parents, would develop a quite different sexuality."[36]

Reich insisted on the importance of understanding sexual repression as a lifelong process. Sexual repression is a process initiated in childhood and reinforced throughout the individual's life. It is a process in which psychological and sociological factors interact with, modify complement, and contradict one another. The Oedipus complex and its mode of resolution in particular have a twofold influence in later life. On the one hand, they are retained as unconscious memory traces which influence conscious thought and behavior. On the other, they are retained as integral components of the individual's character structure. However, character structure is the result not only of infantile conflicts but of later conflicts and repressions as well. That is, the influence of the oedipus complex on character is modified by subsequent social conditions.[37]

The Oedipus complex is the culmination of childhood sexuality and ushers in a period of sexual latency. The Oedipus complex develops from the phallic stage during which the child's eroticism becomes directed at people who are also the object of the child's emotional attachments. Yet the Oedipus complex results in the repression of phallic sexuality and is resolved in the establishment of the superego. Until this point the libidinal impulse was directed toward the parents. Now it is repressed until the emergence of genital sexuality, when libidinal desires are aimed at people outside the family.

Puberty, then, marks the physiological sexual maturity of the individual and becomes a crucial stage in characterological development. The pubescent youth is physically capable of developing mature sexual relationships, but faces tremendous social restraints on the gratification of sexuality. The adolescent living in the parental home experiences a severe conflict between his or her emerging sexuality and the antisexual inhibitions acquired from parents and later other adults, such as teachers. Even if he can resolve this conflict adequately and overcome the guilt associated with sexuality, various social factors actively discourage the adolescent from satisfying his sexual desires. For instance, pregnancy is a real danger associated with sexual intercourse. Only infrequently does the family or school help the adolescent to solve the problem of contraception. The less-inhibited girl may secretively seek help from a birth-control clinic, and the boy may have his responsibility in this regard impressed upon him. But there still will remain the problem of privacy. Without a home of their own, the erotic encounters of adolescents usually assume a tense and clandestine character which can aggravate the unconscious guilt associated with the act.[38]

Reich believed that the ability of the youth to overcome these social barriers depends on the extent to which infantile fixations are overcome, that is, the extent to which the youth is successful in transforming infantile narcissism into emotional attachments and exchanging the infantile objects of erotic impulses for more appropriate objects. If the fixations are not overcome, the expression of sexuality will involve unconscious conflicts provoked by infantile fears. However, social obstacles to the expression of sexuality still may effect a regression to infantile modes of satisfaction even in a youth that has developed normally to puberty.[39] Once again, the expression of sexuality will involve unconscious conflicts. The individual will repress erotic impulses and will seek relief in substitutes or symptoms. Nevertheless, the psychic costs of these processes notwithstanding, regression and fixation prepare the adolescent for later life by accomodating his or her sexuality to the demands of a socially imposed morality.

As an adult the individual confronts this morality as the compulsive monogamy of marriage. The moralistic confinement of sexuality to the family intensifies emotionally the relationships of the family and separates the members of the family from the outside world. That is "sexual inhibition is the basis of the familial encapsulation of the individual . . . the tie to the authoritarian family is established by sexual repression."[40] The affection and support that members of the family may provide for one another is not the issue here.[41] Rather, the issue is the way in which instinctual satisfaction is made to conform to institutional arrangements which require a great deal of repression to maintain. The adult is conditioned to accept this repression in childhood and adolescence. The emotional intensification of family ties that results from this repression is a precondition for the adult's acceptance of family ideology with its notions of family responsibility.

Reich's description of the repression of sexuality in childhood, adolescence, and adulthood supported his belief that the compulsive and authoritarian features of family life are in severe conflict with human sexuality. On the basis of the role of the family in repressing sexuality and the connection between sexual and political repression, Reich attributed to the family a dual political function:

1. It reproduces itself by crippling people sexually. . . .
2. It produces the authority-fearing, life-fearing vassal, and thus constantly creates new possibilities whereby a handful of men in power can rule the masses.[42]

Hence, Reich claimed that his theory of character structure can help to explain the lack of opposition to exploitation and domination. The demands of social institutions, particularly the family, condition the individual to respond to conflict by surrendering a part of his own interest and internalizing the authority he confronts. He is unlikely to resist the sources of the prohibitions and limitations imposed upon him. Reich argued that his theory added a psychological dimension to Marx's theory of ideology, which explained this compliance in terms of the dominance of the ideas of the ruling class. Ideologies are produced socially as the ideas of the ruling class and the expression of its dominance; ideologies are reproduced within individuals through an unconscious association with repressed impulses and emotions. The social conditions which force people to repress basic needs and emotions help to bring about a character structure which readily submits to the relationships of authority that are taken for granted in the dominant ideologies.

In the next section, I will discuss the theory of character structure as a psychological counterpart to the theory of ideology.

CHARACTER STRUCTURE, CLASS STRUCTURE, AND IDEOLOGY

Like the theory of ideology, Reich's theory of character structure is meant to explain not only the systematic distortion involved in the prevailing ways of understanding social life, but also the ability of the exploited classes to overcome that distorted understanding. The material conditions of life among the exploited can lead to a new understanding of social conditions, an understanding in opposition to that of the dominant class.

I will begin this section by further explicating the relationship between character structure and the ideological hegemony of the ruling class. But although social institutions, particularly the patriarchal nuclear family, mold a character structure compatible with class domination, the development of character structure varies between classes. Accordingly, I then will examine the sources of this variation and a dramatic consequence of it: the strong support the German middle class gave to the Nazis.

CHARACTER STRUCTURE AND IDEOLOGY

Reich believed that the character structure molded by the patriarchal family and its ideology was susceptible to excitement and motivation by the ideologies of the dominant class. This is not to suggest that patriarchal authority is the form or basis of all social authority. "From the point of view of social development, the family cannot be regarded as the basis of the authoritarian state, but only as one of the most important institutions that supports it."[43] I believe Reich's thought in this regard can be made clearer by making explicit the psychoanalytic formulations which underlie it.

Freud observed that the child's superego was constructed on the model of his parents' superego rather than the parents themselves. In the course of its development the superego is influenced by the figures of authority appropriate to the individual's stage of development. Freud mentions educators and teachers but we can include work supervisors and political figures as well. Freud concluded from this that the superego becomes "the vehicle of tradition and of all time-resisting judgments of value," and that the ideologies of the superego are formed by the traditions of the race "independently of economic conditions."[44] The patriarchal tradition of the species, which is embedded in the superego via the Oedipus complex, creates the general pattern for the individual's interaction with authority.

Implicit in Reich's analysis is a critical revision of Freud's conclusions. Patriarchy, as both a structure of social relationships and its ideological expression, exerts an influence on human activity which is not reducible to material preconditions. Yet while the ideological significance of the superego may explain the submissiveness of the adult to the authority figures he encounters, it does not explain why, in the first place, the authority figures come to be constituted as such. The authority of the educator, supervisor, or politician derives from the social relationships of particular institutions. Their authority is primarily material and only secondarily psychological. Their influence on the development of the superego represents the conditioning of psychic structures by social structures. It is a materially defined authority that the superego comes to represent. Since the child's superego is based on his parents' superego, the child's superego is influenced indirectly by the social institutions outside the family which condition his parents' superegos. Accordingly, Reich claimed that the authoritarian position of the father is a political role which represents within the family the authoritarianism of the state and the dominant class.[45]

The harsh superego internalizes the authority it confronts. The individual then comes to experience his conflicts with the outer world as internal or psychological conflicts. For example, the internalization of parental authority leads to the repression from consciousness of the conflict between the child's primary impulses and the parental prohibitions. The internalization of political and economic authority activates the mechanisms which repress the consciousness of conflict between the individual's needs and desires and the limitations socially imposed upon them. This pattern of internalization can be overcome by the conscious intervention of the ego, which has the capacity to evaluate the social prohibitions and to resist them when appropriate, as it does with the impulses of the id. But generally the ego succumbs to the severity of the pressures it encounters and begins to identify with the authority that has been internalized in the superego. The ego becomes the agent of repression for the internalized authority and constructs an elaborate system of defenses to maintain the repression. The social structure, from which the internalized authority is derived, thus becomes embedded in the individual's very sense of self.

Identification with the dominant authority impedes recognition among the exploited of a conflict between the dominant and subordinant classes. The individual is psychologically susceptible to ideologies which obscure class structure and mystify class conflict into a symbolic unity, such as the unity of a "nation" or "people" and the ahistorical absolutes of kinship and religion. The individual resists attempts to expose the class structure and the mystifications since any exposure would force him to confront the exploitation and repression he suffers, thereby disturbing the tenuous psychic equilibrium between repressed impulses and characterological defenses.

Reich saw identification as "the psychological basis of national narcissism, i.e., the self-confidence that individual man derives from the 'greatness of the nation.'"[46] Clearly, one does not resist or challenge an authority with which one identifies. It may appear then as if Freud was correct: Social collectivities are formed through the identification with a common leader or symbols of authority.[47]

Yet the leader is the object of identification because he is the leader; he is not the leader because he is the object of identification. The psychological processes of internalization and identification may explain the consensus of the led, or, as the other side of this, the hegemony of the leaders, but it does not explain the derivation of social authority. Reich recognized that social authority cannot be explained with psychological concepts. It derives from the structure of social relationships.

In class societies, social authority embodies the domination of one class over another. The hegemony of the ruling class is expressed in the dominant institutions and ideologies; it permeates society and its classes. Yet along with the hegemonic influence there is the influence of the conditions of life of the particular class. There may be various degrees of contradiction between the influences of hegemony and class position on consciousness and activity. These contradictory influences, in turn, condition the extent of identification with or resistance to the dominant authority. In other words, as we shall see, there is a class differential in the process of the reproduction of the social structure as character structure.

CLASS VARIATIONS IN CHARACTER

Reich emphasized that character structure develops in response to the specific social conditions that the individual confronts. Although he held that social institutions such as the family, church, and government were conditioned by the social relationships of productive activity, he did not posit an immediate relationship between character structure and productive relationships. Instead, the family provided the crucial mediation between the social relations of production and the development of character.

In capitalist societies the patriarchal nuclear family is the prevailing form of family. However, although the patriarchal family permeates all classes, the influence of patriarchal institutions and ideologies varies according to class. Reich identified the source of this variation as the position of the class in the process of production.

Reich believed that the position of the middle class in the labor process resulted in a rigidly patriarchal family structure. This, in turn, conditioned a character structure predisposed to identify with socially defined authority. Actually, when Reich speaks of the middle class he is speaking of three different factions: the rural middle class, the owners of small businesses, and white-collar workers and civil servants. Reich observed that although these individuals were not directly subject to the regimentation of the capitalist production process in the same way as industrial workers, their economic conditions were hardly better than that of the industrial worker. The rural and business middle class worked long and hard for the modicum of comfort they achieved and had little security against the expansion of big business. The white-collar workers and civil servants, especially the lower echelons which comprised 70 percent of this category, often received a smaller paycheck than the skilled industrial worker. Yet these workers were reluctant to organize and to act collectively in pursuit of their interests.[48]

According to Reich, the atomism and individualism of the middle class proceeded from the social conditions of their work, both directly and as mediated through the family. In the rural and business middle class, the family was involved in the individual business enterprise. The economic competition between small enterprises directly impeded both recognition of class interests and their organized articulation. Furthermore, the control exercised by the father in the family enterprise results in a rigidly patriarchal family structure, which in term molds the character structure from which is derived the individual's later attitudes toward authority.[49]

In the other segment of the middle class, the civil servants and white-collar workers, the conditions of work are somewhat different. They are not individual entrepreneurs but workers within a corporate or government division of labor. Yet they work in greater isolation from one another and seem to have more autonomy in their roles than do industrial workers. Socioeconomically, what differentiates them from the workers is not a higher standard of living but the prospect of a career. Since the middle-class employee is dependent upon his employer for the realization of this prospect, "a competitive bearing towards one's colleagues prevails in this class, which counteracts the development of solidarity." The social consciousness of this faction is characterized not by recognition of common interests with coworkers, but by identification with the government or company.[50] This identification is the primary compensation of the lower-middle-class worker for the sacrifice required to pursue his career. Since his living standard is not much better, he differentiates himself from the working class in a sexually moralistic way. He forms notions of honor and duty based upon the dominant ideology, such as the value of hard (alienated) work, self-sacrifice (exploitation), and morality (sexual repression). These notions are what he believes to be necessary to make the most out of life. He imposes them upon his family for what he believes to be their own good. For this reason, Reich believed that the role of the father as the representative of socially defined authority was most rigid among middle-class employees.[51] As in the other factions of the middle class, family structure and material conditions combine to alienate the individual from those in a similar position, whom he looks upon as competitors, and leads him to identify with the socially defined authority.

To claim that patriarchy is most rigid among the middle class is not to neglect its significance in the working class. Religion and conventional morality, the subordination of women, the restriction of the father's role to disciplinarian, and identification with the firm can produce working-class as well as middle-class authoritarianism.[52] Furthermore, Reich believed that the living standard of the working class also had a detrimental effect on sexual development. He emphasized the excessive restrictions imposed upon the sexual activity of working-class individuals, for instance, by the housing shortage. Crowded housing makes it difficult for lovers, especially young people, to be together privately. Couples are often partially dressed while making love, and concerned about being discovered. Also, insofar as working-class people, especially

young people, have less access to birth-control information and
service, the sex act has to be interrupted to avoid unwanted
pregnancy and dangerous abortions.[53] However, the influences
on character structure and ideology are not as homogeneous in
the working class as in the middle class. So although patriarchy
permeates the working class, it is not as rigid there. Working-class
relationships exert an influence in contradiction to the hegemonic
influences.

The capitalist division of labor necessitates cooperation and
interdependence among workers. Workers crowded, impover-
ished, and segregated neighborhoods encourages cooperation and
friendliness among their families. That is, working-class families
are not as isolated from one another as their middle-class counterparts. So, while the relationships of patriarchy promote an
identification with authority, the relationships between workers at
work and in their neighborhoods favor a mutual identification
with one another.[54] Of course, other Marxist theorists including
those discussed in Chapter 2 have described in more detail than
Reich the influences of political and social, as well as economic,
relationships on the development of the working class. Reich's
contribution was to make explicit the implications of at least some
of these relationships on the character and hence ideological
orientation of workers. He argued that the way in which workers
and their families work and live together results in a less-rigid
character structure. Psychologically, as well as socially, workers are
more likely than middle-class employees to resist the authority of
their exploiters.

Reich found support for his comparison of working-class and
middle-class character structures in the success that the German
National Socialists had in mobilizing the middle class. Nazi propaganda focused on the idealized middle class, stressing the tradition
of the family and the virtues of the independent peasant and
businessman. The rural, business, and employee middle class
formed the largest core of the fascists' followers.[55] Reich explained
the Nazis' successful mobilization of the middle class in terms of
the characterological rigidity and authoritarian moralism of the
middle class.

Admittedly, fascism is an extreme form of authoritarian ideology. However Reich saw it as a continuation of class authority rather than a different type of authority. "Fascism's lower middle class is the same as liberal democracy's lower middle class, only in a different historical epoch of capitalism." Reich saw fascism as, in part, a revolt of the middle class prompted by the economic crisis and deteriorating conditions of middle-class life. But it was a distorted and ineffective revolt which actually strengthened the dominance and hegemony of corporate capital by supporting its militaristic, imperialistic policies.[56]

A warning is in order here. Political psychology cannot be used to analyze the emergence of fascist states in a Europe that was economically depressed and scarred by war. That analysis requires attention to the historical dynamics of capitalist world economy and, in particular, the struggle for markets among huge international cartels. Reich focused on a corollary problem: How did fascism become a mass movement; why were large numbers of people mobilized by it?[57] Reich sought an answer at a level of explanation general enough to apply to fascism as an international rather than distinctly German problem.

Reich believed that the strength of the fascist movement resulted from its appeal to the authoritarian character structure molded by the middle-class family. The greatness of the nation and the Fuhrer was a greatness that the fascist masses, being predisposed as a result of their character development, could share via identification. The race theory clearly identified who could participate in this greatness and defined the enemy as impure influences within the nation. The enemy was responsible for compromising the morality of the folk and thereby the greatness of the nation. The enemy was the cause of the deterioration in living conditions; the emergence of a new order was predicated on the elimination of inferior races.[58]

Reich thought it hopeless to argue against the racists and their notion of racial inferiority. "The race theory can be refuted only by exposing its irrational function." Reich interpreted the creed of a "racial soul" and its "purity" as the creed of asexuality or sexual repression. It was the mystical-political expression of a moralism too stern to practice consistently.[59]

Fascism appealed to the secondary character drives and sexual fears which resulted from the effects of a strict moralism on sexual development. It appealed to the secondary drives by the violence and hatred it expressed through its ideology, the spontaneous outbursts of its mobilized adherents, and its aggressive and brutal state policies. The Nazi theory of blood purity and blood poisoning was an example of the appeal to fear. Reich associated the Nazi claim that the pure Aryan blood was poisoned by miscegenation with the fear of syphilis, which Freud considered to be a manifestation of the castration complex.[60] Infantile fixations underlied the irrational fears of racism. This fear is directed at the so-called inferior races thereby isolating them from the fascist mass.

Reich's analysis of Naziism explained how ideology can become the distorted expression of the dissatisfaction experienced in a class society. The extremism of Naziism was a response to the exploitation, domination, and repression that the people endured. Yet fascism could not alleviate these problems, for it never addressed their determinants in the class relationships of society. In fact, it functioned to maintain capitalist hegemony, despite severe economic crisis, through the identification with Aryan greatness and the cathexis of racism. Reich's analysis suggested that extreme nationalism and racism can politically motivate a socially frustrated people whenever a rigid patriarchy and an extreme frustration of impulses molds the requisite character structure. As Gad Horowitz claimed, in his work on the psychoanalytic theory of repression, "Reich's great insight into fascism was that it was the first modern counterrevolutionary strategy able to mobilize the rebellious as well as the submissive impulses of the authoritarian personality."[61] But, in doing so, it became an ideological force more devastating than the material forces it appeared to be challenging.

CONCLUSION: SEXUAL REPRESSION AND POLITICAL PSYCHOLOGY

In Reich's analysis of the psychology of both fascism and capitalist hegemony, the family is the central social institution in the process of the introjection of the social structure. In general, a pattern of submissive reaction to authority is established through the patriarchal relationships of the family. In the fascist, a character structure which expresses its submissiveness through aggressive identification with violent authority is molded by a rigid patriarchy and extreme instinctual frustration. It is only the character of the submissive response that is molded by the family, not the characteristics of the authority or the ideology.

This last distinction is important because Reich has been misinterpreted often. In particular he has been accused of proposing a simplistic relationship between sexual repression and fascism or, conversely between sexual liberation and political freedom. Marcuse, for example, characterized the relationship in Reich's work between sexuality and authoritarianism as follows:

> Wilhelm Reich was right in emphasizing the roots of fascism in instinctual repression; he was wrong when he saw the mainsprings for the defeat of fascism in sexual liberation. The latter can proceed quite far without endangering the capitalist system at the advanced stage. . . .[62]

Marcuse argued that advanced capitalism can accomodate some forms of sexual liberation.[63] However, Reich saw fascism not as a typical consequence of advanced capitalism but as an ideological movement which embodied the *contradiction* of capitalist economic crisis and capitalist cultural hegemony. Nor did Reich consider instinctual repression to be the root of fascism. Rather it was the precondition for the individual's identification with fascism. Reich believed that an understanding of this momentous mass movement required a political and economic analysis of the conditions which led to the emergence and rise of the Fuhrer and his party. It also required a political and psychological analysis of the conditions which produced the secondary drives to which Naziism appealed. Reich saw sexual repression as responsible for those drives. By alleviating sexual misery Reich hoped that the distortions of character necessary for fascist support could be prevented.

Furthermore, there is a looseness of terminology in Marcuse's statement which distorts Reich's meaning. By "sexual liberation" Reich meant something quite different than Marcuse's interpretation. Elsewhere Marcuse claimed that in Reich's work, "Progress in freedom appears as a mere release in sexuality."[64] This is hardly the case. Rather, for Reich progress in freedom was the development of the capacity for self-regulation in work and pleasure. Reich knew well that the mere release of sexuality could occur within compulsively repetitive patterns of interaction and could be associated with infantile conflicts which evoked guilt and anxiety. Reich had ample opportunity to observe allegedly liberalized sexual activity which did not fulfill his criteria of self-regulation.

In fact, Reich could not help but notice that German nationalism and racism developed in a social milieu which was libertine as well as repressive. Postwar Berlin (and prewar Vienna, which has been described as the birthplace of German nationalism) was a city marked by a relatively permissive and promiscuous social life.[65] Prostitution and erotic entertainment were commonplace. The economic strain of inflation made marriage an unlikely prospect for working women who were unable to provide the expected dowries. Consequently premarital chastity was devalued as a social norm. In fact, psychoanalysis itself, with its emphasis on the repression of sexuality in the etiology of neurosis, was better received in Berlin than elsewhere.[66]

Ironically, the very moral liberalization that increased the popularity of psychoanalysis is itself at least perverse and perhaps even pathological by psychoanalytic standards. The cathexis of pornography required a "flight into fantasy" which psychoanalytic theory associates with infantile fixation. Prostitution and promiscuity may somatically engage the individual genitally. However, they lack an important characteristic attributed to the genitally organized libido: the occurrence simultaneously of aim-inhibited, emotional attachment and erotic desire for the same person. Freud attributed the separation of the emotional impulse from the erotic impulse to the fixation of the emotional impulse on the incestuous object of infantile eroticism, the mother, and the redirection of sexuality in relationships that lack emotional attachment.[67] Such sexuality only reinforces the infantile fixations on which this fragmentation is based.

Reich, who lived and practiced in both Vienna and Berlin, maintained that what he meant by sexual liberation was significantly different from the sexual activity that was rampant in those cities. Compulsively repetitive promiscuity and "Don Juanism," which Reich described as "emotionally degrading and sex-economically worthless," is hardly self-regulating sexuality. He polemicized against prostitution as a sexual practice which resulted from women's socially and psychically subordinate position.[68] These activities were hardly self-regulating. Reich associated the potential for self-regulation with orgastic potency, or "the full ability to relate to the partner without blockages to emotional contact caused by neurotic problems." Orgastic potency required the occurrence of both emotional and erotic impulses toward the sexual partner.[69] Yet the relationships of the family as they are economically and ideologically conditioned promote fixations at and regressions to infantile modes of satisfaction and infantile choices of objects. Hence, sexual encounters evoke the guilt and anxiety associated with the infantile fixations. This guilt and anxiety can be expressed in such diverse patterns of behavior as strict repression or the compulsive pursuit of sexual encounters. That is, Reich distinguished sexual activity in terms of human relationships.

Reich's orgastic potency was something quite different than the "pansexualism" or sexual panacea with which Marcuse and other critics have charged him. Typical of the criticism made of Reich was Marcuse's interpretation of Reich's emphasis on sexual liberation as a "sweeping primitivism" which arrested the critical insights of Reich's early works and foreshadowed "the wild and fantastic hobbies of Reich's later years."[70] This criticism misses the mark. True, the critical insights are somewhat arrested and the latter work is foreshadowed in the early. Yet it is a more subtle methodological contradition, rather than a "sweeping primitivism" or "pansexualism," which is responsible for this.

The methodological contradiction in Reich's work is this. After distinguishing such activity as promiscuity and self-regulating sexuality in terms of emotional contact, Reich attempted to measure the quantity of libidinal release involved in each. First he reduced all types of libidinal impulses (partial, genital, incestuous, aim-inhibited, and sublimated impulses) to the abstraction of quantity, then determined that genital sexuality involves a quantitatively greater release than the others. Therefore, he concluded, as long as the genital impulse is satisfied, the other impulses can be sublimated in production.[71] On the basis of this distinction, Reich posited genital primacy as the natural organization of the libido which we achieve automatically as long as society does not impede our development. The partial impulses correspond to different stages of biological development. But once the biological stage passes, the corresponding psychic impulse becomes pathological if it is not sublimated. The repression of genital sexuality does not facilitate this development but rather impedes it by cathecting the partial drives with more energy than can be sublimated effectively. However, if the genital impulse is satisfied, the others can be sublimated in productive activity. Consequently, the conflict between genital sexuality and social activity is not necessary; sexual repression results only from class domination.

In the minds of many of his critics, Reich's belief in the biologically self-generated development of the libido lessened the significance of all his work. This is unfortunate, for his theory of character structure remains the most systematic framework for the examination of the effects of social structures on the expression of human needs. Indeed, Reich argued that our impulses could not even be expressed without social organization. What he failed to recognize is that the interpenetration of needs and means of satisfying them which is fundamental to his description of the social conditioning of character, does not allow for the absolute libido he sought to measure.

In other words, there are two different conceptions of libido in Reich's work: a psychological and a physiological. The psychological conception describes the development, change, redirection, and repression of impulses as the individual makes his way through the institutions he confronts; the physiological describes the natural growth of the instincts as the body matures. In the next chapter, I will consider the problems Reich confronted in maintaining his physiological theory of libido and attempt to resolve these problems within the framework of the theory of character structure.

NOTES

[1] Marcuse, *Eros and Civilization* (Boston: Beacon Press, 1966), p. 239. The increasing conformity among Freud's followers is discussed in Boadella, *Wilhelm Reich: The Evolution of His Thought* (Chicago: Henry Regnery Co., 1973), p. 68; and Jacoby, *Social Amnesia* (Boston: Beacon Press, 1975), pp. 19–45.

[2] Reich, *The Mass Psychology of Fascism*, trans. Vincent R. Carfagno (New York: Farrar, Straus & Giroux, 1970), p. 16.

[3] Ibid, pp. 26–27.

[4] Reich, *Sex-Pol: Essays 1929–1934*, ed. Lee Baxandall, trans. Anna Bostock, Tom Dubose, and Lee Baxandall (New York: Random House, 1972), p. 52 (Dialectical Materialism and Psychoanalysis).

[5] *Mass Psychology*, p. 31.

[6] *Character Analysis*, 3d. ed., trans. Vincent R. Carfagno (New York: Simon and Schuster, 1976), p. xxviii.

[7] Bertell Ollman dates the early period between 1927 and 1936 and refers to it as Reich's Marxist period. See the Introduction by Ollman in *Sex-Pol*, p. xii. In 1933, after the Nazis' victory in Germany, Reich went into exile. He spent the next few years unsuccessfully seeking asylum in various European countries. In 1939, Reich emigrated to America in hopes of pursuing his work in peace. However, 15 years later he was to face in this country the most severe persecution of his life. In 1954 the Food and Drug Administration (FDA) judged his orgone therapy to be fraudulent and ordered him to cease it. The FDA cited articles in which Reich claimed to have had some success with orgone therapy in the treatment of cancer. In fairness to Reich, it should be noted that his claims were taken out of context. The same articles which were cited by the FDA also cited the results of unsuccessful experiments. Also, Reich often treated patients without fee so there was no issue of him attempting to profit off the terminally ill. Reich refused to heed or answer the order. As a result he was served with an injunction which ordered the withdrawal of all his books from the market. This included texts written before he even conceived of the orgone. Perhaps it was the strain of years, but Reich's reaction was even less rational than the injunction. He considered the FDA's campaign to be a Stalinist plot. He refused to answer the injunction, claiming that a court of law was not competent to judge on scientific matters.

On May 25, 1956 Reich was sentenced to two years in a federal prison for violating the court injunction. He was convinced that he would be pardoned by President Eisenhower, and that his imprisonment was "a means of protection against enemies of his work, who would destroy him physically if they could" (Boadella, op. cit., p. 316). On November 3, 1957, after serving eight months of his sentence, Wilhelm Reich died in his cell. He was the victim of a heart condition and the inadequacy of prison health care.

Reich's European exile is recounted in Michael Cattier, *The Life and Work of Wilhelm Reich*, trans. Ghislaine Boulanger (New York: Horizon Press, 1971), pp. 175–184.

Reich's experiences in America are described in Cattier, op. cit., pp. 204–211; Boadella, op. cit., pp. 267–285, 313–319, and pp. 321–337;

and Illse Olandorf-Reich, *Wilhelm Reich* (New York: St. Martin's Press, 1979).

[8] Reich, *Character Analysis*, pp. xviii. See also Reich, *The Sexual Revolution*, trans. Therese Pol (New York: Simon and Schuster, 1974), p. xxvi; and Freud, *A General Introduction to Psychoanalysis*, trans. Joan Riviere (New York: Washington Square Press, 1964), p. 365.

[9] Reich, *Sex-Pol*, pp. 19–20 (Dialectical Materialism and Psychoanalysis).

[10] Despite the fact that Reich had to publish *Character Analysis* privately in 1933, it now is considered a psychoanalytic classic. One reviewer of its English translation called it "an outstanding event in psychoanalysis . . . Reich's contributions to analytic techniques are unparalleled in the literature." Another commentator said that "the practical importance of Freud's *The Ego and the Id* only appeared with the publication of Reich's *Character Analysis* and Anna Freud's *The Ego and the Mechanisms of Defense.* . . ." The first comment appeared in a review in the *Journal of Educational Sociology*; the second, in Guntrip, *Personality Structure and Human Interaction*. Both are cited in Boadella, op. cit., pp. 53–54. Whether or not character structure was a milestone in psychoanalytic theory, it was a major development in political psychology.

[11] The concept of orgastic potency was introduced in a paper on "The Therapeutic Importance of Genital Libido," delivered to the Psychoanalytic Congress in Salzburg. See Boadella, op. cit., pp. 16, 37–38; and Cattier, op. cit., p. 14.

[12] Reich, *Mass Psychology*, pp. xi-xii.

[13] Reich, *Character Analysis*, pp. xxvii, xxx, 53, 90, 226. A similar view has been developed by Erich Fromm through his concept of social character. He claims that the social character consists of those parts of the character structure of individuals common to and forming the nucleus of most members of the group. But the social character is not a statistical concept. It can be understood only in reference to its function, which is to channel and mold human energy within a given society for the purpose of the continued functioning of this society. It develops as a result of the basic experiences and modes of life common to that group. See Fromm, *Escape From Freedom* (New York: Rinehart & Co., 1941), p. 277; and Fromm, *The Sane Society* (New York: Holt, Rinehart & Winston, 1955), pp. 79–80.

Reich's and Fromm's theories about character will be compared in the text, following the discussion of Reich's theory of character structure.

[14] Reich, *Character Analysis*, p. 344.

[15] Tucker (ed.), *The Marx-Engels Reader* (New York: W. W. Norton & Co., 1972), p. 109 (Theses on Feuerbach). By attributing to Reich the Marxian position on human nature, I am suggesting that his view is not simply the opposite of Freud's. The Marxian position is that human nature is formed in interaction with the natural and social environment.

Human nature is socially formed, but it is not necessarily either sociable or antisocial. For a comparison of Freud's and Marx's view on human nature, see Kovel, "The Marxist View of Man and Psychoanalysis," *Social Research,* vol. 43 (Summer 1976), 220–245; and the three-part series of articles by Lichtman, "Marx and Freud," *Socialist Revolution,* no. 30 (October-December 1976): 3-56; "Marx and Freud, Part 2: Antagonistic Themes," *Socialist Revolution,* no. 33 (May-June 1977), 59–82; and "Marx and Freud, Part 3: Marx's Theory of Human Nature," *Socialist Revolution,* no. 36, (November-December 1977), 37–76. In the first article, Lichtman summarizes Reich's contribution to Marxian theory and explores the similarities between Marx's and Freud's thought. In the second part, he reviews Freud's theory of human nature; in the third, Marx's.

Actually, if the notion of "biologic core" is emphasized in Reich's description of character layers, another more mechanistic and utopian version of human nature becomes possible. This other interpretation finds its way into Reich's early works and dominates his later works. Chapter 7 will be concerned with the way in which Reich's emphasis of the biologic core affected his political psychology.

[16] Reich, *Character Analysis,* pp. 177–187, Chapters 8, 10–11.

[17] Ibid., p. 208. See also p. 344.

[18] Ibid., p. 192.

[19] Ibid., p. 205. Furthermore, Reich claimed that the transformation of repressive social institutions is necessary to "create the preconditions for an extensive prophylaxis of neurosis." See ibid., p. xxv.

[20] Fromm, *Man For Himself* (Greenwich, Conn.: Fawcett Publications, 1947), pp. 63–69, 116. The character types are described on pages 70 to 122. In an article first published in 1932 in the journal of the Institute for Social Research in Frankfurt, Fromm advances a characterology much more similar to Reich's. See "Psychoanalytic Characterology and its Relevance for Social Psychology," *The Crisis of Psychoanalysis* by Erich Fromm (Greenwich, Conn.: Fawcett Publications, 1970), pp. 163–189. However, in works such as *Character Analysis,* Reich developed the theoretical and clinical implications of the relationship between character and social life much more fully and systematically than Fromm. Furthermore, it is the later theory on character, developed in America, for which Fromm is best known. For a short discussion of developments in Fromm's work and its changing relationship to Marx's and Freud's, see Jay, *The Dialectical Imagination* (Boston: Little, Brown & Co., 1973), pp. 95–100.

[21] Fromm, *Man for Himself,* p. 86.

[22] Adorno, "Sociology and Psychology, Part II," *New Left Review,* no. 47 (January-February 1968), 89.

[23] Fromm, *Man for Himself,* p. 90. For Fromm's description of the general characteristics of this healthy character, which he refers to as the productive orientation, see pp. 89–102.

[24] See for example, Reich, *Mass Psychology,* p. 30.

[25] Engels, *The Origin of the Family, Private Property, and the State*, ed. with Introduction by Eleanor Burke Leacock (New York: International Publishers, 1972), p. 139.

[26] Ibid., p. 137.

[27] Reich, *Sexual Revolution*, p. 173.

[28] Engels, op. cit., p. 137; and Reich, *Sexual Revolution*, p. 174.

[29] Reich, *Sex-Pol*, pp. 304, 312 (What is class Consciousness).

Contemporary sociologists have described, in greater detail than Reich, the daily discourse through which attitudes toward politics and work were communicated in the family. See for example Richard Sennet and Jonathan Cobb, *The Hidden Injuries of Class* (New York: Random House, 1972). See especially pp. 125–146.

In a series of interviews with students from working class families, Sennett and Cobb found that family pressures hindered these students from deviating from conventional lifestyles. Fathers dissatisfied with their own work pressured their sons to become qualified for those jobs which were most valuable on the labor market—especially professional careers. But these families were also fearful of their upwardly mobile children abandoning them. Through what one son perceived as the imposition of a "guilt trip," the values of hard work and sacrifice for the family are transmitted to the children. In other words, the atomistic ideology of the family directs the children toward private solutions (that is, "upward mobility") for social problems. Consequently, they try to adapt to the social structure rather than change it. As Sennett and Cobb concluded, "The psychological motivation instilled by a class society is to heal a doubt about the self rather than create more power over things and other persons in the outer world" (p. 171). See also Herbert Gans, *The Urban Villagers: Group and Class in the Life of Italian-Americans* (New York: The Free Press, 1965), pp. 27–30, 122–128.

[30] Reich, *Mass Psychology*, pp. 30, 104; and *Sexual Revolution*, pp. 86–89. Reich stressed the transmission of moralistic sexual attitudes within the family and the political consequences of this.

[31] Reich, *Mass Psychology*, pp. 30–31, 56–57. See also the discussion of "The Establishment and Preservation of Infantile Patterns of Relationships" in Chapter 4, above.

[32] Reich, *Sex-Pol*, p. 43 (Dialectical Materialism and Psychoanalysis).

[33] Ibid., p. 26.

[34] Ibid., p. 47. Reich discusses the political-psychological implications of Malinowski's work in his essay "The Imposition of Sexual Morality" in *Sex-Pol*, pp. 89–249. Although Reich's venture into anthropology was necessary to support his claim that the oedipus complex was peculiar to the nuclear family, Reich attempted to use the Trobrianders as an example of a natural state of self-regulating sexuality. Consequently he implicitly reformulated the social potential for self-regulation as a biological fact. The problems with this will be discussed in the section on "Sexual

Repression and the Relationships of Production and Reproduction" in Chapter 7, below.

[35] Quoted in Mitchell, *Psychoanalysis and Feminism* (New York: Pantheon Press, 1974), p. 174.

[36] Reich, *Sexual Revolution*, pp. 90–91. Reich sought confirmation for this view in the work of Vera Schmidt, a Soviet psychoanalyst who founded an experimental children's home in 1921. Schmidt's home operated on the principle that for every primitive desire which the child must learn to renounce (for example, oedipal desires) other "reasonable rational pleasures" should be substituted. Thus masturbatory activity was tolerated and the children even had "the complete freedom to satisfy their sexual curiosity with each other." Reich was convinced that these children would grow to be healthy adults. Unfortunately, less than a year later the Soviet authorities stopped maintaining the home and the experiment came to a premature end. See *Sexual Revolution*, pp. 296–302.

[37] Reich, *Character Analysis*, pp. 177–187.

[38] Reich, *Sexual Revolution*, pp. 134–136. Of course the repression of adolescent sexuality and problems such as birth control and privacy were more severe in Reich's time than at present, but many of these problems continue to hinder the sexual expression of adolescents.

[39] Ibid., p. 100.

[40] Reich, *Mass Psychology*, p. 56. In *Sexual Revolution*, Reich cites data which indicates an inverse correlation between marital fidelity and premarital sex (pp. 88, 100, 121).

[41] Reich stressed that he was not criticizing the family itself, but only its most compulsive and repressive features. *Sexual Revolution*, p. 32. Reich's predominantly negative evaluation of family life will be discussed in the section on "Sexual Repression and the Relationships of Production and Reproduction," in Chapter 7, below.

[42] Reich, *Sexual Revolution*, p. 95.

[43] Reich, *Mass Psychology*, p. 104.

[44] Freud, *New Introductory Lectures on Psychoanalysis*, trans. and ed. James Strachey (New York: W. W. Norton & Co., 1965), p. 67.

[45] Reich, *Mass Psychology*, p. 53. Compare Sartre's suggestion that we first experience alienation and reification not in our own work, but in our parents' work. Sartre, *Search For a Method* (New York: Random House, 1963), p. 62.

[46] Reich, *Mass Psychology*, p. 63.

[47] Freud, *Group Psychology and the Analysis of Ego*, trans. and ed. James Strachey (New York: Liveright Publishing Corp., 1967), pp. 32, 48. See also the section on "The Psychology of Group Dynamics" in Chapter 5, above.

[48] Reich, *Mass Psychology*, pp. 11–13 and Chapter 2, especially pp. 44, 46.

[49] Ibid., pp. 46, 51.

[50] Ibid., p. 46.

[51] Ibid., p. 53. See also pp. 46–47, 51–53.

[52] The father's role as disciplinarian is described in greater detail by contemporary sociologists. See Sennett and Cobb, op. cit., pp. 127–132; and Gans, op. cit., pp. 47–53.

[53] Reich, *Sex-Pol*, p. 237. (The Imposition of Sexual Morality); Reich and Teschitz, *Selected Sex-Pol Essays: 1934–37* (London: Socialist Reproduction, 1973), p. 44–48 (History of the German Sex-Pol Movement; The Editorial Group); and Reich, *Sexual Revolution*, pp. 134–137.

[54] Reich, *Mass Psychology*, pp. 55, 65–66. More specific descriptions of the social ties of contemporary working-class neighborhoods may be found in Sennett and Cobb, op. cit., pp. 105–108; and Gans, op. cit., pp. 45–47, 74–103. Although neither deal with attitudes toward sexuality as such, Gans suggests that in the working-class subculture that he observed, people were *more* anxious about sexuality than in the middle class. However, these relationships still may provide an important aim-inhibited release, as Reich suggests.

[55] Reich, *Mass Psychology*, p. 13.

[56] Ibid., pp. 41, 433.

[57] Reich stressed the hegemony of imperialistic and capitalistic interests in fascism but emphasized that its mass support could not be explained in terms of those interests. See ibid., p. 43. Even as severe of a critic of Reich as Mitchell emphasized the originality and significance of Reich's project. (Mitchell, op. cit., p. 214). Some of Mitchell's criticisms will be discussed in Chapter 7.

Clearly, political psychology can add little to the analyses of historians and political economists on the role of German and foreign corporations and cartels in creating a social crisis of tremendous magnitude. German business offered a great deal of support to the Nazis. Foreign business, particularly the French, helped to bring about a severe economic crisis in Germany by actions such as the extraction of huge reparations and the expropriation of the Saar Mining region. See Otto Friedrich, *Before the Deluge* (New York: Harper & Row, 1972), pp. 53–54, 133–135, 144. For a collection of discussions and bibliographic essays on the political, economic, and social antecedents of fascism, and the class alignments expressed within the movement, see the issue on "Critiques of Fascism Theory from the German New Left," *International Journal of Politics*, vol. 2 (Winter 972–73).

[58] Reich, *Mass Psychology*, pp. 75–79.

[59] Ibid., pp. 78, 84.

[60] Ibid., pp. 81–82; and Freud, *New Introductory Lectures*, p. 88.

[61] Horowitz, *Repression* (Toronto and Buffalo: University of Toronto Press, 1977), p. 127.

[62] Marcuse, *Counterrevolution and Revolt* (Boston: Beacon Press, 1972), p. 130.

[63] Ibid., pp. 130–133; and Marcuse, *One-Dimensional Man* (Boston: Beacon Press, 1966), Chapter 3.

[64] Marcuse, *Eros and Civilization* (Boston: Beacon Press, 1974), p. 239.

[65] Janik and Toulmin, *Wittgenstein's Vienna* (New York: Simon and Schuster, 1973), pp. 50–58.

[66] Ibid., pp. 46–48, 70; Friedrich, op. cit., pp. 64, 74, Chapters 7 and 8; and Mitchell, op. cit., pp. 420–435.

[67] Freud, "On the Universal Tendency to Debasement in the Sphere of Love," discussed in Horowitz, p. 128. Actually Freud's description was stated in terms of a male redirecting the erotic impulse toward women who cannot be identified with mother. But this process is important for female sexuality as well. On the one hand, women, as well as men, may come to express their sexuality as distinct from emotional attachments. On the other, the social categories of emotional object and sexual object (or mother and whore) must be at least as important in the social conditioning of women as men. A woman who even exhibits the alienation of emotional and sexual impulses and who indulges in sex with men to whom she is not emotionally attached in many situations will have to bear the consequences of being assigned to the morally undesirable side of the dichotomy. Even the woman who is not dependent on one man and who is capable of establishing emotional attachments with more than one lover may be socially chastised.

A distinction between psychic and somatic genitality is discussed by Horowitz, op. cit., pp. 62–64.

[68] Reich, *Sexual Revolution*, pp. 142–143, 40–41, 167; and Reich and Teschitz, op. cit., p. 46 (History of the Sex-Pol Movement).

[69] Boadella, op. cit., p. 22. See also *Reich Speaks of Freud*, ed. Mary Higgins and Chester M. Raphael, trans. Therese Pol (New York: Farrar, Straus, & Giroux, 1967), p. 24.

[70] Marcuse, *Eros and Civilization*, p. 239. See also Mitchell, op. cit., pp. 163–164, 171; and Rycroft, *Wilhelm Reich* (New York: The Viking Press, 1972), pp. 62–65.

[71] Reich, *Character Analysis*, pp. 206–211, 231.

7

LIBIDO AND SOCIAL
RELATIONSHIPS:
A CRITIQUE OF
REICH'S LIBIDO THEORY

IN a discussion of the psychoanalytic theory of the instincts, Reich favorably cited Freud's formulation that "the instinct is a borderline concept between the psychic and the somatic." Reich believed that the primary contribution of his own work was to increase our understanding of this ambiguous juncture. Those who sought to understand human impulses as biological facts he criticized with the admonishment that this position

> . . . is not rooted in the heart of psychoanalysis, which is specifically dialectical, but in the mechanistic thinking of psychoanalysts which, as usual, is supplemented by metaphysical theses. Drives emerge, change and disappear.[1]

Even late in his career, while he was preoccupied with developing a biophysical theory of sexual energy, Reich was to insist, "It is not either libido or society. The libido is the energy which is molded by society." That is, as Reich stated elsewhere, "There was never any doubt but that the biological drives were molded by the social forces at work in the particular period."[2] Unfortunately, these insights were overwhelmed by the logic of Reich's libido theory. The separation of biology and social existence was presupposed in his procedure of reducing socially conditioned human impulses to their quantifiable, physiological source. Reich seemed to believe that the libido is its own biological energy source. As early as 1919 Reich interpreted Freud as claiming that the libido was the energy of the sexual instinct, not the instinct itself. Reich added that some day this energy might very well be measurable, like electrical energy. This was no metaphor; Reich saw definite structural similarities between the two types of energy.[3] Furthermore Reich seemed to believe that if he could measure sexual energy, then he would have evidence that the critics of the psychoanalytic theory of sex could not refute. Reich saw the psychoanalytic mainstream as too willing to compromise with these critics.

Freud excluded the somatic source of psychic energy from the immediate concerns of psychoanalysis. He sought to understand the psyche in terms of the topography of structures, the dynamics of repression and resistance, the economics of cathexes and anti-cathexes, and the consequent instinctual vicissitudes. Since Reich's theory of character analysis was intended to fit the framework of psychoanalysis, it also can be understood in these terms and it is in these terms that I presented it in the preceding chapter.[4] There we saw how Reich described in much greater detail than Freud how human needs are conditioned in a class society. Yet Reich insisted on going beyond Freud in studying the biological source of psychic energy. He claimed this was necessary to develop the libido theory.

Ilse Olendorf Reich, a colleague, wife, and biographer of Reich, noted that the "energy concept" was the central concept of all of Reich's work.[5] Indeed, it is hard to exaggerate Reich's fascination with the sources of energy in human beings. Yet when Reich pursued the sources of libido, he approached the study of energy from two different perspectives: that of psychology and that of physiology. Since psychology is concerned with the mental representations of instincts and physiology with their somatic sources, Reich ran into trouble when he confused the two. His physiological perspective on the libido manifests itself in Reich's political psychology as a double-edged reductionism. On the one hand, human sexuality was reduced to the biophysical energy associated with stimulations in the erogenous zones. On the other, the social modification of sexuality was reduced to a simple manifestation of class domination.

In this chapter, I will examine, in turn, each of these tendencies. In doing so, I will attempt to make explicit the contradictions between Reich's theory of character structure and his theory of libido. I then will suggest a critical reconstruction of Reich's libido theory. I will not endeavor to evaluate Reich's biophysical theory of sexual impulses, but only to demonstrate how it resulted in contradictions and uncritical formulations in his political psychology.

THE REICHIAN LIBIDO: THE SOMATIC SOURCE OF SEXUAL ENERGY

Freud examined the processes by which the child comes to adapt his or her sexuality to the specific demands of his culture. He revealed how the child expresses his sexuality through diverse erogenous zones and psychic representations and how the child progresses from autoerotic activity to object-directed sexuality. He described how the partial impulses, through their association with the self-preservation impulses, develop into the genital sexuality of the adult.

Reich viewed the development of genital sexuality as a less-complicated, more-natural process. The child does progress through erotic stages which are distinguished by their corresponding partial impulses and the dominance of a particular erogenous zone, but the passage from one stage to another is not primarily a matter of psychological development. Rather it is the natural consequence of biological maturation. The quantity of libido used in the excitation of the genital zone and discharged in orgasm makes the genital impulse, in terms of libidal release, the most vital impulse. Hence genital primacy is the natural result of sexual development. Reich believed that psychological disorders can be overcome only when genital impulses are satisfied. The partial drives, insofar as they distracted from genitality, are perverse or disturbed.[6]

What Freud suggested and Reich denied was made explicit by Reimut Reiche three decades later. In genital sexuality the partial drives are not rejected but at least subordinated and ideally integrated into the pattern of sexual development.[7] In this respect Freud better appreciated the socio-historical influences on the libido than did Reich. For Freud genital sexuality, while socially repressed, is also culturally achieved. It is the culmination of the process of the sexual maturation of the child within social institutions, particularly the family. The secondary processes of the reality principle express the demand for the repression of erotic strivings. Yet they also initiate the development of genital primacy. The psychological development of the child within the family results not only in the internalization of social authority, but also in the development of the capacity of the ego to test reality. For Reich, however, culture only represses sexuality. Sexual maturity can be achieved only in spite of cultural demands. Genital primacy is derived from the very source of the libido. It is particularly ironic that a thinker who rejected the absolutes of "Freudism" could hold such single-minded views of genital primacy and cultural repression. The cultural demands imposed upon the impulses cannot be explained in terms of class domination alone as Reich attempted to do. The unconscious is dominated by the sexuality of the pleasure principle which is expressed in dreams and infantile fantasies. This primary sexuality must be directed outward and modified before it can find expression in ways that are socially accepted. Furthermore self-preservation requires that erotic energy be sublimated in self-protective and socially necessary or valued activity. Sublimation is brought about through basic repression. The repression necessary to maintain relationships of exploitation and domination is surplus repression. While Freud failed to address himself to surplus repression Reich reversed the error. Reich did not recognize the dual origin and function of repression and used the term repression to refer only to surplus repression, that is "repression seen as interfering with natural growth."[8] However, the critical question is not whether there is an underlying harmony or conflict between the primary processes and social life, but whether the specific modification demanded by the reality principle promotes self-regulation or moralistic repression. In other words, the issue is not a specific conception of "human nature" but a specific mode of social conditioning.

Freud insisted that the modification of the primary processes was a social necessity. His conception of the primary processes actually parelleled Marx's conception of human nature as an embodiment of the history and structure of the social relationships within which it finds and expresses itself. While Reich's theory of character structure also was a theory of the social conditioning of human needs, desires, beliefs, and responses, the essential nature of this conditioning is obscured in Reich's libido theory. Instead of a historically conditioned character structure, Reich posits a naturally self-regulating libido. Self-regulation is conceived not as a human potential realizable through the processes of individual and social development, but rather as a natural law of the pleasure principle which was expressed in more natural, prehistoric societies and continued to be expressed until the emergence of class relationships. That is, in the theory of character structure self-regulation is a feature of the interaction between the ego and id as they develop socially; in the theory of the libido, a feature of the instincts themselves as they strive for discharge naturally and automatically.

Reich could not reconcile his belief in the social molding and transformation of instincts and needs with his biological perspective on the libido. If human sexuality is a natural, biophysical energy which is released most efficiently, indeed, qualitatively more efficiently, in genital sexuality, then sexuality can only be expressed or repressed, not mediated and molded. For Reich, whether social institutions allow the expression or demand the repression of sexuality depends entirely on whether or not the social structure is based on class exploitation. Patriarchy, as a structure of social relationships and its ideological expression, emerges in a society in which a social surplus is produced collectively but expropriated by a ruling group. Previous to this, Reich alleged, matriarchal family forms allowed the free expression of sexuality.[9]

Since Reich's speculation on the relationship between class society and sexual repression is hardly confirmed by empirical evidence, it has been a major target of his critics.[10] In the following section, I will not attempt to defend Reich's position on the emergence and dynamics of patriarchal repression, but to demonstrate that even while rejecting his speculation, his theory of character structure can be utilized to examine the role of family relationships in conditioning the individual's patterns of response to authority.

SEXUAL REPRESSION AND RELATIONSHIPS OF
PRODUCTION AND REPRODUCTION

Reich's attempts to trace the historical development of kinship and family structures suffered greatly from his one-sided view of the association between class relationships and sexual repression. Reich claimed that the repression of sexuality was a distinct feature of patriarchal societies, which in turn were a consequence of the institution of private property. Furthermore, as property accumulated in private hands, the patriarchal family became increasingly repressive. In this section, I first will discuss the difficulties involved in maintaining Reich's views on the relationship between patriarchy, private property, and sexual repression. Then I will show that even while rejecting Reich's conclusions on patriarchal repression, the theory of character structure can be utilized to examine the part played by the nuclear family in the social conditioning of the individual. Had Reich approached these problems from the perspective of character structure, he would have been led to more defensible, and more useful conclusions.

PATRIARCHY, PRIVATE PROPERTY, AND SEXUAL REPRESSION

Reich developed his theory of the emergence of patriarchal repression in his work, "The Imposition of Sexual Morality." The work was based on Bronislaw Malinowski's anthropological field work among the Trobriand Islanders of Melanesia. Reich saw the Trobrianders as a society in transition from matriarchy to patriarchy. Reich's primary concern in describing Trobriander life was to explicate the relationship between the institutions and repressive morality of patriarchy, and the institution of private property.

Reich followed Engels in associating the emergence of patriarchy with the economic interests of the male, particularly the chief and other notables who were allowed to be polygamous, and the developing institution of private property. Reich claimed that Malinowski's observations supported this hypothesis by revealing the mechanism by which the male's social and economic position is enhanced by marriage: the marriage dowry. A consequence of the dowry is that marriage becomes imbued with the contradiction between "sexual interests, which point to relationships of limited duration, and economic interests, which aim at permanent relationships."[11]

For Reich, the practice of providing a dowry became the basis for making the transition from a matriarchy to patriarchy. That is, the transferral of marriage tribute from the wife's brother to the prospective husband places the wife in a subordinant position to the men who are the dispensers and receivers of the family wealth. Reich also saw in this custom the basis of class divisions. The chief's family uses the kinship structure to accumulate wealth in two ways. First, the chief is allowed many wives and thus can receive many dowries. Second, though the chief must give a dowry to his sister's husband, this tribute is returned to the chief's family by the imposition of the cross-cousin marriage on the chief's son. That is, the daughter of the chief's sister must marry the son of the chief, thereby returning to the chief's family the dowry that the chief paid to his sister's husband. Through the cross-cousin marriage matrilineal inheritence (inheritence through the woman's family) is circumscribed, the chief's wealth returns to his son, and wealth is accumulated within the chief's family. All clans "become subordinate to the chief's clan and ultimately to the chief's family." The accumulation of wealth and, consequently, power in the chief's family leads to the creation of hereditary patriarchy.[12]

Reich saw in the relationship between the chief's clan and the maternal clans an early form of class exploitation. He also saw these relationships as the source of repressive sexual morality. He claimed that two of Malinowski's observations confirmed this. One was the contradiction between the sexual liberty allowed in childhood and adolescence, and the repression of sexuality after marriage, which already had been transformed into an economic arrangement by the dowry. The other was the chastity demanded only of those youngsters destined for cross-cousin marriages. The demand for childhood and adolescent continence is associated with the form of marriage in which material interests most clearly are evident.[13]

Reich interpreted Malinowski's description of the freer expression of sexuality among the Trobrianders as an indication of an unrepressive society. He associated their freer sexual expression to matriarchal relationships within which the women of the clan were not yet subordinated to the men. Reich described the marriage dowry as the means by which matriarchal, primitive communism is transformed into a patriarchal system based on private property. It is within the latter that the demand for adolescent asceticism is articulated, presumably in the interest of molding the character structure necessary for permanent, mono-gamous marriage. In Reich's analysis that which is affirmative of sexuality is associated with the moribund matriarchy; that which is repressive, with the nascent patriarchy.

However, the associations between kinship structures and sex-uality that Reich described are not so much conclusions as as-sumptions. Reich noticed both sexually affirmative and repressive features in Trobriander sexual life and assumed that these features had to be associated with different kinship structures. He did not consider that the specific relationships of the patriarchal family, and the corresponding restraints and taboos placed upon sexual activity, may vary with the structures of kinship and class relation-ships. Charles Rycroft noted that the following assumption un-derlies Reich's hypothesis of a transition from matriarchy to patriarchy: "that the conventions governing kinship and the tracing of lineages reflect the structure of a society and the nature of power relationships existing within it." Yet even in societies in which inheritence is traced through the mother's family, property can be controlled by men; that is, matrilineal societies still may be patriarchal.[14] Unwittingly, Reich's own discussion of the role of the maternal uncle in Trobriander society constituted an example of this. Reich described the relationship between brother and married sister as similar, except for the sexual component, to that between husband and wife in patrilineal societies. Reich claimed that "the brother of the wife is her real provider and the guardian of her children." Women still are dependent upon and subordinate to men, only the brother rather than the husband exercises the authority of the male in each family.[15]

The maternal uncle seemed, for Reich, to have the most obvious power in Trobriander society before the Trobrianders began the transformation to patriarchy. And, by his own description, women were placed in a subordinate position to the men of the clan. Furthermore, Reich recognized that the position of the maternal uncle is the mark of an exogamous society, that is, a society which forbids marriages within the clan. Although there may be more repression involved in the cross-cousin marriage, which Reich associated with the rights of the father and private property, repression already was exerted once marriage within the clan was forbidden. Juliet Mitchell, one of Reich's most severe critics, followed Claude Levi-Strauss in arguing that all culture is exogamous and patriarchal, since culture is based on the exchange of women.[16] Reich's own descriptions of the role of the maternal uncle and the institution of the marriage dowry tend to support rather than undermine Mitchell's position. To maintain his view on the association between patriarchy, private property, and sexual repression, Reich must follow Freud in reconstructing a primal hord.[17] If Freud's concept of the primal horde justifies strict repression, Reich's reveals a naturally self-regulating libido, which is repressed only for class domination.

By Reich's own description, sexuality already was restricted in Trobriander society. The transformation from the alleged primal hordes to matrilineal societies was the transformation from an incestuous society to an exogamous society. Yet Reich claimed that the sexuality which is dominant in matrilineal societies is quantitatively different from that which is dominant in patrilineal societies. Sexual taboos exist in both, but within matrilineages more expression is allowed than within patrilineages. In Reich's description of "The Imposition of Sexual Morality" his conception of the libido as a natural energy source contradicts the psychoanalytic conception of psychic energetics. Reich made the degree of satisfaction of the sexual instinct a major distinction between patrilineal and matrilineal societies. From the viewpoint of psychoanalytic theory, however, the social significance of sexuality lies not as much in the extent of the release as in its mediation through objects, restrictions, and sublimations that are defined as socially acceptable. Reich, in his speculation on the etiology of patriarchy, obscured, more than he revealed, these mediations. He considered the expression of sexuality allowed within the presumably matriarchal culture of the Trobriand Islands only in terms of the opportunity for release, and not in terms of the development of sexuality within specific family relations. Reich was aware of the existence of a distinctly matrilineal taboo on incest, yet he assumed that since a sufficient amount of libidinal release is allowed in the childhood and adolescent relationships of Trobriander life, the restrictions are hardly felt. While he described the way men control kinship exchange through the role of the maternal uncle, he considered that role to be a social institution which preceded the patriarchy based on private property. It is difficult to see how he maintained these positions, unless he was equating patriarchy with sexual repression and matriarchy with sexual freedom. The logic of this argument is the logic Reich used to formulate his libido theory. In this logic, the multi-faceted relationship between character structure and social structure is reduced to a contradiction between natural needs and class domination. Reich concluded not only that the reality principle of class societies imposes an overly harsh modification on the primary processes for achieving pleasure, but that the reality principle modifies the pleasure principle only in class societies. Yet Reich could not claim the Trobrianders as an example of a society in which sexuality is governed by the natural law of self-regulation. As Mitchell asks, "If intergeneration sexuality is tabooed and sibling sexuality allowed . . . could we not legitimately call this an 'extended oedipus complex' much on a par with the extended family?"[18]

Despite his denial, Reich did seem to posit a natural sexuality which is allowed varying degrees of expression within different societies.[19] Reich's discussion of the relationship between sexuality and social institutions in matrilineal kinship societies emphasized the greater opportunity for genital release in sexual relationships that exists in these societies. He failed to recognize that these opportunities are compatible with the repressions demanded by the matrilineal relationships. Moreover, he failed to consider that, as his own analysis implied, these opportunities are provided in support of the dominant social relationships. He himself claimed that the taboos on and direction of sexuality imposed by the kinship structure are made tolerable by permissiveness in regard to premarital sexuality. Since Reich was following the quantitative logic of his libido theory, the amount of release was all-important. He did not consider the consequences of the social direction of sexuality on character development. In contrast, Reich considered the permissiveness and promiscuity of his own society, as we have seen in the preceding chapter, to be an expression of repressed and alienated sexuality. There probably are valid distinctions to be made between the sexual promiscuity of the Trobriand Islands and that of the Berlin cabarets, but nowhere does Reich address himself to this point. Here again Reich's attempts to compare the ways in which sexuality is expressed in different social structures as amounts of libidinal energy distorted his analysis.

In his analysis of Trobriand society, Reich failed to substantiate his claim of a naturally self-regulating sexuality which is allowed expression up to the transformation of social relationships that resulted from the accumulation of property, through the marriage dowry, in private hands. Had Reich been more careful in drawing conclusions from his description of Trobriander life, he would have contended that before the accumulation of property sexual morality was less repressive, not unrepressive. Furthermore, after positing this idealized state of sexually permissive kinship, Reich seemed unconcerned with identifying historical differences in the forms of "permanent monogamous marriage."[20] If the family is seen only as the setting in which natural sexuality is opposed by patriarchal repression, it becomes hard to distinguish the ways in which the family functions to condition character in different social structures. So, if Reich made a contribution to the study of the family, he did not do so when he relied upon his theory of libido and its distinction between natural sexuality and patriarchal repression; he did when he applied his theory of character structure with its emphasis on the political consequences of the emotional conditioning of family members, to the study of family life.

THE NUCLEAR FAMILY AND CHARACTER STRUCTURE

In a series of review essays on several works of family history, Christopher Lasch suggested that what is of importance in the study of family history is the consideration of the interaction between social relationships and family relationships and the effect of this interaction on the emotional content of family relationships.[21] Lasch based his suggestion on the observation that the contemporary family is an organized unit in a socially atomized society; as such, it serves ideally as a private retreat from the frustrations of the outer world. The class relationships which underlie a mass society, however, also result in an organization of work and leisure which erodes and penetrates the privacy of the family. Lasch maintained that the transition to capitalism resulted in changes in the family's relation to the outside world, such as the separation and hence isolation of the nuclear family from the extended family and the social organization of work. As a consequence of the increasing isolation of family life, the family became a "private retreat" or "safe haven" from the pressures and frustrations of social life. At the same time that capitalist cultural hegemony undermines many of the traditional functions of the family, as we have seen in Chapter 2, the family comes to provide the intimate space necessary to recover psychically from struggles of social life. The establishment of this intimate space requires the emotional intensification of family relationships. A psychic consequence of this emotional intensification is a strengthening of the child's identification with parents which "at once sharpened the struggle necessary to achieve autonomy and gave it a stronger basis by forcing the individual to develop inner resources instead of relying on external direction."[22]

However, if social forces lead to an intensification of family relationships, which in turn promote the development of the individual's sense of self, other forces at the same time lead to the loosening of relations, which undermine this sense of self. For example, the withdrawal of the father into the world of work weakens the sons identification with his father. The growing influence of the statements made by organizations concerned with mental health have had an increasing influence on family patterns of child rearing. The statements have stressed the need to condition the child for the depersonalized relationships of the labor market and corporate and governmental bureaucracies, as well as easygoing interpersonal relations. Parents raising children in the child-centered family seek to avoid painful confrontations with their children. Consequently, the child does not internalize parental authority as completely and therefore does not need to struggle as hard to overcome it. Yet psychic independence is not achieved so easily. The individual spared the painful struggle for independence is susceptible to dependence on authority outside the family. Lasch suggested that family historians consider the extent to which the changed relationships within the family have contributed to psychic injury and then the extent to which this injury results from sources outside the family.[23]

Lasch's criticism of family histories which emphasize changes in family structure can be directed against Reich's work on patriarchal repression. However, Lasch's proposal for a new direction in family history which stresses the emotional conditioning of family members suggests the efficacy of Reich's description of the political function of the family in industrially advanced societies. Reich's concept of character structure and the mode of explanation it implies is central to Lasch's new direction; he claims that family historians "need to study changes in emotional life and character structure, the contribution of the family to these changes, and their relation to changes in the organization of work and economic activity."[24] Reich described these changes and relationships in his political and psychological analysis of the family in capitalist societies. His description of the process by which the repression of sexuality within the family molds the character structure necessary for capitalist hegemony is a trenchant political psychology concerned with specifying the myriad interconnections between character structure, family and class relationships, and the dominant ideologies.

Reich's most powerful application of a political and psychological analysis of the family was, as we have seen, his examination of the success of fascism. He examined how the middle-class family molded a character structure susceptible to Nazi ideology. He did not distinguish the middle-class family in terms of its structure; the middle-class family was structurally similar to the working-class family. Rather he distinguished the middle-class family in terms of the intensity of the expression of patriarchal ideology within it, which he related to the atomization of the middle class in the process of production and in social life. He recognized that the ideological distinction between the working-class and middle-class family was reduced both by the conditions of the labor market, which still maintained although not as completely, the role of the male as head of the household, and also by religious morality. In his analysis of fascism Reich also acknowledged that the capacity to resist authority depended on the modification of primary processes and the development of partial drives. Narcissism, fixation, and regression defined the unconscious content of fascist ideology. In his political psychology Reich emphasized more than Freud the specific historical form of the interpenetration of social structure and character structure in class societies. Reich argued effectively that in differentiating himself from the outer world the individual psychically reproduces the demands imposed by the structure of social relationships and dominant ideologies. He conceptualized the relationship between the psychic processes described by Freud and the ideological and cultural hegemony of the politically and economically dominant class. He formulated the role of the family as the mediator in the relationship between psychic processes and hegemony. In short, Reich searched for the social sources of repression and the mechanisms of its introjection.

The theory of character structure demands a rigorous examination of the social sources and mechanisms of introjection. Reich's theory of the libido, however, demands much less rigor. The repression of sexuality is associated historically with the patriarchal accumulation of property. The distinction between matriarchal natural expression and patriarchal repression makes it unnecessary to explore the way in which the conditioning of character is influenced by variations in family and class relationships.

Hence as critics of Reich have recognized, taking the psychoanalytic approach to the study of the libido gives a more sensitive description of the relationship between sexuality and social institutions than does taking Reich's biological approach. For Freud, the individual's sense of self begins to develop at that time that the absence of the objects of needs leads the narcissistic infant to differentiate himself from the outer world. Mitchell, for example, is right to criticize Reich for the notion of a "separate, pre-existent self" which underlies his view of sexuality.[25] What she and other critics fail to appreciate, however, is the extent to which Reich's biological approach is incompatible with his approach based on character development. The individual's character develops as a psychological defense against frustrations he encounters as he must deal with the institutions that structure his life. Reich's treatises on the opposition between natural libido and patriarchal repression shed little light on the social processes which condition character.

The central thesis of Reich's political psychology is that the social structure is psychologically reproduced during character development to permit the individual to interact socially and to modify the instincts. Yet while he developed a systematic framework to try to understand the way in which the individual is conditioned to accept his or her social position, Reich did not contribute that much to our understanding of instinctual modification. He failed to recognize the modification of sexuality in Trobriander life. He was unconcerned with the changes in character that might result in changes from the family's relationship with the outside world. He certainly never suggested, as did Lasch, that more permissive child-rearing may lead to a greater reliance on depersonalized social authority. In short, Reich failed to develop a consistent perspective on the libido as a source of energy which is conditioned by the dominant social relationships.

In contrast to Reich, who spoke of sexual liberation as the ability to satisfy genital instincts, Marcuse spoke of it as the transformation of libido. Marcuse stressed a qualitative distinction in sexual activity which Reich neglected: whether the apparent increase in freedom involves a contraction or extension and development of instinctual needs. Marcuse claimed that the satisfaction of a contracted need can work "*for* rather than *against* the status quo of general repression." Marcuse recognized that once social conditions have preconditioned and affected the articulation of human needs, the satisfaction of those needs, no less than their repression, can lead to the psychological reproduction of the social structure. "Pleasure, thus adjusted, generates submission."[26]

Marcuse's formulation of the problem of repression is particularly important for those interested in political psychology. Rather than concerning themselves with the quantity of libidinal release, political psychologists have more to gain from studying the interactions of people when they express their impulses through their character. Accordingly, it is to Marcuse's theory of the interaction between sexual expression and the material conditions of existence that we now turn.

LIBIDINAL CONTRACTION AND CAPITALIST RELATIONSHIPS

Marcuse followed up on both Freud's description of basic repression and Reich's description of surplus repression. According to Marcuse, all social life demands some instinctual modification, but class societies demand much more than this. Marcuse described the effect of the social relationships of the labor market and the consequent alienation and fragmentation of existence on libidinal organization as follows:

> Under the rule of the performance principle, the libidinal cathexis of the individual body and libidinal relations with others are normally confined to leisure time and directed to the preparation and execution of genital intercourse; only in exceptional cases, and with a high degree of sublimation, are libidinal relations allowed to enter into the sphere of work. These constraints, enforced by the need for sustaining a large quantum of energy and time for nongratifying labor, perpetuate the desexualization of the body in order to make the organism into a subject-object of socially useful performance. Conversely, if the work day and energy are reduced to a minimum, without a corresponding manipulation of the free time, the ground for these constraints would be undermined. Libido would be released and would overflow the institutionalized limits within which it is kept by the reality principle.[27]

In this passage, Marcuse was attempting to analyze a process that Reich only alluded to: the way in which "sublimated libido is turned into working capacity and hence into a productive force."[28] Reich was preoccupied with examining the psychic effects of the release and repression of genital sexuality. In contrast, Marcuse emphasized the amount of libidinal energy desexualized in work more than the libidinal cathexis of genital sexuality. His concern was with the way libido is desexualized and the psychic consequences of this. What is most significant for Marcuse about this process of desexualization is not that the impulse is diverted from its genital aim but that it is diverted from its broader aim— gratification. Alienated labor leaves the individual with little choice between preestablished functions which must be performed, not much control over the work process, and few opportunities for aim-inhibited gratification. This involves a surplus repression since there is not anything intrinsic to the nature of work which

necessitates such a drastic renunciation of gratification. Nonalien-
ated labor would allow the attainment of modified libidinal gratification through work. Aim-inhibited emotional relationships with
coworkers may be one source for this. Work which involves both
displaced libidinal energy and the neutralized energies of the
cognitive ego functions, such as artistic sublimation, may be
another.[29]

Marcuse followed Reich in suggesting that genital primacy made
possible the sublimation (desexualization) of the energy of the
partial impulses for use in work. But rather than defining this as
sexual health, Marcuse described this sublimation as surplus
repressive, since the partial drives are not integrated into object-
directed sexuality and not allowed to strive for modified (basic
repressive) expression. Instead they are reduced to subservient
functions.[30] They are limited in expression to sexual foreplay or
desexualization in alienated labor.

The desexualization of work energy results in a deeroticization
of the body. The energy of the impulse has been employed, but
the aim of the impulse (gratification or even modified gratification)
has been repressed. Within the constraints imposed by the use of
energy in nongratifying work, the release of contracted libido in
genital intercourse may be socially tolerated. Reich was wrong to
assume that the establishment of genital primacy would result in
overcoming a submissive character. Genital sexuality may be a
socially acceptable manner for release in a society based on
nongratifying labor. Limiting the expression of the pleasure
principle to sexual encounters alters the nature of sexuality; "from
an autonomous 'principle' governing the entire organism it is
turned into a specialized temporary function, into a means for an
end."[31]

Sexual repression goes much deeper than Reich described.
Sexual repression is enforced partly through psychological and
physical obstacles to the release of tension in genital sexuality. But
more fundamentally, sexual repression is enforced by the repression of the aim of gratification in the energy spent in social activity
and social relationships. Insofar as genital primacy is associated
with the outward direction of sexuality, it is a necessary modification of the narcissistic partial impulses. Insofar as it is associated

with a libidinal organization that seeks gratification only through genital activity, it is surplus repressive.

The repression of the aim of gratification in the realm of alienated labor results in the contractive restructuring of the libido. The individual is preconditioned to renounce—not just modify—the aim of the pleasure principle in all activity and in all bodily functions that are not directly (genitally) sexual.[32] After renunciation the lack of enjoyment and creativity in work seems tolerable. The sole exceptions to this renunciation are the aim-inhibited relationships of the family and, to a lesser extent, of friends and lovers. But as a realm of "personal relationships" or "private life," these exceptions are fragmented from social activity.

As long as the socially dominant modes of sublimation precondition the libido, the desublimation or resexualization of repressed libido can be adjusted to the repressive demands of the reality principle. The present contents of the reality principle are compatible with liberalization of sexual restriction within the constraints of alienated labor and contracted libido. Since these constraints embody a surplus repression of the libidinal aim of gratification, Marcuse described the liberalization involved as repressive or institutionalized desublimation.[33] Desublimation can overcome surplus repression only when the use of libidinal energy in social activity is aimed at gratification, even in a modified form.

Marcuse's conception of repressive desublimation explains how advanced capitalism can allow a great deal of contracted instinctual pleasure and still retain its most exploitative and repressive features. Marcuse went beyond Reich in arguing that real instinctual liberation is not the mere release of libidinal strivings but the transformation of the libido which has been shaped by the class society within which it exists. "It is a spread rather than explosion of libido—a spead over private and societal relations which bridges the gap maintained between them by a repressive reality principle."[34]

The transformation of the libido Marcuse describes will be possible only in a social system in which sexuality is expressed in social activity as well as personal relationships, through the entire body as well as in the various erogenous zones. Marcuse speaks of the "reactivation of all erotogenic zones" and a consequent "resurgence of pregenital polymorphous sexuality." Horowitz suggests that Marcuse's meaning can be made clearer if, "Marcuse's term polymorphous perversity is taken to mean polymorphous genitality." That is, Marcuse is envisioning not a regression to the partial erotic stages, but a supercession of the genitally contracted libido. Polymorphous genitality would refer "to genitality that combined psychically genital object relations with freedom of expression for the pregenital component instincts within a genital organization of libido."[35]

Marcuse saw the emergence of a new sexuality as dependent upon the achievements of capitalist society (especially the conquest of scarcity), and the overcoming of its exploitative aspects. Although capitalist production has relieved scarcity for many, at least at times, and thereby alleviated some of the basic repression necessary for social life, surplus and detailed labor still require a surplus repressive sublimation of libidinal energy in work, and a contraction of the libido in time and bodily space. The expansion of libido would be possible only when surplus labor is minimized, and labor made less repetitive, more involving of the workers' interests and talents. The libido would be allowed a broader "cultural" expression. "The instinct is not deflected from its aim; it is gratified in activities and relations that are not sexual in the sense of 'organized' genital sexuality and yet are libidinal and erotic." (Of course, this does not deny genital gratification. Marcuse seemed to believe, as did Reich, that repressed sexuality cannot be creatively sublimated, only repressively desublimated.) The reality principle and the pleasure principle would be brought together in an activity that is both work and play, that serves simultaneously the ends of self-preservation and pleasure. The living organism will exist in an environment which no longer is perceived as a mere object of domination (which was historically necessary for industrial progress) and a source of profit but rather in an environment which "partakes of and invites libidinal cathexis and tends to be eroticized." In such an environment the libido will transcend "beyond the immediate erotogenic zones. . . ."[36] Pleasure and the release of tension will be a function of the total person and not an isolated realm of existence complementing the individual's function as an alienated laborer.

Hence Marcuse believed that contracted instinctual liberation can proceed quite far without endangering the capitalist system at an advanced stage. Beyond this, instinctual liberation can become a force of social liberation only to the degree to which sexual energy is transformed into erotic energy, striving to change the entire mode of life. It becomes a political force only when it is accompanied and guided by the rebellion of reason, the absolute refusal of the intellect to support the establishment. R. Reiche (without referring explicitly to Marcuse) makes this criticism more specific. He points to the failure of the German student movement in the 1960s to develop a more widespread political organization from a strategy which emphasized the "sex issue."[37]

Politically Reich was careful not to raise the sex issue in isolation from the struggles of the working class. He believed that no real sexual reform was possible without political activity because the political relations of the social system would not allow the implementation of reforms suggested by sexual research. Furthermore, Reich argued that the conflict between work and pleasure was not a necessary conflict but the result of the capitalist organization of work. Yet, even while recognizing that a more pleasurable existence is possible only with a radical reorganization of the relationships of work, Reich failed to recognize that a reorganization of human sexuality also will be necessary.[38]

Nevertheless Reich's theory of character structure is supported rather than undermined by the concept of repressive desublimation. Character structure is the historically specific expression of "human nature." Freud believed that the psychic structures and processes that he described were immutable and universal. Arguing against Freud, Reich examined the extent to which the historically specific social relationships penetrated the depth of human psychology. But at that very depth Reich himself posited an immutable and universal nature, the self-regulating libido. Marcuse's critical revision of Freud's libido theory emphasized the role of social relationships in the organization of the impulses. The release of tension is contracted both temporally and in terms of bodily space by the nongratifying desexualization of libidinal energy required for work. Genital primacy is the culmination of a process of psychic maturation, but this process itself is conditioned by exploitative social relationships. The potential for self-regulation, which Marcuse called "self-sublimation", is realizable not within the restructed genital organization of the libido, but in a polymorphously genital organization which overcomes this restriction.[39]

Character develops in response to the moralistic repressions imposed by such institutions as religion and the family. It also develops in response to those relationships of work which preclude the sublimation of erotic energy in at least mildly pleasurable activity and thus restrict the expression of the pleasure impulse. Reich analyzed the institutions through which sexual repression is imposed most directly and the role of sexual repression in conditioning a characterological submissiveness and resignation to those institutions. Marcuse showed more fully than Reich how the individual can be conditioned to accept alienated labor through sexual promiscuity. However, character structure is not only a preconditioned instinctual apparatus. It also is the way the individual learns to absorb the anxiety that results as the authoritarian institutions of a class society frustrate his instincts throughout his life. Character is comprised of defenses and resistances that the individual employs to block the awareness of the way in which his needs are being socially repressed. The preconditioning of the instincts is only one way in which character is formed. Accordingly, with all Reich's emphasis on the libido, it is not to our understanding of the libido that he made his major contribution. Even though Reich's critics expose the problems in his description of the libido, they fail to provide as systematic a framework for the analysis of the psychology of social conditioning and its political consequences, as the theory of character structure.

Reich stressed the interpenetration of character structure and social structure mostly when he was involved in socialist politics. This connection between his theory and practice was a logical one. The socially conditioned character could be overcome only by transforming the system of social relationships which was its precondition. When he abandoned socialist activity, Reich abandoned the only means to close the gap between the repressive present and self-regulating future. In the concluding chapter, I will describe the evolution of Reich's work and politics as an example of the relationship between theory and activity, and make explicit some of the more general implications of the relationship between political activity and political psychology.

CONCLUSION: CHARACTER, LIBIDO, AND SOCIAL STRUCTURE

While criticizing Freud's social theory, I claimed that the psychoanalytic method enables theorists to replace the impressionistic formulation of human nature in traditional theory with a psychology of human needs and desires. The problem that arises is that Freudian psychoanalysis, like traditional liberal theory, fails to appreciate the depth to which "human nature" is conditioned by the social structure within which it is expressed.

Freud's conception of human nature precludes a critical analysis of social structures. His belief in a fundamental conflict between individual needs and the demands of social life precludes the possibility of this conflict being alleviated by political activity aimed at restructuring human character and social relationships. Political activity is doomed to repeat compulsively the pattern of the oedipal conflict. The struggle against authority is conditioned by the struggle against the father. The resolution of the conflict is successful only when the prevailing authority is internalized and consciousness of the conflict is repressed. Thus Freud's social psychology justifies strict rulers and passsive citizens.

Reich offered a systematic revision of Freudian theory which stressed the interpenetration and mutual conditioning of character structure and social structure. Reich followed the Freudian method of raising the unconscious to consciousness and discerning in conscious thought the distorted expression of socially repressed and manipulated needs and desires. Reich's revision of Freud was informed by Marx's thesis that human nature is constituted by the ensemble of social relationships.

The process of psychic maturation includes the internalization of the authority expressed in the dominant social relationships. The psychic agency of the internalized authority is the superego. As the individual's dependency on parents decreases, the superego comes to respond to the demands of a more abstract social authority, but continues to be based on the situation of infantile dependency. The individual's adjustment to these demands is accomplished through a characteristic pattern of defense and resistance which functions to impede recognition of the repression forced upon him. The individual confronts authority not through an ego with a developed capacity to evaluate the imposed demands but rather through an elaborate system of defense mechanisms which absorb the pain and frustration which results from the socially imposed repressions.

Reich's theory of character structure remains the most-developed framework for examining the development of the ego, or the individual's understanding of himself and his social position. The ego develops its character in response to both the demands of society, as those demands are imposed and internalized, and the strivings of the id. Character determines the individual's pattern of response to the institutions he confronts. The frustrations and restrictions imposed upon the individual condition a character structure which submits to authoritarian relationships and is susceptible to authoritarian ideologies.

In contrast to modern societies, in which character is conditioned by repression, Reich attempted to prove the existence of societies in which libidinal energy, unrestrained by the surplus repressions of class domination, was self-regulated in its release. What he described instead was a society in which manipulation and direction of the libido appears to be less repressive than our own. Reich's analysis of the Trobrianders supported his claim that the reality principle manifests the historically specific structure of social relationships. It did not support his claim that social activity was possible without the modification of the pleasure principle by the reality principle.

By claiming the latter, Reich argued against Freud's conception of human nature only to introduce an equally impressionistic conception of human nature. For Freud, humans were naturally aggressive and insatiable, naturally in conflict with the instinctual restrictions necessary for social activity. For Reich, humans were naturally self-regulating. The fundamental conflict was not the conflict between the pleasure principle and the limitations necessary for social activity, but between the reality principle and human needs.

In terms of critical Marxism, the difference between Freud's and Reich's conception of human nature is less significant than it may appear. More important is the fact that in Freud's social psychology and Reich's libido theory, human nature is conceived in isolation from the social relationships within which it is expressed. Reich's theory of character structure is an alternative to both these abstract modes of explanation. The theory of character structure is a theory of the psychological response of a pleasure-seeking and self-preserving organism to specific social conditions. Character structure is the historically specific expression of "human nature."

However, Reich's preoccupation with genital sexuality obscured the way the instincts are preconditioned by the social structure. Since the preconditioned instincts can be satisfied through the desublimation that is allowed, their satisfaction, no less than their repression, can lead the individual to accept the social relationships he confronts. However, libidinal sublimation in activity such as work and cathexis in nonsexual relationships, may retain the recognition of conflict between the individual's needs and the social structure. The manipulation of libidinal energy into socially acceptable roles and onto socially acceptable objects, no less than its repression, can result in the psychic reproduction of the social structure.

Critics of Reich such as Marcuse and Mitchell who otherwise have a firm grasp of the issues of political psychology and have made significant contributions of their own, fail to appreciate his insights into character after they react so forcefully to his claims on libido. Nevertheless much of the criticism of Reich's theory of the libido is valid and useful. In particular, Marcuse's critical analysis of Freud's theory of the libido allows us to resolve the problems that arise as a result of Reich's physiological conception of libido. Not only are psychic structures and processes socially conditioned, so too are the impulses themselves. Reich was never fully able to incorporate this into this thought. Marcuse followed Freud in emphasizing the need to redirect libidinal energy into socially necessary work. According to Freud, this could be done in two ways, sublimation and repression. Sublimation entailed a displacement of the object of the impulse and modification of its aim. Repression involved the unconscious abandonment of the aim and object of the instinct while its energy was being partially discharged in work. Freud argued that human civilization required a great amount of instinctual repression since most people were psychologically incapable of sublimation. In my critique of Freud's social theory, I argued that the possibility of sublimation was precluded by the structure of work, the detailed operations and surplus labor that most people performed. Marcuse's criticism of Freud's (and implicitly, Reich's) libido theory contained an even more fundamental criticism. Marcuse did not deny the incapacity that Freud observed. Rather, Marcuse argued that it was a socially conditioned rather than psychologically innate incapacity. Since detailed and alienated labor greatly impeded the possibility of sublimation, the libido of the worker contracted. As a result, Marcuse claimed, the aim of satisfaction is associated with the discharge of energy only in the realm of "personal relationships." Pleasure in sexual and aim-inhibited relationships is the compensation for the abandonment of sublimated satisfaction in work. The individual is psychically preconditioned to seek satisfaction in personal relationships, while accepting surplus instinctual repression in the realm of work.

Reich investigated the relationship between instinctual repression and the social structure as mediated through ideology. Marcuse, concentrating on the sublimation of impulsive energy in work, attempted to describe a more immediate association. Insofar as the moralistic ideology of the middle-class family (which, as we have seen, pervades the working class as well) contributes to the psychological reproduction of the authority expressed in social relationships, Reich's analysis of the political function of the repression of genital sexuality has much to offer political psychology. As the strength of the moralistic "New Right" suggests, Reich's analysis of sexual repression still may be timely. However, the alleged liberalization of sexuality, or its desublimation, already had proceeded quite far in Germany between the wars and has proceeded since in advanced capitalist countries. So, desublimation coexists with moralist repression. Therefore a critical political psychology also must examine the way in which the libido is preconditioned through the nongratifying sublimations of work, and the extent to which the individual participates in his own domination and exploitation by accepting immediate contracted gratifications through socially accessible objects.

Theodor Adorno claimed that within the context of repressive social institutions, the ego must participate in the social struggle or retreat into the libido.[40] The retreat into the libido is the retreat from the social struggle. The individual is conscious of the satisfaction derived from sexual activity and the resexualization of perverse impulses. He is not aware that these desublimations also evoke psychic conflicts which manifest themselves in feelings of guilt, anxiety, and frustration. Nor is he aware that desublimation may function to maintain an exploitative structure of work. Thus in terms of character structure it seems as if desublimations and alienated labor as well as sexual repression may provoke the character to develop defenses. That is, the individual develops psychological patterns of response to the anxiety that results from the repression of the aim of gratification in work and the guilt and anxiety provoked by contracted sexuality. This character defense functions to block awareness of the conflict between the individual's needs and the restrictions imposed by social institutions. The social system appears to allow satisfaction. If the individual still is not content, he must search within himself for the source of the dissatisfaction. The individual thereby is psychologically conditiond to accept without question the structure of social relationships.

It is to Reich's credit that he did not attempt to describe the fascistic character of his time. Rather he described the character structure which prevailed among the followers of Naziism and the psychological processes that make people susceptible to repressive and authoritarian movements. If we assume that moralistic repression as a form of social conditioning has been superceded by desublimation, as Lasch has claimed that the "authoritarian personality" has given way to a "narcissistic personality," we lose much of what is of value in Reich.[41] Desublimation and narcissism may be rampant in contemporary societies. Yet processes similar to those that Reich described as underlying the identification with fascism appear to be occurring among the mobilized followers of overtly racist groups and also among the significant number of followers of the moralistic right. I do not mean to suggest that Reich's analysis of fascism can be applied to all authoritarian movements. I do mean to emphasize that Reich's analysis of fascism was based on a method that can be used to analyze contemporary authoritarian movements in terms of the social dynamics of class societies and the psychological processes which result in the internalization of and identification with social authority.

In the theory of character structure the process of psychological development is grounded in specific social institutions. Through character structure the existing mode of life becomes embedded in human unconsciousness. As a result, unconscious processes become a major support of that way of life. Yet while the interpenetration of social structure and character structure militates against the transformation of either, the transformation of both can be accomplished concurrently in practice. That is, the potential for self-regulation can be realized only through political activity.

Beginning from Reich's own practice, the concluding chapter of this study will be concerned with the relationship between political psychology and political activity.

NOTES

[1] Reich, *The Sexual Revolution*, trans. Therese Pol (New York: Simon and Schuster, 1975), p. xxiv. See also Reich, *Sex-Pol: Essays 1929–1934*, ed. Lee Baxandall, trans. Anna Bostock, Tom DuBose, and Lee Baxandall (New York: Random House, 1972), pp. 14–15, 13n (Dialectical Materialism and Psychoanalysis); and Freud, *Three Contributions to the Theory of Sex*, trans. A. A. Brill (New York: E. P. Dutton and Co., 1962), p. 30.

[2] *Reich Speaks of Freud*, ed. Mary Higgins and Chester M. Raphael, with translations by Therese Pol (New York: Farrar, Straus and Giroux, 1967), p. 23. The editors cite the latter quote in a footnote.

[3] Cattier, *The Life and Work of Wilhelm Reich*, trans. Ghislaine Boulanger (New York: Horizon Press, 1971), pp. 189–192; and Boadella, *Wilhelm Reich: The Evolution of His Work* (Chicago, Ill.: Henry Regnery Co., 1973), p. 19.

[4] Freud, *General Psychological Theory*, ed. Phillip Reiff (New York: Macmillan Publishing Co., 1974), p. 88 (Instincts and Their Vicissitudes). See also the section on "Psychic Structures" in Chapter 3 above; and Reich,

Character Analysis, 3d ed., trans. Vincent T. Carfagno (New York: Simon and Schuster, 1976), p. xix.

⁵ Olendorf-Reich, *Wilhelm Reich* (New York: St. Martin's Press, 1969), p. 9.

⁶ Reich, *Character Analysis*, pp. 231, 206–211. See also Horowitz, *Repression* (Toronto and Buffalo: University of Toronto Press, 1977), pp. 133–134; and Mitchell, *Psychoanalysis and Feminism* (New York: Pantheon, 1974), p. 163.

⁷ Reiche, *Sexuality and Class Struggle*, trans. Susan Bennett (New York: Praeger Publishers, 1971), p. 77.

⁸ Horowitz, op. cit., pp. 15–19, 126. The distinction between basic and surplus repression is developed in Herbert Marcuse, *Eros and Civilization* (Boston: Beacon Press, 1974), p. 235.

⁹ *Sex-Pol*, p. 238 (The Imposition of Sexual Morality).

¹⁰ See for example Mitchell, op. cit., pp. 174–178; and Rycroft, *Wilhelm Reich* (New York: The Viking Press, 1972), pp. 41–52.

¹¹ *Sex-Pol*, p. 144–146 (The Imposition of Sexual Morality).

¹² Ibid., pp. 148–155, 188–189.

¹³ Ibid., pp. 162–165

¹⁴ Rycroft, op. cit., pp. 49, 51.

¹⁵ *Sex-Pol*, p. 119, 138 (The Imposition of Sexual Morality). See also Mitchell, op. cit., p. 178. Mitchell presents a stronger version of the criticism I am making.

¹⁶ Mitchell, op. cit., pp. 370–377.

¹⁷ *Sex-Pol*, p. 198–203 (The Imposition of Sexual Morality).

¹⁸ Mitchell. op. cit., p. 176.

¹⁹ Reich denied this in response to a criticism of his "Freudo-Marxism" by a French Marxist reviewer. See *Sexual Revolution*, pp. xxvii–xxix. Leaving aside the accuracy of the criticism, Reich cannot have it both ways. That is, he cannot have a natural (that is, ahistorical) science of the libido and a critical psychology of the social conditioning of human impulses.

²⁰ *Sex-Pol*, p. 226 (The Imposition of Sexual Morality).

²¹ Lasch, "The Emotions of Family Life," *New York Review of Books*, vol. 22 (November 27, 1975), 37. The other articles in the series are "The Family and History," *New York Review of Books*, vol. 22 (November 13, 1975), 34–38; and "What the Doctor Ordered," *New York Review of Books*, vol. 22 (December 11 1975), 50–54.

²² "The Emotions of Family Life," p. 39. See pp. 39–40, and "What the Doctor Ordered," pp. 50–51.

²³ "What the Doctor Ordered," p. 54. See also "Emotions of Family Life," p. 40; and Lasch, "The Narcissistic Personality of Our Times," *Partisan Review*, no. 1 (1977), 13–14.

²⁴ Lasch, "Emotions of Family Life," p. 37.

²⁵ Mitchell, op. cit., p. 384.

[26] Marcuse, *One-dimensional Man* (Boston: Beacon Press, 1966), pp. 74–75.

[27] Marcuse, *Eros and Civilization* (Boston: Beacon Press, 1974), p. 236. The performance principle is Marcuse's term for the content of the reality principle in capitalist societies.

[28] Reich, *Sex-Pol*, p. 47 (Dialectical Materialism and Psychoanalysis).

[29] Marcuse, *Eros and Civilization*, pp. 45, 212–214, 84. See also Horowitz, op. cit., pp. 30–37.

[30] Marcuse, *Eros and Civilization*, pp. 38, 48.

[31] Ibid., p. 41.

[32] Ibid., pp. 41–48.

[33] Marcuse, *One-Dimensional Man*, pp. 71–77.

[34] Marcuse, *Eros and Civilization*, p. 208.

[35] Ibid., p. 201; and Horowitz, op. cit., p. 72. The change in terminology suggested by Horowitz can be useful since polymorphous perversity is a concept stressed by thinkers with a more naturalistic viewpoint than Marcuse's. See for example Norman O. Brown, *Life Against Death* (Middletown, Conn.; Wesleyan University Press, 1959). See expecially the chapter on "Death and Childhood." An exchange between Marcuse and Brown may be found in Marcuse's collection of essays, *Negations* (Boston: Beacon Press, 1968).

[36] Marcuse, *Eros and Civilization*, pp. 208, 214–215; and *One-Dimensional Man*, p. 73.

[37] Marcuse, *Counter Revolution and Revolt* (Boston: Beacon Press, 1972), pp. 130–133; and Reiche, op. cit., p. 17.

[38] Reich, "The Sexual Misery of the Working Masses and the Difficulty of Sexual Reform," *New German Critique*, no. 1 (Winter, 1973), 93; and *Mass Psychology*, p. 288.

[39] Marcuse, *Eros and Civilization*, p. 204.

[40] Adorno, "Sociology and Psychology, Pt. II," *New Left Review*, no. 47 (January–February 1968), 89.

[41] Lasch, *The Culture of Narcissism* (New York: Warner Books, 1979), p. 22.

8

POLITICAL PSYCHOLOGY AND POLITICAL ACTIVITY

ALTHOUGH socialists and psychoanalysts practice in different arenas, the theoretical traditions that emanate from Marx and Freud each demand that the theorist take an activist perspective. Marx studied the structure of social relationships in order to intervene in class conflicts and to reverse the exploitation and domination of workers. Hence socialists act collectively to intervene in social processes. Freud studied the unconscious to intervene in the processes which bring about neurotic and pathological symptoms in patients. Thus psychoanalysts act on the individual to intervene in psychological processes. Reich, in turn, realized that an effective synthesis of Marx and Freud required that therapeutic practice also take the form of collective action and that collective action address itself to the insights resulting from therapeutic practice. Consequently, Reich attempted to articulate the political issues which underlie psychic conflicts and the social conditions which breed pathologies.

Reich's Sex-Pol movement was discussed, in Chapter 3, as a strategy for the development of class consciousness. As such Sex-Pol was discussed in terms of cultural hegemony and the everyday life of workers, and compared with the strategy to which it responded and which still dominates the organized Left: the strategy of a vanguard party. This comparison was intended to show how a political psychology could improve the traditional Marxist explanations of how consciousness is socially conditioned and how working class consciousness develops.

Yet Sex-Pol was more than a strategy for the development of the class consciousness of workers; it also was a strategy for the development of the self-regulating character. The Sex-Pol leadership attempted to develop the capacity for self-regulation through the struggle to overcome exploitation and repression. Politically progressive movements cannot make the process by which character is changed subsidiary to that of social change, for without the capacity for self-regulation, people will continue to accept authoritarian institutions and ideologies and fail to act consistently with their class interests. Furthermore the capacity for self-regulation must be developed in order for people to act responsibly if the struggle succeeds and institutions are made less repressive.

As a Marxist, Reich emphasized that it is not enough to understand how character is socially conditioned. The point is to oppose the processes by which character structures which submit to or violently identify with authority are formed, and to support the development of self-regulation. This requires political action since institutions such as the family, religion, schools, and government foster feelings of dependency which impede the development of self-regulation. Reich believed that people were developing the capacity for self-regulation whenever they struggled for more control over their lives. Workers struggle against domination not only at work but in their personal lives as well. In the theory of character structure Reich sought to explain the relationship between class structure and the institutions of personal life, particularly the family. He analyzed how authoritarian family relationships are conditioned by class relationships and in turn, condition submissive and dependent characters. Through Sex-Pol, Reich confronted class domination in terms of the issues that workers were raising about the institutions that structure their personal lives.

The Sex-Pol movement was an attempt to address in practice the issues that workers were raising. Its program advocated adequate, low-rent housing; sexual education, birth control and abortion rights; and changes in the relationships of family life. It took a stand against prostitution, and for the improvement of the social position of women. Some of these issues had already been raised by traditional Marxian theory and are still being raised by antipoverty and minority organizations, feminists, and counter-cultural youth groups. As some "New Left" journalists have recognized, the Sex-Pol movement eventually inspired, among other practices, youth politics, women's liberation, and building rational coalitions among diverse groups.[1] The strategy Sex-Pol relied upon to form political coalitions focused on locating and assailing the roots of these diverse issues in the class relationships of society. Unlike the New Left, where diversity led to diffusion, the Sex-Pol movement sought to advocate these positions all at once, while working within the organized working-class movement.

Reich focused on these issues as a strategy for attacking the social conditions which promote psychic conflicts and pathologies. Nevertheless, he was not concerned only or even primarily with expanding the arena for the therapeutic confrontation with unconsciousness. He also was concerned with expanding the arena for the political confrontation with class domination.

In this chapter, I will consider some of the issues involved in developing a strategy for a working-class sexual politics. I will begin from Reich's attempts to implement his theory of character structure into political practice. Here I will distinguish the Sex-Pol strategy from Reich's later theory of work democracy (c. 1936). I will argue that the later theory does not belong in the history of struggles for workers' control since it is based on some idealistic presumptions about social structures and the processes of social change. For example, work democracy reversed the activist perspective of character structure and thereby abandoned the only means to bring about institutions which promote self-regulation. Accordingly, Reich left his mark on critical Marxism as a psychologist of character and not a sociologist work. The struggle against the social antecedents of psychological repression is an important aspect of the broader struggle against capitalist hegemony. Sex-Pol would be most at home in a movement which is organized variously at multiple levels of social practice, yet coordinated in a struggle against capitalist hegemony and its mystification of social life. Therefore a possible strategy is to organize Sex-Pol groups within the framework of council communism. I will conclude this study with a consideration of some difficulties activists still must confront in relating political psychology to political activity.

REICH'S POLITICS

Reich's involvement in working-class politics provided him with direct observations of the effects of class structure on the living conditions of workers. His involvement provides us with a case study of the interaction between political activity and theory. Reich developed a trenchant political psychology while he was active in the working-class movement. Then, as he became increasingly estranged from organized political activity, his work turned increasingly toward natural science, and his politics became increasingly utopian. In this section I will discuss the development of Reich's politics and his relationships with different organizations, in an attempt to make explicit the practical implications of his development.

Early in his career, Reich joined a medical group affiliated with the Communist party. From this position he was invited to give party-sponsored lectures which were attended by progressive students and workers. Initially Reich lectured on the principles of psychoanalysis, but his audiences had difficulty grasping these. When he began to discuss the sexual conditions of the working class, his audience reacted much more favorably. He then realized that he had to relate his ideas to the life experience of his listeners. Reich already had been familiarized by his clinial experience with the difficulties confronting working-class patients. The new setting gave him a broader perspective on the sexual hygiene problems of the working class. Reich believed that the resulting sexual and psychological problems, which seemed to him to have reached the epidemic proportions of the medieval plagues, could best be treated preventively. By 1928, Reich, with the help of some colleagues, opened the first sexual hygiene centers in Vienna, thereby initiating the Sex-Pol movement.[2]

In 1930 Reich left Vienna for Berlin. There he convinced the German Communist party (KPD) to organize a section for the implementation of his program for a working-class sexual politics. The program included the establishment of centers for advice on sexual hygiene, birth control, and abortion, and for lectures and discussions on the relationship between psychological problems, sexual repression, and class hegemony. Through the KPD, the Sex-Pol activists carried their program to the workers and Communist youth groups, and seemed to have received a favorable response.[3]

Reich held no illusions concerning the movement's success. He did not believe meaningful sexual reform could be achieved within capitalist, patriarchal institutions. The goal of the Sex-Pol movement was not sexual reform per se. Rather, it was the treatment and prevention of widespread disorders of the character and raising the individual's consciousness of the conflict between human needs and the social structure. In 1930 Reich split with the World League Of Sexual Reform because it refused to adapt his radical political perspective. The Communists, however, approved Reich's political program and the German National Association for Proletarian Sexual Politics was established under party auspices. Its manifesto proclaimed:

> Sexual politics prior to the socialist revolution is essentially characterized as a revolutionary critique of the prevailing social order and as propagandistic activity seeking to overthrow the entire system. It can only achieve its true constructive purpose when the economic basis for this has been created.[4]

The manifesto proceeded to link sexual problems directly with class conditions. It presented a political program meant to alleviate sexual problems, but it "clearly recognized that the manifesto cannot be fulfilled within the capitalist state."[5] Its demands had to be raised to consciousness, discussed, and struggled for in capitalist society. But they could not be achieved within a system in which the needs of the living worker were repressed for his use in surplus and detailed labor. The main priority of the Sex-Pol movement while capitalism remained intact was the politicization of the sexual question.

The Sex-Pol movement marked the peak of Reich's political theory and practice. However, despite a favorable response among workers themselves, Reich found the organizational basis for his activity declining. While Reich attempted to reconcile the socialist and psychoanalytic movements, each rejected rigorously any attempt to associate them with the other. "Sexology to the Communists had become a bourgeois heresy, a distraction from the economic struggle. Sexual politics for the psychoanalysts was a 'Communist red herring," a bolshevik fallacy of Reich's."[6]

The psychoanalysts were worried that Reich's association with radical politics would make their work more controversial than it already was. In 1934 the International Psychoanalytic Association disassociated itself from Reich.[7] The Communists were particularly disturbed by Reich's criticism of the party's inadequate and vacillating response to fascism and his support of a Communist-socialist united front at a time when the party opposed such an alliance.[8] In addition, they began to oppose his emphasis on the politicization of the sex question, claiming that it alienated many workers from the movement. Reich's advocacy of sexual freedom was considered a "manifestation of bourgeois decadence" and a "Jackpot for Hitler's propaganda." Reich's pamphlet on the "Sexual Struggle of Youth," which criticized party policies, was particularly upsetting to the party hierarchy.[9]

Just as Reich refused to compromise with the psychoanalysts on the questions of masochism and the death instinct, so Reich refused to compromise with the Communists. Reich held fast to his view that the exploited class had to confront the sources of their submissiveness and passivity. Besides, the Communists' advocacy of the abolishment of the private ownership of the means of production itself allowed their opponents to characterize them as immoral and could alienate workers imbued with bourgeois ideology. Clearly the Communists were not willing to foresake this demand. Reich believed that compromises on sexual issues were no more tolerable.

By 1934 Reich and his small but loyal supporters were completely isolated. Reich had been expelled from both the party and the International Psychoanalytic Association. The victory of the Nazis in Germany the previous year forced Reich into exile. But instead of finding refuge, Reich encountered harassment and persecution. He moved from country to country. His professional colleagues avoided him and his work, not wishing to be associated with the controversy they provoked.[10]

Reich attempted desperately to continue his Sex-Pol work. Since both the psychoanalytic and Communist presses were closed to him, a *Journal of Political Psychology and Sexual Economy* was established. For the next several years, Reich continued to advocate his perspective on sexual politics. He attempted to maintain the movement without an organized base. This affected his theory as well as practice. Despite the dogmatism of the party's leaders and the inadequacy of their position, Reich's involvement in the party enabled him to recognize the forces within the class system which influenced the formation of character structure. After he lost contact with the working-class movement, Reich relied less and less on the method of class analysis in his social criticism. In its place Reich developed his theory of natural work democracy.

"Work democracy" as conceived by Reich was meant to supercede all existing political movements. Disillusioned by Communist politics, he, at first, correctly directed his attacks against economistic historiography. However, from the late 1930s to the end of his career, he abandoned working-class politics in general. As he did so, Reich lost the perspective of historical specificity which had helped him to criticize productively both Marxist and psychoanalytic theory. Instead Reich posited the existence of the eternal forces of orgone energy and work democracy. Reich came to define orgone energy as the transhistorical negation of the psyche divided against itself; work democracy, as the negation of the class contradictions which underlay the existing social structure. Reich still accepted the validity of "dialectical materialist" methodology, yet the crucial historical contradiction for him was no longer the contradiction between class interests but that between the organically necessary free flow of human instinctual energy and its social repression. As he states, the theory of class man "on the one hand was set against the irrational nature of the society of the animal 'man' on the other hand."[11] That is, people do not always rationally pursue their social and class interests.

The Sex-Pol movement emphasized the impossibility of achieving sexual liberation and self-regulation within capitalist society. But while Sex-Pol was based on a strategy of class struggle to produce the new individual and social order, this strategy was not applied to achieve work democracy. Reich came to believe that although it is possible to divide a population into those who possess capital and those who sell labor power, this division did not correspond with the division of the population by psychology, ideology, or value of work done. Within each class there were individuals afflicted by and others who resisted reactionary ideologies and authoritarian character structures. Furthermore, there are capitalists who perform vital work and there are functionaries of working class-parties who are social parasites. Reich's abandonment of class struggle resulted from his belief that politics and work are antithetical; work supports life and politics deters it. Work democracy is always present and functioning, whether individuals are conscious of it or not. It is based not on "conditions that must be created but from natural processes that have been present and have been developing from the very beginning."[12]

Reich's attempts to unify the fundamental contradictions of a class society into an eternal but dormant form of organization led him to obscure the social processes he sought to explain. The realization of a work democratic society was placed in the future when the dominant character structures will allow the work process to function without authoritarian regulation. Yet, if the social order which produced the existing character structure remains unchanged, how is the new character to be produced? Reich could not address himself to this problem. With his utopian abandonment of class struggle, the historical practice necessary to effect social and characterological change, and to secure it against the reaction of those who benefit from the existing social and psychological structures, is lost.

Since Reich emphasized the democratization of the work process and the social responsibility of workers, Bruce Brown, in his book on the Marxist and psychoanalytic critiques of everyday life, noted that Reich's later program had strong similarities with that of the syndicalists and council Communists, who saw "the struggle for workers' control as the most fundamental element of the whole revolutionary process, as both its form and its content, its principal means and its irreducible ends." Actually, in his denial of the value of political activity, Reich is closer to the syndicalists, whom he earlier had dismissed as utopians for their failure to recognize that individuals are conditioned to be incapable of dealing with freedom.[13] However, the council Communists, even while emphasizing workers' control, recognized the tremendous obstacles that a class society placed in the way of its attainment. These obstacles could be surmounted only by the collective social practice of the exploited class. Since the political organization of society was used by the ruling class to maintain the existing property and work relationships, political activity was no less necessary than economic activity.

Work democracy was marked by its explicit effort to minimize the importance of class relationships in the struggle for control over the work process. That is, work democracy could be achieved by the unified wills of individuals and required no irreconcilable confrontation between collective wills. Accordingly, whereas work democracy retains some of the most crucial insights of critical Marxism, it is even more conspicuous for those that it omits. Brown would have done better to establish a distinction between the Sex-Pol movement and the theory of work democracy and to cite the similarities of the former to council Communism.

In the next section, I will follow through on Brown's comparison of Reich and the political figure and theorist who was perhaps the formost advocate of council communism, Antonio Gramsci. However I will be concerned with relating the council movement to the Sex-Pol movement rather than work democracy. The worker's movement must organize issues of sexual politics as the Sex-Pol groups attempted. It also must develop the forms of organization necessary to relate the diverse struggles of workers, as the council movement attempted.

ORGANIZATION AND THE STRUGGLE FOR HEGEMONY

Like Reich, Gramsci argued that the struggle for the development of a politically conscious working class could be attained only if workers gained control not only of the means of production, but also of the means for gaining an understanding of the world and their place within it. The struggle to gain hegemony in civil society (which cannot be achieved from a subordinate position in relation to the state or the forces of production) is the struggle of a subordinate social group to become conscious of its potential. This means, for example, that the members of the subordinate group must see the futility of confronting a repressive social order individually and instead pursue their class interests collectively. That is, in terms of political psychology, workers must overcome the conditioning of their character and ideological beliefs and identify with each other rather than with symbols of authority and the lifestyles of the rich, famous, and powerful.

Gramsci was very much concerned with developing the organizational structures of the workers' struggle for hegemony. He was no less aware than Reich of the authoritarian tendencies of political parties and that the leadership of the political parties might impose its will on its followers. Yet this did not reduce the need for conscious leadership. Gramsci believed that the spontaneous emergence of a revolutionary movement was impossible, although a conscious and directly accountable leadership could be established, which was necessary to educate, direct, and consolidate the elements of spontaneity in the workers.[14]

Gramsci's desire to avoid authoritarian organizations led him to distinguish bureaucratic and democratic forms of centralized parties. The proletarian party must be well organized if it was to have the focus and discipline necessary to be effective in the struggle against capital. The party was to have as its aim the transformation of the state and all its values.[15] This socialism would have as its purpose the active participation of the workers in the process of directing and coordinating their own basic activities. Accordingly, socialism could not be realized simply by replacing capitalist bureaucrats with party bureaucrats, or by formulating, a priori, the organizational principles of democratic centralism. For Gramsci, democratic centralism was not a matter of formal institutional procedures but of widespread political mobilization.

In attempting to mobilize the workers, the party would be confronted with a contradiction between exercising leadership and remaining on an equal basis with the workers. If the party was to remain the disciplined and focused center of the anticapitalist movement, the party "cannot throw open its doors to an invasion of new members, unused to the exercise of responsibility and discipline."[16] Yet if it was to create the forms of a socialist society in its practice, it had to involve the masses of workers actively. Gramsci believed that the difficulties faced by the movement in its attempt to mobilize large numbers of workers while developing disciplined leaders could be overcome if the workers attempted to organize themselves as a social force, while the centralized organization of the party directed and focused the anticapitalist struggle.

Workers could organize themselves because they formed relationships with each other arising from the process of production. Productive labor is properly organized into workers' councils representing the different divisions of work. Workers' councils are the negation of wage labor as organized by capitalists. That is, through these councils workers organize themselves on the basis of their mutual needs, and free themselves from the restrictions of the capitalist labor market.

However, as wage labor, workers in their direct struggle against capital, organize not into councils but into unions, which aim to bring about changes in working conditions. Though unions could do this, they could not go beyond the established social order to gain their objectives.[17] They could not overcome their dependence on wages and their reduction to the status of a commodity to be consumed by the employer in the production of surplus value. They could only attempt to increase the value of labor as a commodity. In terms of political psychology, unions would not be able to overcome the repression of the aim of modified gratification associated with the libidinal energy sublimated in work. Unions only could attempt to increase the ability of workers to sublimate and desublimate through commodity consumption and private life. That is, the unions were to be the organizations through which workers defended themselves against capital. In contrast workers' councils are the organizations through which the workers prepare themselves to expropriate capital. Both involve the workers directly.

Yet, neither unions nor councils could provide the focus and discipline necessary for the struggle against capital. This was impressed upon Gramsci by the events of 1920. Then, even after having occupied the factories, the main preoccupation of the Italian workers remained the concern to maintain production rather than to mobilize their forces to meet the resistance of the expropriated industrialists. As a result, the political arm of the

ruling class had no problem in violently suppressing their insur-
rection. This convinced Gramsci that an organization which
stressed the need for revolutionary political activity was indispensable to the success of any movement to organize the work process
more rationally. While the unions and councils would mobilize the
workers, the function of the party would be to coordinate the
activities of workers in a broad and flexible system that would
include and order the entire class.[18] The party would provide the
perspective from which a particular struggle of workers would be
understood as a manifestation of the general struggle of workers.

The workers' struggle had to be organized politically and
economically. But the struggle should not be subsumed under
either the party or the councils, for the party, as a highly disciplined
and centralized organization, would have little contact or involvement with most workers. The councils, as the representative organs
of the working class, would not be politically or ideologically
prepared to lead an aggressive anticapitalist struggle. So each
would require the other. Furthermore, the party and the councils
did not include all of the organizations of the working class.
Gramsci noted that working class life is rich in institutions. For
example, workers had formed ward committees which represent
different factions of workers by place of residence.[19]

The significance of Gramsci's council communism is not that a
mass, economic organization would be counterposed to an elite,
political, organization. Rather, he conceived that organizations,
such as the factory councils and the ward committees, would be
the organizational forms of socialism planted in the soil of capitalism. They would also serve as the liason between the disciplined
party and the unorganized workers. Reformist organizations, such
as unions and parliamentary parties, could not maintain this
relation, for they neither provided an alternative to capitalist social
relationships nor attempted to mobilize the mass of workers. Only
through organizations in which workers asserted their demand to
control their own activity, and developed their capacity to do so,
could the workers become prepared for involvement in a leadership party.

The Sex-Pol organizations were not intended, as were the
workers' councils, to be the institutional foundation for socialism.

Rather, they were intended to be the media, within capitalist society, for the workers to develop a political and psychological self-awareness and to reappraise the consequences of social institutions that people took for granted. The Sex-Pol leaders were concerned with preparing people for the long and difficult struggle necessary to overcome class exploitation and domination and for the social upheaval that would be unleashed in that struggle. This preparation required the individual to develop the capacity to resist authority and to regulate his behavior after the old forms of social repression had been abolished. By involving large numbers of workers, the Sex-Pol organizations, no less than the councils, helped to establish a practical relationship between the revolutionary leadership and the mass of unorganized workers.

Although the Sex-Pol movement was not concerned with organizing workers at the point of production, it also followed a strategy of attempting to develop workers' responsibility and discipline through their participation in political organizations. Reich believed that the direct involvement of workers in a struggle against the psychological repression demanded by the institutions of civil society in capitalism was the only way to overcome their psychological and ideological attachment to capitalist institutions. Just as workers must demand the right to organize the production process for themselves, so too, they must demand the right to organize their entire lives in accordance with their own needs. If people are brought up to sacrifice a part of their own interests to avoid a painful conflict with the demands of authority, they would not be able to offer the resistance to authority, including the authoritarian tendencies of political parties, required for a collective struggle. The significance of the Sex-Pol movement was to realize that, although necessary, it is not sufficient for the working-class movement to develop socialist institutions in capitalism. The success of socialism requires the development of the workers' ability to regulate their character.

The Sex-Pol movement remains one of the best examples of a serious and systematic attempt to organize and coordinate workers' social struggles and to politicize their personal frustrations. It also is an example of the role of political psychology in clarifying our understanding of the struggles of workers for greater control over their lives. For example, Sex-Pol suggests the psychological dynamics implicit in the strategy of council communism. Gramsci recognized that if workers were mobilized in political struggles and involved in organizations of opposition, they would develop an awareness of their social interests and their ability to organize their own lives. Reich made explicit the psychological processes and social conditions which hindered the development of this awareness and this ability.

From a purely contemplative perspective, progression from the repression of the workers at present to their self-regulation in the future is impossible to conceive. Like the gap between the organized leadership and unorganized workers, the gap between the present and future can only be overcome by disciplined and directed action. The commitment to action connects the struggle for psychological self-regulation with the struggle for workers' self-management. Reich's concept of a work democracy contributes little to either the social or psychological struggle, since his solution to the problem of social exploitation and repression is a contemplative one: enumerate the formal criteria of a democratic work process and wait until the world is rational enough to accept them. In contrast, the Sex-Pol and council movements recognized that the ideological and cultural hegemony of the ruling class would not be broken by rational discourse. The new society must be struggled for and developed within the old. Although socialism presupposes a shift in the control over production, the struggle against capitalist hegemony, upon which existing production depends, must be fought on several fronts. The development of character and the problems of personal life is a front that has not received the attention it deserves in socialist theory and practice.

POLITICAL PSYCHOLOGY AND POLITICAL ACTIVITY

As we have seen, the crucial problem for Reich was not that the ruling class disseminated its ideology but the readiness with which the working class accepted it. He explained that as a function of the social repression of sexuality and the submissive character structures produced by repression. The individual, existing in an environment which frustrates his pleasure-seeking drives, alleviates the resulting anxiety by withdrawing into himself and identifying with the authority which has brought about the frustration. In his treatment of the problem Reich shed light on the ways in which unconscious processes mediated the process of the conditioning of consciousness by social conditions. The struggles against the ruling ideologies cannot be subsumed under the struggle for political and economic reorganization because the character structures of the exploited classes renders them incapable of assuming the responsibility such a reorganization would demand.

Workers develop character structures which leads them to internalize and identify with the authority they confront. The primary impetus for the development of character is the perceived threat of parental abandonment within the context of the nuclear family. The infant comes to internalize, in the forms of the superego, ego ideals, and characteristic defenses, the patriarchal authority expressed in the family. This authority is itself conditioned by the distinction between domestic and social labor, and by moralistic ideology. The formation of character structure establishes the lifelong pattern for interaction with authority. As the individual grows older, however, it is not so much parental authority as social authority that influences the character structure. In a class society, the authority which is introjected is ultimately the authority of the dominant class.

By politicizing the psychological impact of the family, Reich hoped to ameliorate the authoritarian features of family life, as well as the authoritarian character structures that they produced. The aim of the Sex-Pol movement was to prepare people for socialism by weakening "the inhibiting influences of character structure in adults through the constant encouragement of their social responsibility and capacity for self-organization. . . ." This was its short-term strategy. Beyond this, the Sex-Pol movement was concerned with altering the patterns of child-rearing which resulted in the formation of an authoritarian character structure.[20] If socialism is to be established by workers organizing themselves and participating in social institutions directly, then they must be brought up to regulate their own activity. Reich and Sex-Pol recognized that such maturation is not just a matter of psychological development. Self-regulation cannot be realized if the workers are repressed and dominated by capitalist institutions.

Reich's contribution to critical Marxism was to develop the most systematic framework for analyzing the processes of social conditioning. He was able to do so only by attempting to implement his strategy to politicize personal problems within the working-class movement. In the Sex-Pol movement, theory informed practice by teaching the leadership to recognize the way in which social experiences are transformed by the unconscious before being expressed in consciousness, thereby enabling the leaders to explain the social and psychological antecedents of issues to workers. Practice informed theory by providing the context of an active working class to challenge capitalist hegemony and to raise the major social issues.

Activists must understand the processes by which the individual's character reacts to extremely repressive authority if they are to intervene in these processes. Specifically, they must recognize when people are resisting the social pressures which condition an internalization of and identification with authority. These forms of resistance must be brought under the direction of the organizations of the working-class struggle against exploitation, for the relationships of capitalism are the hegemonic relationships of our society. They are hegemonic in the sense that the relationships of traditional institutions are shaped in the interest of the dominant class. For example, the family adapts to the pressures of the labor and commodity markets much more readily than these markets react to family pressures. The development of the mass labor market and mass commodity market create the conditions for the integration of women into the labor market and a lightening of the domestic labor demanded of them, if not a fairer division of domestic labor. The relationships of the classes also are hegemonic in the sense that demands can be raised against the class that controls the power and resources of society only from the opposition between labor and capital. Without this unifying perspective oppressed and exploited groups make their demands against society as a whole, including other oppressed and exploited groups.

There is, however, a basis in fact that conflicts exist between subordinate groups, since the authoritarian character structures resulting from psychic development within the institutions of class domination pervades all classes and groups in society. Those most affected by the processes and institutions of social repression cannot be expected to suppress their interests until this authoritarianism is overcome. They must be supported in their efforts to assert their interests even if working-class institutions cannot accommodate their struggles.

Currently issues concerning the nature of the authority exercised within the institutions of personal life are being articulated most explicitly and politically not as much by workers' groups, as by women's groups. In their organized activity women assert their interest in overcoming their economically and socially subordinate position and in defending the victories of the women's movement against the challenges of moralistic reactions. Women also have been asserting in practice their interest in overcoming the phallocentric expression of contracted sexuality within patriarchal institutions and ideology, as well as moralistic repression which always falls most heavily upon women. Thus the women's movement not only defends the reproductive freedom of women, but also attacks the exploitative and brutal sexual images of pornography, advertising, and mass media as well. By attacking exploitative relationships between men and women feminists may be creating the basis for an attack on the character structures which underlie these interactions. Yet to be effective, an attack on these character structures must also attack the class relationships which condition character.

Nevertheless the Sex-Pol strategy cannot be imposed upon the struggles of women against social and sexual exploitation. It is up to the worker's movement as a whole, and not the organizations of those who are particularly vulnerable, to develop such a strategy. That is, it is not reasonable to expect a class perspective to develop when women are organized in their struggles for their rights in isolation from men. To develop a Sex-Pol strategy on these issues women will have to be supported by and work with male workers concerned with relating issues of sexual politics to issues of class domination. Through united action an effort can be made to overcome characterological dependence on existing institutions.

The problems involved in raising social and sexual issues separately from class issues is highlighted by an interesting dynamic which is developing around these issues. Against the transformations of family life being promoted by market relationships, a moralistic reaction advocates the values and lifestyle of the idealized middle-class family. In this sense, the moral movement can be seen as a challenge to capitalist hegemony. Hence this moralism can be opposed even while supporting the economic, ideological, and characterological functions of the family in a capitalist social system which can be maintained with more flexible family relationships. Opposition to the moral movement that seeks to make explicit such broader issues as patriarchal repression and class exploitation must understand that movement as an ideological force which itself expresses a contradiction of capitalist hegemony, and not as a direct expression of that hegemony.

Yet as Reich argued so persuasively, ideology can become a material force when it can mobilize large numbers of followers for political movements. Thus the moral movement cannot be ignored in favor of focusing activity on market relationships. In their activity on such issues as abortion, sex education, and equal rights, the moralistic reaction undermines the gains that women make in their struggle for justice. The reaction also seeks to impose the strict repression that conditions the characterological acceptance of authoritarian ideologies. The fact that the repressive right recognizes this in practice makes the failure of the anti-authoritarian left to recognize it that much more crucial. The moral movement has broadened its attack on liberalized attitudes toward sex and increased options for women into an attack on the expression of nonmoralistic, nonauthoritarian outlooks in the schools and other social institutions. Groups across the country seek to censor material that describes social as well as sexual problems, contains "obscenities," or fails to distinguish "right" from "wrong." Some groups make the connection between moralism and class domination explicit by demanding that the schools educate students for the competition demanded by capitalism.[21]

The ground must be laid in practice for workers and other exploited groups to intervene likewise in the process of social conditioning. The forces of repression cannot be opposed effectively in their own terms. That is, opposition to the moralistic reaction cannot be forced into a position in which it merely responds to the moralists' attacks. Although it may often be valuable to respond directly, opposition also must expose the exploitation and repression inherent in the relationships of work, consumption, and the institutions of personal life. Other groups besides exploited workers have a vested interest in this struggle. I already have mentioned the special interests of women in this regard. Minority groups have an interest in exposing the connections between moralistic repression and racism in ideology and character. Professional educators who do not hold moralistic views currently are being attacked by the repressive right. Furthermore, educators and mental health professionals are in a position to take a leadership role in the opposition to moralism by relating their professional activities to the political activities of exploited groups. Educators can help people who oppose authoritarian repression to become aware of the processes by which their thoughts are socially and psychologically conditioned, and to understand the connections between these processes and the issues they raise. Mental health professionals can focus attention on problems of character and attack the character armor that the individual has been socially conditioned to form. Of course if professionals such as these are to act progressively they must resist institutional pressures to adaptation.

As groups struggle to overcome exploitation and repression, the value of theory asserts itself. Since daily activity is so structured as to make class relationships appear as commodity relationships, a theoretical understanding of class relationships is necessary to overcome class exploitation and domination. Since the conditioning of character through moralistic repression and desublimations may make social conflicts appear as psychological conflicts, a theoretical understanding of the conditioning of character is necessary to overcome capitalist psychological and ideological hegemony. Theoretical examinations of economic and hegemonic struggles serve also to keep theory informed by the events of practice. However, the practical implications of theory are drawn out most effectively only when activists are also theorists; and theorists, activists.

NOTES

[1] Gabree, "Politics: Reich Now," *Fusion*, no. 10 (January 7, 1972), 49; and "Wilhelm Reich: a Brief Biography," *Liberation*, vol. 16 (October 1971), 50. (This issue of *Liberation* is devoted to Reich's essay "What is Class Consciousness"). The platform of the Sex-Pol movement is contained in Reich and Teschitz, *Selected Sex-Pol Essays: 1934–37* (London: Socialist Reproduction, 1973), pp. 48–50 (History of the Sex-Pol Movement: The Editorial Group).

[2] Cattier, *The Life and Work of Wilhelm Reich*, trans. Ghislaine Boulanger (New York: Horizon Press, 1971), pp. 77–79.

[3] Ibid., pp. 77–80, 88–89, and 150–163; and Reich and Teschitz, op. cit., pp. 41–42, 51 (History of the Sex-Pol Movement).

[4] Reich and Teschitz, op. cit., pp. 41–43 (History of the Sex-Pol Movement).

[5] Ibid., p. 49. See also pp. 44–50 and the section on "Class Variations in Character" in Chapter 5 above.

[6] Boadella, *Wilhelm Reich* (Chicago: Henry Regnery Co., 1973), p. 85.

[7] Ibid., pp. 111–114.

[8] Cattier, op. cit., p. 162.

[9] Reich and Teschitz, op. cit., p. 37. (History of the Sex-Pol Movement); and editor's note to "Politicizing the Sexual Problem of Youth," Reich, *Sex-Pol: Essays 1929–1934*, ed. Lee Baxandall (New York: Random House, 1972), p. 237.

[10] Cattier, op. cit., pp. 175–188.

[11] Reich, *The Mass Psychology of Fascism*, trans. Vincent R. Carfagno (New York: Farrar, Straus and Giroux, 1970), p. xxii. The quote is from Reich's preface to the third edition, 1942.

[12] Ibid., p. 314. See also Chapters 11 and 13. It may seem as if I am contradicting the distinction I made between Reich's early and later works by citing the *Mass Psychology* in this context. However, Reich revised all his texts before allowing them to be translated (Cattier, op. cit., p. 205). The terminology and ideas of the last several chapters of *Mass Psychology* make it obvious that they were written by Reich later in his career.

[13] Brown, *Marx, Freud, and the Critique of Everyday Life* (New York: Monthly Review Press, 1973), p. 136; and Reich, *Mass Psychology*, pp. 229–230.

[14] Gramsci, *Selections from the Prison Notebooks*, ed. and trans. Quintin Hoare and Geoffrey Nowell Smith (New York: International Publishers, 1976), p. 198.

[15] Pozzolini, *Antonio Gramsci: An Introduction to His Thought*, trans. Anna F. Showstack (London: Pluto Press, 1970), p. 76.

[16] Gramsci, "The Soviets in Italy, 1919–1920," *New Left Review*, no. 57 (September–October 1968), 27.

[17] Ibid., pp. 31–41.

[18] Ibid., p. 30. See also carl Boggs, *Gramsci's Marxism* (London: Pluto Press, 1976), p. 97; and Perry Anderson, "Introduction to Gramsci, 1919–1920," *New Left Review*, no. 57 (September–October 1968), 27.

[19] Gramsci, "Soviets in Italy," p. 30.

[20] Brown, op. cit., p. 138.

[21] Keiman, "Parents Groups Purging Schools of 'Humanist' Books and Classes," *New York Times*, May 17, 1981, Sec. 1, p. 1.

BIBLIOGRAPHY

ARTICLES

Adorno, Theodor. "Sociology and Psychology: Part 1," *New Left Review*, no. 46 (November–December 1967): 67–80.

——. "Sociology and Psychology: Part II," *New Left Review*, no. 47 (January–February 1968): 79–97.

Freud, Sigmund. "Civilized Morality and Modern Nervous Disorders," *The Standard Edition of the Complete Psychological Works of Sigmund Freud*, vol. 9. Edited by James Strachey. London: Hogarth Press, 1962.

——. "The Dissolution of the Oedipus Complex," *The Standard Edition of the Complete Psychological Works of Sigmund Freud*, vol. 19. Edited by James Strachey. London: Hogarth Press, 1962.

Lasch, Christopher. "The Emotions of Family Life." *New York Review of Books*, vol. 22 (November 27, 1975): 37–42.

Rabinback, Anson. "The Politicization of Wilhem Reich," *New German Critique*, no. 1 (Winter 1974): 90–97.

Reich, Wilhelm. "The Sexual Misery of the Working Masses and the Difficulties of Sexual Reform," *New German Critique*, no. 1 (Winter 1974): 98–110.

Reiff, Phillip. "The Authority of the Past: Sickness and Society in Freud's Thought," vol. 2, *Social Research* (Winter 1954): 428–450.

——. "History, Psychoanalysis, and the Social Sciences." *Ethics*, vol. 63 (1952–53): 107–120.

——. "Psychology and Politics: The Freudian Connection," *World Politics*, vol. 7 (January 1955): 293–305.

BOOKS

Abendroth, Wolfgang. *A Short History of the European Working Class.* New York: Monthly Review Press, 1972.

Aronowitz, Stanley. *False Promises: The Shaping of American Working Class Consciousness*. New York: McGraw-Hill Book Co., 1973.

Baron, Paul A., and Paul M. Sweezy. *Monopoly Capital: An Essay on the American Economic and Social Order*. New York: Monthly Review Press, Modern Reader Paperbacks, 1966.

Boadella, David. *Wilhelm Reich: The Evolution of His Thought*. Chicago: Regnery Co., 1973.

Boggs, Carl. *Gramsci's Marxism*. London: Pluto Press, 1976.

Braverman, Harry. *Labor and Monopoly Capital*. New York: Monthly Review Press, 1974.

Castles, Stephen, and Godula Kosack. *Immigrant Workers and Class Structure in Western Europe*. London: Oxford University Press, 1973.

Dubofsky, Melvyn. *Industrialism and the American Worker, 1865–1920*. The AHM American History Series. Arlington Heights, ILL: AHM Publishing Corp., 1975.

Engels, Frederick. *The Origins of the Family, Private Property and the State*. Edited with an introduction by Eleanor Burke Leacock. New York: International Publishers, 1972.

Freud, Sigmund. *Beyond the Pleasure Principle*. Translated by James Strachey. New York: Liveright Publishing Co., 1967.

——. *Civilization and Its Discontents*. Edited and translated by James Strachey. New York: W. W. Norton & Co., 1961.

——. *The Ego and the Id* in *The Standard Edition of the Complete Psychological Works of Sigmund Freud*, vol. 19. Edited by James Strachey. London: Hogarth Press, 1962.

——. *The Future of An Illusion*. Translated by James Strachey. New York: Doubleday & Co., n.d.

——. *A General Introduction to Psychoanalysis*. Translated by Joan Riviere. Prefaces by Ernest Jones and G. Stanley Hall. New York: Washington Square Press, 1964.

——. *General Psychological Theory: Papers on Metapsychology*. Edited with an Introduction by Phillip Reiff. New York: Macmillan Publishing Co., 1963.

——. *Group Psychology and the Analysis of the Ego*. Translated and edited by James Strachey. The International Psycho-Analytical Library, no. 6. New York: Liveright Publishing Corp., 1967.

——. *Group Psychology and the Analysis of the Ego*. Translated and edited by James Strachey. The International Psycho-Analytical Library, no. 6. New York: Liveright Publishing Corp., 1967.

——. *Three Contributions to the Theory of Sex.* Translated by A. A. Brill. Introduction by Hendrik M. Ruitenbeek. Forewards by James J. Putman and A. A. Brill. New York: E. P. Dutton & Co., 1962.

——. *Totem and Taboo.* Translated by James Strachey. New York: W. W. Norton & Co., 1950.

Friedrich, Otto. *Before the Deluge: A Portrait of Berlin in the 1920's.* New York: Harper & Row, 1972.

Fromm, Erich. *The Crisis of Psychoanalysis: Essays on Freud, Marx, and Social Psychology.* Greenwich, Conn.: Fawcett Publications, 1970.

——. *Escape From Freedom.* New York: Rinehart & Co., 1941.

——. *Man For Himself: An Inquiry into the Psychology of Ethics.* Greenwich, Conn.: Fawcett Publications, 1947.

——. *Marx's Concept of Man.* With a translation of *Marx's Economic and Philosophic Manuscripts* by T. B. Bottomore. New York: Frederick Unger Publishing Co., 1961.

——. *The Sane Society.* New York: Holt, Reinhart & Winston, 1955.

Giddens, Anthony. *The Class Structure of the Advanced Societies.* New York: Harper & Row, 1973.

Gramsci, Antonio. *Selections From the Prison Notebooks.* Edited and translated by Quintin Hoare and Geoffrey Nowell Smith. New York: International Publishers, 1976.

Habermas, Jurgen. *Knowledge and Human Interest.* Boston: Beacon Press, 1971.

Hempel, Carl G. *Fundamentals of Concept Formation in Empirical Science.* International Encyclopedia of United Science, vol. 2, no. 7. Chicago: University of Chicago Press, 1952.

Horowitz, Gad. *Repression: Basic and Surplus Repression in Psychoanalytic Theory: Freud, Reich, and Marcuse.* Toronto and Buffalo: University of Toronto Press, 1977.

Jacoby, Russell. *Social Amnesia: A Critique of Conformist Psychology From Adler to Laing.* Boston: Beacon Press, 1975.

Jay, Martin. *The Dialectical Imagination: A Social History of the Frankfurt School.* Boston: Little, Brown & Co., 1973.

Kaplan, Abraham. *The Conduct of Inquiry: Methodology For Behavioral Science.* Scranton, Pa.: Chandler Publishing Co., 1964.

Lasch, Christopher. *The Culture of Narcissism: American Life in an Age of Diminishing Expectations.* New York: Warner Books. 1979.

Lenin, V. I. *Essential Works of Lenin.* Edited by Henry M. Christman. New York: Bantam Books, 1966.

Lukacs, Georg. *History and Class Consciousness: Studies in Marxist Dialectics*. Translated by Rodney Livingstone. Cambridge: MIT Press, 1971.

Marcuse, Herbert. *Counterrevolution and Revolt*. Boston: Beacon Press, 1972.

——. *Eros and Civilization: A Philosophical Inquiry into Freud*. New York: Beacon Press, Beacon Paperback, 1974.

——. *One-Dimensional Man: Studies in the Ideology of Advanced Industrial Society*. Boston: Beacon Press, 1966.

Marx, Karl. *Capital*, vol. 1. New York: International Publishers, 1972.

——. *A Contribution to the Critique of Political Economy*. Edited by Maurice Dobbs. New York: International Publishers, 1970.

The Marx-Engels Reader, Edited by Robert C. Tucker. New York: W. W. Norton & Co., 1972.

Mitchell, Juliet. *Psychoanalysis and Feminism: Freud, Reich, Laing and Women*. New York: Pantheon, 1974.

Ollendorf-Reich, Ilse. *Wilhelm Reich*. With an Introduction by Paul Goodman. New York: St. Martin's Press, 1969.

Ollman, Bertell. *Alienation: Marx's Concept of Man in Capitalist Society*. Cambridge: Cambridge University Press, 1971.

Osbert, Reuben [Reuben Osborn]. *Freud and Marx*. New York: Equinox Cooperative Press [1937].

Reich Speaks of Freud. Edited by Mary Higgins and Chester M. Raphael. Translations by Therese Pol. New York: Farrar, Straus and Giroux, 1967.

Reich, Wilhelm. *Character Analysis*. 3d ed., enl. Translated by Vincent R. Carfagno. New York: Simon & Schuster, 1976.

——. *The Mass Psychology of Fascism*. Translated by Vincent R. Carfagno. New York: Farrar, Straus & Giroux, 1970.

——. *Sex-Pol: Essays 1929–1934*. Edited by Lee Baxandall. Translated by Anna Bostock, Tom Dubose, and Lee Baxandall. Introduction by Bertell Ollman. New York: Vintage Books, Random House, 1972.

——. *The Sexual Revolution: Toward a Self-Regulating Character Structure*. Translated by Therese Pol. New York: Simon & Schuster, 1975.

Reich, Wilhelm, and Karl Teschitz, *Selected Sex-Pol Essays: 1934–37*. London: Socialist Reproduction, [1973].

Reiche, Reimut. *Sexuality and Class Struggle*. Translated by Susan Bennett. New York: Praeger Publishers, 1971.

Reiff, Phillip. *Freud: The Mind of the Moralist*. New York: Anchor Books, 1961.

Roazen, Paul. *Freud: Political and Social Thought*. New York: Alfred A. Knopf, 1970.

Rycroft, Charles. *Wilhelm Reich*. New York: The Viking Press, 1972.

Selsam, Howard, and Harry Martel, eds., *Reader in Marxist Philosophy: From the Writings of Marx, Engels and Lenin*. New York: International Publishers, 1971.

Thompson, E. P. *The Making of the English Working Class*. New York: Pantheon, 1963.

Wolheim, Richard, ed. *Freud: A Collection of Critical Essays*. New York: Anchor Books, 1974.

ACKNOWLEDGMENTS

From *Eros and Civilization* by Herbert Marcuse. Copyright © 1955, 1966 by The Beacon Press. Reprinted by permission of Beacon Press.

From The Sexual Revolution: *Toward a Self-Regulating Character Structure* by Wilhelm Reich. Copyright © 1975 by Farrar, Straus and Giroux, Inc. Reprinted by permission of Farrar, Straus and Giroux.

From *Sex-Pol: Essays 1929–1934* by Wilhelm Reich, edited by Lee Baxandall, translated by Anna Bostock, Tom Dubose, and Lee Baxandall. Copyright © 1972 by Random House, Inc. Reprinted by permission of Random House, Inc.

INDEX